THE NUN IN THE SYNAGOGUE

The Nun in the Synagogue

Judeocentric Catholicism in Israel

EMMA O'DONNELL POLYAKOV

The Pennsylvania State University Press
University Park, Pennsylvania

Library of Congress Cataloging-in-Publication Data

Names: Polyakov, Emma O'Donnell, author.
Title: The nun in the synagogue : Judeocentric Catholicism in Israel /
    Emma O'Donnell Polyakov.
Description: University Park, Pennsylvania : The Pennsylvania State
    University Press, [2020] | Includes bibliographical references and index.
Summary: "A study of Catholic perceptions of Jews, Judaism, and Israel,
    offering an exploration of biographical narratives and reflections on
    Holocaust trauma, conversion, Zionism, and religious identity"—
    Provided by publisher.
Identifiers: LCCN 2020020550 | ISBN 9780271087252 (hardback)
Subjects: LCSH: Catholic Church—Relations—Judaism. | Judaism—
    Relations—Catholic Church. | Catholics—Israel. | Philosemitism.
Classification: LCC BM535.P5725 2020 | DDC 261.2/6095694—dc23
LC record available at https://lccn.loc.gov/2020020550

The Pennsylvania State University Press is a member of the Association of
University Presses.

It is the policy of The Pennsylvania State University Press to use acid-free
paper. Publications on uncoated stock satisfy the minimum requirements
of American National Standard for Information Sciences—Permanence of
Paper for Printed Library Material, ANSI Z39.48-1992.

This book is dedicated to all those whose voices are heard in these pages and also to those whose voices could not be heard here, each of whom navigated their own way along the many borderlands between Judaism and Christianity, from within their monasteries and within the land of Israel. To all of these lives on the border and in memory of Sr. Paula.

CONTENTS

ACKNOWLEDGMENTS

The research that eventually resulted in this book initially began with a very different focus. In 2015, I had begun a series of interviews with Christians in Israel and the West Bank, studying their understandings of the holiness of the land commonly called the Holy Land. However, after interviewing approximately eighty Catholic clergy, nuns, and monks, I began to notice a remarkable phenomenon linking the testimonies of a number of those who lived in Israel. When I realized that was I was witnessing was a distinct form of post-Holocaust thought, which I refer to here as a Judeocentric Catholic phenomenon, I set aside the initial research plan and began again with this new focus. I owe the eventual realization of this phenomenon to each and every person whom I encountered in the process of this research—not only to those who exhibit this Judeocentrism but also to the many others who do not share these views and who expressed their perspectives so generously. The candid and thoughtful reflections of every person I encountered in this long and winding process of research have contributed immeasurably to this book, and my gratitude to each of them is deep and sincere.

I would like to thank the colleagues who supported me in this work and who made this research possible. The majority of the research for this book was conducted during my term as a postdoctoral fellow at the Centre for Theological and Religious Studies at Lund University, and I would like to thank all of my colleagues in Lund, particularly Alexander Maurits, Blazenka Scheuer, and Johanna Gustafsson Lundberg. I would like to express my gratitude to the Crafoord Foundation, which generously funded my postdoctoral position at Lund University and made the research in Israel possible. I am immensely grateful to the Swedish Theological Institute in Jerusalem, which often served as a home base during my research in Jerusalem, and particularly to Maria Leppakari, whose enthusiastic support has been invaluable. I'd also like to thank my colleagues at Merrimack College, particularly Joseph Kelley, Karen Ryan, and Sean Condon, for so generously supporting my ongoing research in Israel. I am grateful to Gavin D'Costa for his remarkably generous and thoughtful reading of the manuscript and for his pressing questions. I wish to acknowledge Kathryn Yahner and the editorial staff at Penn State Press for their work in bringing this book to completion.

I'd like to express my sincere gratitude to the many people who so warmly opened the doors of their homes to me in Jerusalem, whether to offer me a place to stay, to speak about my research, or to host me for Shabbat dinner. The many individuals I encountered in Israel who helped me in so many ways, through both collegiality and friendship, are too numerous to mention, but their generosity has not been forgotten. Finally, I'd like to express my gratitude to my husband, Valery, for his tireless and unwavering support.

A small, unassuming sign set at knee height reads, "La Solitude." Beyond it, a narrow trail winds between carefully tended garden beds blooming amid sun-bleached stretches of dust and stone. The trail leads to a door set in a low, humble building, which opens to a series of shadowed rooms. Inside, a nun in a pale-blue habit sits in a chair by a window and gestures to the sweeping vista outside, to the plunging valleys and steeply soaring hillsides of Ein Kerem. A few kilometers to the east, she points out, is the Yad Vashem Holocaust Museum, and a few kilometers to the west is the Hadassah Medical Center. She believes that living precisely between these two points is spiritually significant to her because she sees the two points as centers of suffering and healing for the Jewish people. From this hilltop perch, where she lives a life of solitude and contemplation, she sends out prayers in both directions. She prays for the people mourning as they visit Yad Vashem, and she prays for healing for those in the hospital.

Over those hills, in the center of West Jerusalem, another nun lives alone in an apartment in a middle-class Jewish neighborhood. She dresses in secular clothes, and the cross that she always wears is kept carefully tucked inside of her clothing. She speaks Hebrew fluently and goes by a Hebrew name. From her home, she steps out onto a balcony that overlooks the grounds of the Israeli president's residence. From there, she prays for the president and for all the leaders of Israel—that they may lead well and wisely. When she prays for them, she is careful to never use the name of Jesus; instead, she prays in Hebrew and addresses her prayers only to God, to "ha kadosh baruch hu" (the holy one, blessed be he).

On a hillside just outside of a village in the mountainous region west of Jerusalem, up a long winding footpath, a Catholic nun lives as a hermit in a single room in a compact one-story concrete structure. Here she spends her days in solitude and prayer. The purpose of her life of solitude, as she expresses it, is simply to live for God and to be a presence of love in the land of Israel, with and for the Jewish people.

Down the steep hill from where she lives, in the center of the town below, a monastery stands behind high stone walls. Here a community of nuns and monks live side by side, and their purpose, as they express it, is "to be a presence of prayer, for listening to the mystery of Israel." In the women's quarters lives a nun whose religious name, drawn from the name of Michael the archangel, symbolizes her desire to gather together and hold up the prayers of all the people of Israel. She says that her call to religious life and her call to the people and land of Israel are unified, a call within a call.

Fifteen kilometers to the east, in Jerusalem, another set of high stone walls encloses a different monastery. The walls stand along the edge of Hebron Road, which runs from Jerusalem into the West Bank, and a person walking alongside these walls would be unlikely to know that a monastery lies behind them unless she stopped to read the very small print next to the doorbell that flanks the unadorned door in the center of the long wall. Inside these walls live nuns of the order of Poor Clare. They remain inside the monastery in a life of contemplative prayer and very rarely step outside the walls. Among them is one woman who has felt a deep spiritual connection to Judaism ever since she first arrived in Jerusalem thirty years ago and experienced a mystical insight when watching Jews pray at the Western Wall. Night and day she prays, contemplating the spiritual role of the Jewish people, whom she believes are a laboratory of hope for the entire world.

On top of the Mount of Olives, behind the walls of a Benedictine monastery, a nun's eyes are damp as she tells the story of what led her to that place. She speaks of living in the woods to escape the Nazis, of hiding for months in a cellar, of wanting to die rather than become a Christian, of eventually converting and becoming a nun, and of finally coming to Israel. She says that she had never stopped praying to die until the day she heard that the State of Israel had formed. She believes that God kept her alive through the war and keeps her alive today for Israel.

PART 1

The Jewish People Through a Christian Lens

CHAPTER 1

Behind the Monastery Walls

PRAYING FOR THE JEWS

The concept of "praying for the Jews" has historically been linked with proselytism, evoking the image of Christians fervently praying for the conversion of Jews. The Christian desire for Jewish conversion is as old as Christianity itself, which began as a movement within Judaism and only later shifted its missionary efforts outside of the Jewish community to target Gentiles. Despite its origins as a movement within Judaism, deeply ingrained anti-Jewish theologies took root as Christianity expanded over the following centuries, and the desire to convert Jews to Christianity became one of the many expressions of this anti-Judaism.

As Christianity increasingly defined itself in contrast to Judaism, a theology of supersessionism developed that claimed that Christianity had abrogated Judaism. As supersessionist theologies took root, much theological discourse portrayed Jews in vilified forms. Jews were seen as a sign and remnant of the fundamental sin of refusing to acknowledge Jesus as the messiah and, even worse, as a people accused of deicide, culpable for the death of God on the cross. This theological anti-Judaism spread insidiously through Western society and eventually influenced the development of racial antisemitic tropes.[1] While Christian anti-Judaism is by no means the sole cause of antisemitism, which also predates Christianity and can be seen in ancient Greco-Roman culture, the sizable contribution of Christian theology to antisemitism is clear. However, in a world still struggling to reckon with the senseless horror of the Holocaust, the malevolence of Christian anti-Judaism has been brought to light. Christians have begun to acknowledge that Christianity is implicated in a long history of violence against Jews and to recognize the culpability of Christianity in the antisemitism that made the Holocaust possible.

In the last half-century, Christian attitudes toward Judaism have changed radically, and theological and liturgical revisions have been enacted to attempt to erase teachings of contempt for Judaism from Christian thought. Christian-Jewish dialogue initiatives have become increasingly common, and many Christians have made great efforts toward atonement and reconciliation, particularly in Western contexts, where the legacy of Christian anti-Judaism weighs heavily on the historical conscience.

In the Catholic Church, this change has been particularly profound, and in an ecclesiastical institution known for being extraordinarily slow to change its teaching and traditions, the Second Vatican Council initiated a groundbreaking reform in Catholic understandings of Judaism.[2] Fueled by the theological reforms in the second half of the twentieth century, Christian concepts of Jews and Judaism have shifted substantially, acknowledging the anti-Judaic elements of Christian thought through the centuries and seeking new ways to understand Judaism through Christian theological lenses. However, anti-Judaic theologies still linger within the Catholic Church and throughout Christian thought, and even the most progressive statements still frame Jews and Judaism firmly within a Christian vision of faith and salvation. In short, given this history, the notion of Christian practices of praying for Jews remains entangled with the potential for conversionary motives and remnants of anti-Judaism.

A JUDEOCENTRIC CATHOLICISM

Despite the persistence of Christian anti-Judaism, in the new atmosphere inaugurated by these midcentury theological shifts, the controversial practice of Christian prayer for Jews has taken new forms. This book identifies a new religious and cultural phenomenon that has arisen from post-Holocaust reflection on the part of Christians and is characterized by developments of "praying for the Jews" that depart from earlier precedents. It designates this phenomenon as a new Judeocentric Catholicism,[3] and the following chapters trace its development within the specific context of Catholic monastic life in Israel.[4]

I propose that this Judeocentric Catholicism reflects new patterns in Christian perceptions of Jews and Judaism. These patterns have arisen from efforts to comprehend the shock of the Holocaust and have taken shape within the theological worldview developed in the past half-century of Catholic theological reforms and within the context of contemporary Israel. This distinctly post-Holocaust, post–Vatican II Catholic phenomenon often takes philosemitic forms, but they are notably different from earlier forms of philosemitism, many of which aimed at proselytization. In contrast, this new phenomenon is characterized by the study of Jewish texts and traditions, by the contemplation of the theological relationships between Christianity and Judaism, and by practices of praying for the ongoing thriving of the Jewish people.

This Judeocentric Catholicism can be observed in two main forms: the first can be found in Catholics whose spirituality is immersed in Jewish life and thought; the second in Jews who have converted to Catholicism and yet maintain a strong sense of Jewish identity. If wordplay may be forgiven here, these two approaches may be distinguished as that of the philo-semites and the fellow-semites. For the former, this Judeocentrism often manifests as a Christian philosemitism, characterized by a powerful attachment to Jews and Judaism. The latter, on the other hand, find themselves on the border between Judaism and Christianity in a very different way, through choosing to maintain a Christian faith and a Jewish identity. This includes those who were raised Jewish and later converted to Christianity as well as those raised in mixed Jewish-Christian families. Many express that they find themselves continuously dwelling along the border between Judaism and Christianity, often feeling suspended between two identities.

Through a close study of Catholic nuns, monks, and religious sisters and brothers who live in Israel today, the following chapters explore how this Judeocentric Catholic phenomenon is lived out, experimented with, and transformed in the Jewish milieu of Israel.[5] The Catholics whose narratives are shared here do not self-identify as a group, and they share no mutually agreed-upon set of principles, beliefs, or practices other than those of the Christian faith. A number belong to a congregation or monastery within which the focus on Christian-Jewish relations is shared and made explicit. Others, however, find themselves alone in their community in this sense and have developed this focus entirely on their own. Yet despite this lack of cohesion, a pattern is evident across their narratives. They are all originally from Europe and North America and have made long-term or lifelong commitments to remain in Israel. Whether they lead solitary lives in monasteries or are busy with directing educational programs or other work outside of the monastery, each engages deeply and intentionally with Judaism. This engagement takes the form of studying, teaching, participating in Christian-Jewish dialogue, or practicing forms of prayer for the Jewish people motivated by a post-Holocaust desire for atonement and for reconciliation and for greater understanding between Christians and Jews.

The theological views held by those who evidence this Judeocentric Catholic phenomenon are diverse. Some maintain philosemitic views with a Christocentric focus, basing their adoration of Jews and Judaism on beliefs about the role and nature of Jesus. According to this line of thought, Jesus is the universal savior of all people, and yet "salvation is from the Jews" (John 4:22),[6] and Christians share in the covenantal relationship that God established with the Jewish people. Others, however, have radically moved beyond a Christocentric basis in their interpretations of Judaism and hold a pluralist view that sees Judaism as a path to God that is separate from Christian faith and yet equally valid. Yet despite their decentered and diverse traits, together they contribute to a small yet notable contemporary phenomenon in Christian understandings of Jews and Judaism.

This book listens to and analyzes the narratives of these nuns and monks and traces the societal, theological, and personal influences that give rise to this phenomenon. It explores encounters along the border between Christianity and Judaism, including forays across this border in both directions, through conversion and other forms of immersion into the two religious traditions. It follows the lives of individuals navigating and negotiating these borders, from Jewish Holocaust survivors who converted to Catholicism and entered monastic life, to those who have been Catholic all their lives and yet attend synagogue services every Shabbat. These chapters analyze the contexts and histories of these border negotiations, with attention to where the boundaries become permeable and where they are reinforced.

Many of the people whose narratives are heard in these pages are advanced in years, and there are others discussed here who passed away before my research began and whose experiences can only be surmised through letters, interviews, or other documentation that remains. The interviews for this book were conducted in 2015 and 2016, and in the few years that have passed since then, a number of those whose voices are heard here have encountered struggles with health that required them to leave Israel after many decades of life there to live in the retirement communities of their congregations overseas. The living situations, careers, and other biographical details of those interviewed here reflect their positions when they met with me and shared their stories, and these narratives now serve as windows into the time, just a few short years ago, in which they were all vigorous and in good health, living in Israel.

The individual voices and narratives heard here reflect developments in Catholic understandings of Judaism that are not found within official Church documents but arise in personal experiences and interpersonal encounters. While this new Judeocentric Catholic phenomenon is far from widespread, it serves as a significant case study in hermeneutical shifts in Christian conceptualizations of Judaism. When viewed from within the context of a church still just beginning to grapple with the Holocaust and with the contribution of Christian theology to the history of antisemitism, this phenomenon becomes more than a few individuals praying alone in monasteries. It serves as an indication of developing Christian perceptions of Jews and Judaism in a time of swiftly changing theological and cultural contexts and as a view onto contemporary Catholic negotiations of identity and faith in relation to the Jewish people, Jewish history, and Jewish religious traditions.

This Judeocentric Catholic phenomenon is equivocal; its value and impact on Jewish-Christian relations and Catholic theologies are ambiguous and can be interpreted in many different ways. Although the impetus behind its development has been the eradication of anti-Judaism from Catholic thought and improved relations between Christians and Jews, it is also complicated by a few problematic issues. When it swings toward philosemitism, it tends to cast Jews in an idealized light, reinforcing essentializations about Jews. These stereotypes are positive, and yet they are stereotypes nonetheless and preclude the perception of Jews as people like any else. Claims of hybrid Jewish-Christian identity can also be problematic and often encounter resistance in Jewish communities, for Jewish conversion to Christianity is heavy with cultural and religious taboos, reflecting a traumatic history of forced conversions. And yet, despite these and other problematic issues, this phenomenon has also contributed to greater education about Judaism and Jewish experience for Christians and to a fuller recognition and acknowledgment of the history of Christian anti-Judaism.

This book does not seek to provide a final evaluation of this phenomenon's cultural or theological value. Its purpose is not to persuade; it does not promote this phenomenon as positive, nor does it indemnify it. The purpose, rather, is to explore this Judeocentric phenomenon as it takes shape in the lives of Catholic nuns and monks in Israel and to investigate the complex and diverse cultural, religious, historical, political, and personal factors that influence it. This book is also an exploration through personal narratives, which invites the reader to listen to intimate reflections on faith, conversion, Holocaust trauma, Zionism, and religious identity. In this way, it is both an analytical investigation of a contemporary phenomenon and a meditation on faith and identity.

Together, the following chapters speak of intimate spiritual experiences and personal relationships and of the interplay of faith and uncertainty. They tell the stories of lives on the border: on the border between Christian identity and Jewish identity, on the border between Christian belief and Jewish practice and culture, on the border between Israeli life and life within a monastery, and on the border between old, ingrained Christian patterns of interpreting Jews and Judaism and new directions in Christian-Jewish relations.

STRUCTURE AND THEMES

This is a book about people and about relationships. For this reason, it cannot speak properly if it remains entirely within the standard academic format of analysis. To speak properly, it must also take a form suited to communicating the depth of feeling and the complexity of the informants' experiences and relationships, and capable of expressing the ambiguities of the heart of which the informants speak. Therefore, I have composed a patchwork of two distinct components: chapters of analytical discussion, and narrative "portraits" of individuals interspersed between the analytical chapters. The latter consists of descriptive passages about the participants and the contexts in which they live, featuring excerpts of their personal narratives and reflections gathered during interviews. Like poetry or other arts, which, if done well, communicate through their aesthetic form something that cannot be communicated otherwise, the descriptive portraits are intended not to simply transcribe our meetings but to communicate the subtleties of interpersonal encounters that elude standard academic writing.

I have divided this volume into four parts. The first part, "The Jewish People Through a Christian Lens," introduces the scope and method of the book and situates the specific phenomenon discussed here within its greater social context. This section investigates the image of the Jew in the Christian imagination, examining how a religiously formed Christian worldview draws on scriptural narratives to construct understandings of the Jewish people. It surveys the phenomenon of philosemitism as it has been observed and theorized in a range of forms and places this new Judeocentric Catholic phenomenon in contrast to other Christian responses to Israel, such as Palestinian Christian perspectives and Christian Zionist thought.

The narrative descriptions of individuals begin with the opening of the second part, "A Judeocentric Catholicism," presented in a format of analytical chapters alternating with descriptive portraits of individuals. This section describes and analyzes current expressions of this phenomenon found in Israel today and traces its roots in a number of individuals and institutions that set the groundwork for it in the mid-twentieth century. Following this is a discussion of responses to the State of Israel expressed by the Catholics whose voices are heard throughout this study, many of whom feel a strong emotional attachment to Israel and yet also feel torn by what they see as injustices in the political conflict.

The third part, "Religious Identity After the Holocaust," examines the influence of the Holocaust on self-understandings of religious identity, drawing together a number of related discourses revolving around Holocaust trauma, conversion, hybrid religious identities, and post-Holocaust theology. It shares the narratives of Jews who survived the Holocaust and who converted to Catholicism in the midst of the war or in the immediate aftermath. Each of them chose to enter monastic life, and eventually "made aliyah" by immigrating to Israel, motivated by a desire to be in the Jewish homeland.[7] This section considers the impact of the trauma of the Holocaust on these radical life decisions and discusses the persistence of the desire to belong to the Jewish community that many express even after their conversion to Christianity. This section closes with a critical look at the problematic issues involving attempts to theologize about the Holocaust using Christian concepts and beliefs.

The final part, "Praying for the Jews," addresses the specifically religious issues of prayer and ritual practice, and theological debates about evangelization and Christian truth claims. It begins with a discussion of the role of interreligious dialogue in monastic life and then moves to an analysis of Christian participation in Jewish liturgies and ritual life, considering the controversial issues that can arise. The final chapter addresses the central theological issues at play in these Christian perceptions of Jews and Judaism, examining the soteriological and Christological views expressed by the informants. It engages in a critical consideration of the practice of praying for the Jewish people in an age when Jewish conversion to Christianity is no longer accepted as an appropriate goal of dialogue. At the core of Christian belief is the necessity of recognizing Jesus as the universal savior, and this chapter discusses how this belief becomes a point of theological irresolution, and even paradox, for Christians who are also convinced that Judaism is a theologically valid religion. At the heart of this inquiry is the question of whether this philosemitic Christian gaze on Jews continues to maintain traces of implicit hope for conversion and, if it does not, how this is reconciled with essential Christian truth claims.

LIVED RELIGION

The remainder of this introductory chapter explores the methodological underpinnings of this study. Here I make an argument for the importance of the study of lived religion and individual experiences, and following this, I consider researcher reflexivity and ethical issues in the representation of human subjects. Readers who desire to move directly to the central content of the book may wish to skip ahead to the second chapter, which explores the phenomenon of philosemitism in its historical contexts. Any readers who might prefer to entirely forgo the methodological, historical, theoretical, and sociological chapters and to move directly to the narrative descriptions of individuals may wish to turn to part 2 of this book.

While most scholarship on Christian-Jewish relations focuses on historical studies or on the interpretation of scriptural texts or church documents, this book explores a phenomenon that exists not in the form of texts and public statements but within the lives and spiritual experiences of individuals. At the heart of this book is the encounter; it is a meditation on encounters between Christians and Jews and also encounters among memories, hopes, and religious worldviews. But why do the experiences and reflections of these people matter? When prayers are made in silence and solitude, alone in a room as dusk falls outside a small window, of what interest are they to others and of what relevance to scholarship on religion? Arguing against the idea that private experiences such as these are irrelevant to the academic study of religion, Robert Orsi criticizes "the idea that real-world significance is public and political whereas lived religion is preoccupied with the intimate (and therefore politically irrelevant) domains of family, relationships, imagination, and so on."[8] This book, too, rejects this polarized mapping of the world, in which what is public is important and what is private is insignificant. Public and institutional forms of religion are only structures that house the vast interior array of personal, intimate, and often very private experiences. As Meredith McGuire asks, "What might we discover if, instead of looking at affiliation or organizational participation, we focused first on individuals, the experiences they consider most important, and the concrete practices that make up their personal religious experience and expression? What if we think of religion, at the individual level, as an ever-changing, multifaceted, often messy—even contradictory—amalgam of beliefs and practices that are not necessarily those religious institutions consider important?"[9] Religions take as many shapes as there are people who practice them, in multiple and diverse expressions of religiosity. This becomes particularly evident in the specific context explored in this volume, for the voices heard here express views that do not always seamlessly align with many Christian teachings.

These observations also point to why the study of antisemitism and other patterns in Christian perceptions of Jews continues to be so crucial even after the theological reforms of the twentieth century. The institutional Church has revised its teachings about Judaism, but this does not ensure that these new teachings have broadly become a part of the lived religion. For example, despite the emphasis that recent Christian teachings have placed on the Jewish roots of Christianity, many Christians still do not realize that Jesus was a Jew—not only that he was born as a Jew but also that he died as a Jew—and at no point became a Christian. Antisemitic sentiments still run through the lived religiosity of many, and at times they are so subtle that they are not recognized as such.

METHODOLOGICAL REFLECTIONS ON REFLEXIVITY

The issues addressed in this book are explored through personal histories and narratives using an ethnographic method that, while in demand in other areas in religious studies, has yet to be popularized in studies of Christian-Jewish relations. This method necessitates the consideration of not only *what* to portray but also *how* to portray it, and it raises a host of questions regarding the ethics of representation. In any discipline, the effort to understand the object of study is tangled in layers of perception, interpretation, and communication, and this is even more challenging when the objects of study are living people. The ethnographer "reads" the subject based on his or her own perception and identity, and the ethnographer's representation can sometimes mislead or fail to be understood. The very presence of the ethnographer can also make the context "nonauthentic" through introducing an outside presence. The struggle for correct representation is not solely the researcher's problem either; at times, the subjects may present—or misrepresent—themselves according to their desired view of themselves.

The notion that it is possible for ethnographic fieldwork to be fully objective began to crumble in the last decades of the twentieth century. This began with the postmodernist critique of objectivity, which argued that the anthropological gaze all too often displays much of the exploitation characteristic of the colonial era, and pointed to the potential for fieldwork to become imperialistic.[10] This discourse brought the position of the ethnographer into the forefront, carefully drawing attention to the ways in which the ethnographer's position, identity, and hermeneutical lens influenced the collection and interpretation of the data. The self-conscious awareness implicated in this reflexive turn allowed the supposedly rigid imperialism of the anthropological gaze, convinced of its own objectivity, to break down.

The reflexive turn brings the researcher into the picture, or more precisely, it finally acknowledges that the researcher has always been in the picture. This brings greater transparency to fieldwork, but it does not solve the problem of how to represent the object of study as truthfully as possible, with the greatest integrity, given the impossibility of absolute objectivity. Behind every participant's statement is the context in which it was made, which in this project involved face-to-face encounters between the participant and me as we discussed intimate spiritual experiences while a digital voice recorder blinked beside us. My own identity, biography, and participation inevitably became part of the participants' narratives whether I intended it or not, for not only does my own context influence my interpretation of their narratives, but in addition, the first-person narrations were addressed to me personally in a conversational format.

The following chapters detail my interpretations of the informants and their narratives, but what did they see when they spoke, looking at me? A few said that they were surprised that I was so young (as they saw it), and I wondered if their comments reflected their expectations of a researcher's authority and power—had they expected someone with more of an air of authority, signaled by age? Some inquired about my own religious affiliation as soon as we sat down, before I had time to ask any questions of them, and the pressing way in which they asked it seemed to indicate an anxiety: Was I one of them, would I understand, could I be trusted to not misrepresent them? I generally answered with an honest although brief and opaque description of my own rather complex religious identity. When the interview was held at a monastery, I would often flesh out my biography just a bit by adding that I had spent some time in the past as a long-term guest at a Benedictine monastery. This admission allowed our conversation to go deeper; if they knew that I was familiar with monastic life, they would move into more complex, reflective, and probing topics.

In my role as a researcher, I remain an outsider to the personal narratives shared in this book. However, the boundary between the outside and inside is somewhat porous in this case, and I remain an outsider with the ability to "visit" the world of the insider. My scholarly training is theological, allowing me to be conversant in the language of faith even though I do not speak it as my own. As an outsider, I use theological language only as a tool of scholarly inquiry and not as a confession of faith.

This book quite intentionally does not take any theological position as its own, whether Christian or Jewish. It analyzes this topic from a scholarly distance, all the while recognizing that researcher neutrality is an impossibility. And given that impossibility, I recognize that the presentation and analysis of the phenomenon in this book occur through an interpretative lens with a specific worldview, one that may be characterized as inherently liberal and pluralist. This pluralist perspective is not a theological perspective because it makes no claims about the nature of God. Indeed, a pluralist perspective is at times at odds with, and perhaps incompatible with, some of the religious convictions and traditions discussed in these pages, which

stand upon a foundation of Christian truth claims that are not easily reconciled with pluralism.[11] This book does not support or argue against these
religious convictions or any others; it aims simply to present them from a
position of scholarly inquiry that, while categorically incapable of being
fully objective or neutral, nevertheless maintains a scholarly distance and
refrains from arguing for any religious truth claims.

THE ETHICS OF REPRESENTATION

In many cases, the process of interviewing also became a process of developing a relationship, and as this connection was forged, the participants often
opened up more. By welcoming me into the possibility of understanding
their experience, the participants invited me to become less of an outsider,
or perhaps a guest insider.

In openly speaking with me and giving me permission to publish their
private thoughts and experiences, the informants in this study placed a great
deal of trust in me as a researcher and as a confidant. The lives of these nuns
and monks are marked by solitude and interiority—even those with active
apostolic religious lives who engage with the outside world through teaching
or other vocational activities. All of them, from the cloistered nun in a full
habit to the religious sister in an apartment in central Jerusalem, have made
vows to a life of prayer and spiritual introspection. Their lives are deeply
interior and private, and yet they welcomed me into their homes. Those
who live in monasteries welcomed me inside the stone walls surrounding
the cloister of their monasteries; hermits invited me to enter their solitary
dwelling places, where few others enter; those who live in apartments hosted
me in their sitting rooms and offered me food and drink.

The issue of trust arose again and again in this fieldwork, and when
trust was lacking, it was the biggest obstacle that I faced. Without trust,
the participants would rarely speak openly, and their answers would often
reflect the "official" response of the Catholic Church rather than their own
perspectives. They would often make this clear by prefacing their answer
with a response such as "Well, the answer to that has already been decided
by the Church. We are taught to believe . . ." Sometimes they would point
me to their congregation's website to seek the answers even if my question
specifically asked about their personal experience. At other times, they

would ask that I not record the conversation and, in some cases, that I not share it in writing at all. When trust was established, all else flowed smoothly. This was accomplished in a number of different ways: in some cases, it was established after the participants asked me questions about my own religious views, family background, education, or the goals of research; in other cases, it unfolded naturally as the conversation progressed, signaled through nonverbal communication such as eye contact and body language.

Once trust had been established and the participants had opened up to me and shared intensely personal spiritual reflections, I needed to achieve two seemingly contradictory aims. On the one hand, I felt compelled to portray the informants as they would like to be portrayed, with respect to their own self-understanding, and to not betray the trust they had invested in me. On the other hand, as a scholar I must place critical analysis first, which can involve deconstructing and challenging the informants' own self-understanding.

In the course of a conversation with one of my informants, I brought up this issue and spoke to a nun by the name of Sr. Talia about the challenge of sharing her words through an academic study and subjecting them to analysis and publication while also respecting the intimate and hidden nature of her spiritual experiences. I wanted to let her know that I was trying to be conscientious about how to portray her in my analysis and to respect her own self-understanding in my representation of her. I was particularly concerned with this challenge in her case because Sr. Talia often speaks like a mystic; she expresses wordless spiritual experiences through evocative language that suggests meaning without explicitly defining meaning, and this way of communicating does not translate easily into a scholarly discussion. However, Sr. Talia was unperturbed at the prospect of having her words appear in an academic study. She explained that although her spiritual experiences are indeed private and hidden, "'Hidden' does not mean that it should not be published. I don't mind publishing; I really don't mind." Reflecting on the way she understands the privacy of her spiritual experiences, she continued, "I think it's important that people should know. . . . They will have words, but words will not transmit the secret. The secret will still be here. Like your secret, you cannot transmit your secret, the secret of your life. You just cannot. So it's not a problem; you can publish it." In other words, she does not see the exposure through publication to be threatening to her privacy, for she believes that the innermost meaning of her spiritual experiences will remain protected and ultimately inaccessible to others.

As a researcher, I intruded into private spaces and private lives and asked the participants to speak about their spiritual experiences and to put words to thoughts that they rarely (if ever) shared. They shared openly, and some told me that the experience of speaking with me had been emotionally exhausting for them. The trust that they eventually placed in me was not just as an offer of information that allowed me to write this book but also a gift of sincerity, openness, and emotional generosity. In exchange, I consider it my responsibility to represent the informants and their testimonies as accurately as possible and, in addition, with empathetic respect.

The demands of scholarship require a hermeneutic of unbiased critical thinking, and yet criticism and analysis do not always mesh well with empathetic relationships. However, perhaps the notion of accuracy itself should be critically rethought. If accuracy indeed cannot be based on disinterested, machinelike objectivity, as the postmodern and reflexive turns of the twentieth century have proposed, of what then does it consist? I argue here that empathy is a necessary component of accuracy in the interpretation of all things human—and particularly in the interpretation of oral testimonies.[12] An intensely critical interpretative strategy can fall short of a deep and nuanced understanding of testimonies if it fails to understand the speaker in his or her humanity. It is all too easy to present participants as disembodied data. A hard-edged intellectual critique lacking in empathy is not necessarily good scholarship; one can end up instead with a representation stripped of all emotive nuances and devoid of compassion. Interpreting and representing human subjects with the greatest accuracy requires empathetically seeing participants in all their humanity.

The following chapters aim to listen carefully to the voice of human experience, often choosing to forgo critical conclusions in favor of allowing multiple perspectives to coexist—as they often do in first-person narratives—weighing conflicting thoughts and feelings within a single narrative, twisted and intertwined in the dance of memory and reflection. In this exercise in listening, these pages offer a meditation on faith and identity, uncovering and following the experiences of many who continually walk, in some form or another, along the border between Judaism and Christianity.

CHAPTER 2

A New Philosemitism

A POST-HOLOCAUST CATHOLIC PHILOSEMITISM

The Judeocentric phenomenon that this book explores is highly contextual, reflecting the cultural and religious context of Israel today. Yet while it takes a unique shape in the context of contemporary Israel, the roots of this phenomenon lie in Western theological and social contexts and in Western models of interreligious relationship. Westerners who express this line of thought bring the memory of a dark history of European Christian anti-Judaism into a social and religious context entirely different from that in which it originated. In Israel, these European and North American Catholics live within a Jewish milieu and, for the first time in history, find themselves in a context in which they are a minority within a Jewish majority. In this context, they interpret Judaism and Zionism through the lenses of their own theological and cultural traditions, and all of this comes together to result in unique forms of Christian-Jewish encounter.

A point of clarification is due: this Judeocentric phenomenon is evident only in an extremely small portion of the Christians in Israel and is in no way characteristic of Christian residents and citizens of Israel as a whole.[1] In both Israel and the Palestinian territories, the majority of Christians are Arabs who primarily identify as Palestinian, and for these Christians, perceptions of Judaism are colored by the political conflict, which sets the stage for tense relations between local Christians and Jews. In addition, the vast majority of Palestinian Christians in Israel and the Palestinian territories do not see themselves as inheritors of the history of European Christianity, and they associate instead with the ancient history of Middle Eastern Christianity. Therefore, they identify not with the history of antisemitism that took root in European Christianity and the history of Christian power in Europe but rather with a Middle Eastern Christianity that throughout much of history has been a minority population.[2] The phenomenon explained here, therefore, is found not within Palestinian Christian communities but rather among some—but certainly not all—Western Christians whose views are shaped by a sense of collective Christian culpability for the violent history arising from Christian anti-Judaism.

The phenomenon explored here is one specific manifestation within a wider range of forms of contemporary philosemitism. Many of these other forms of philosemitism are responses not to post-Holocaust reflections but to religious and nationalist interpretations of the State of Israel. This is seen most clearly in the movement identified as Christian Zionism, which emerges from evangelical Protestant Christianity. However, the Catholic philosemitism explored here takes a very different form, one without the central organization, political affiliation, or ideological sway of Christian Zionism. It is less a public movement than a private experience born of interpersonal relationships and contemplative prayer.

The philosemitic aspects of this phenomenon arise in response to prevailing Christian views of Judaism, which, despite major theological reforms in the last half-century, still bear remnants of anti-Judaism and the historical legacy of antisemitism. However, in an effort to reject anti-Judaism and antisemitism, it at times walks along a close line with this history and dances with its shadow. Although this phenomenon is a reactionary response against antisemitism, it is not simply the polar opposite of antisemitism; rather, thriving in reaction to antisemitism, it is intricately and at times uncomfortably intertwined with it. As a direct reaction against a history of antisemitism, it swings toward philosemitism, and in doing so, it inevitably engages aspects of the tropes perpetuated by anti-Judaism. Through the process of constructing idealized notions of Jews, it at times reinforces essentializations of Jews not unrelated to those perpetuated by antisemitism. So while post-Holocaust Catholic philosemitism is often motivated by very good intentions—by recognition of the contribution of Christian theology to antisemitism, by a desire to atone and seek forgiveness, and by the search to more fully recognize the ways that Christianity is indebted to Judaism—it is still entangled in this troubled legacy of antisemitism, and when these impulses are expressed as philosemitism, they become linked, whether wittingly or unwittingly, with a legacy that has historically been very problematic.

PHILOSEMITISM AND ANTISEMITISM: A CLOSE RELATIONSHIP

The introduction to Karp and Sutcliffe's volume *Philosemitism in History* begins with a joke: "Q: Which is preferable—the antisemite or the philosemite? A: The antisemite. At least he isn't lying."[3] The dark humor of this joke points to the ambivalence with which philosemitism is received and the suspicion that philosemitism may be nothing more than an iteration of antisemitism.

No uncontested definition of philosemitism exists, but in his volume *Between Philosemitism and Antisemitism*, Alan Levenson defines it very broadly as "*any* pro-Jewish or pro-Judaic utterance or act."[4] A definition as broad as this one suggests that philosemitism is not always or only an expression of anti-antisemitism, nor is it necessarily bound to contexts in which antisemitism is prevalent. It can arise in any context and can arise from a variety of impulses, but it is rarely found in contexts in which antisemitism has not existed. It is generally reactive, and yet it does not always successfully disengage itself from antisemitism. As Levenson observes, "While antisemitism usually provided the first prompting of philosemitic sentiment, that does not mean that all philosemites liberated themselves from prejudices regarding Jews or Judaism."[5] Philosemitic tendencies often coexist with antisemitic ones not only in general cultural contexts where both are operative but even within the same person, for the two are tightly interwoven. Despite this complicated relationship, in the cases where the philosemitic impulses became dominant, Levenson argues that "we have a philosemite—even if antisemitism prejudices remained."[6]

Noting the blurred line between philosemitism and the rejection of antisemitism, Jonathan Judaken proposes that "anti-antisemitism" is a more accurate term for what is often called philosemitism. He argues that anti-antisemitism is a broader category than philosemitism and that it can be used to refer to any action that opposes antisemitism based on basic ethical attitudes. What is termed "philosemitism," in his appraisal, is often no more than anti-antisemitism, and he finds that this term better describes "the defenders of Jews and Judaism in contexts where they are under assault."[7] He argues that "the usage of 'philosemite' is often conflated with those who do not share a philosemitic viewpoint, but who commit to opposing antisemitism; frequently these are people who lack a profound understanding or appreciation of the history, culture, and religion of Jews. Anti-antisemitism more clearly denotes an opposition to prejudices and stereotypes related to Jews, Judaism, and Jewishness."[8]

The origin of philosemitism is disputed by scholars. Some argue that philosemitism can be found in ancient Greek and Roman culture, reflecting a notion of the distinctness of the Jewish people that came to be expressed in both philosemitic and antisemitic stereotypes in antiquity.[9] However, while philosemitic and antisemitic views preceded Christianity, the impact of the close historical relationship between Christianity and Judaism cannot be underestimated, and antisemitic and philosemitic phenomena developed in greater definition after the development of Christianity. Most scholars agree that philosemitism as a distinct worldview arose in a diverse range of contexts, though primarily European and primarily in the modern era.[10] Although the origins of philosemitism are disputed, each of the many theories regarding these origins points to the close relationship between philosemitism and antisemitism and to the impact of Christian theology in shaping cultural views of Jews.

In the nineteenth century, philosemitism was often viewed negatively even by those who were defined by others as philosemites. As Karp and Sutcliffe explain, "Almost all late nineteenth-century opponents of antisemitism strenuously sought to defend themselves from the charge of philosemitism, insisting instead that they regarded the Jews neutrally and were untainted by prejudice either for or against them."[11] This insistence on retaining a neutral, disinterested attitude toward Jews was fueled by the desire to stay far away from any essentializations of Jews. "This normalization of attitudes toward Jews," Karp and Sutcliffe continue, "has remained the aim of almost all liberal engagements in the field of Jewish–non-Jewish relations, both by Jews and by non-Jews, and from this dominant perspective philosemitism is almost always regarded as deeply suspicious, sharing with antisemitism a trafficking in distorted, exaggerated, and exceptionalist views of Jews and Judaism."¹²

One of the core traits of philosemitism is the tendency to view Jews as a distinct people bearing inherent traits that set them apart from all other people. The concept of the distinctiveness of Jews, in which they are seen as exceptional and essentialized, has been called "allosemitism," a term first coined by literary historian Artur Sandauer and later brought into discourse by Zygmunt Bauman. Whereas philosemitism denotes the love of Jews and antisemitism the hatred of Jews, allosemitism refers to "the practice of setting the Jews apart as people radically different from all the others, needing separate concepts to describe and comprehend them and special treatment in all or most social intercourse."¹³

This notion of the Jews as distinctive from other people is noncommittal, as Bauman puts it—that is, it does not clearly indicate either a positive or negative evaluation of Jews. Yet Bauman observes that this ambiguity holds within it the capacity for both love and hate and can lead to intensified expressions of either, easily taking the form of philosemitism or antisemitism: it "contains the seeds of both, and assures that whichever of the two appears, is intense and extreme."¹⁴

PHILOSEMITISM AND CONVERSION

Philosemitism has historically walked hand in hand with missionary efforts. This discomforting alliance can be traced to a central theological question that lies beneath Christian expressions of philosemitism. This question arises from the Christian belief that Jews have failed to recognize Jesus as the true messiah, and it asks how Christians are to make sense of Judaism theologically in light of this "refusal." This is particularly pressing for many Christian philosemitic views, which paradoxically idealize Jews while seeing Judaism as theologically errant.

In fact, this same question haunts both Christian philosemitism and antisemitism, as each attempts to assess the Jewish religious tradition in light of Christian truth claims. For the antisemite, the theological question takes the form of an accusation: Jews do not recognize Jesus as the messiah. For the philosemite, the question takes root in the tension between the essential Christian truth claim of the identity of Jesus as the messiah and the Christian philosemitic impulse to express adoration for a people who explicitly reject that Christian truth claim.

In the early development of Christianity, this particular issue served as the main point of division between Judaism and Christianity, when Christianity established itself as a distinct movement arising within Jewish circles and eventually claimed distinction as a separate religious movement. At the same time, rabbinic Judaism defined itself partially in contradistinction to this Christian claim. The result was that each tradition asserted its difference from the other largely on this one point. To this day, this issue of the identity of Jesus remains a point of distinction and tension between Christianity and Judaism, and it shadows philosemitic expressions with the suggestion of possible intentions to proselytize.

Implicit in the philosemitic view that sees Jews as spiritually elevated and bestowed with an important eschatological task is the belief that their ultimate goal will be reached with conversion to Christian faith; thus, missionary movements have often gone hand in hand with philosemitic movements.[15] The intention behind this proselytization—at least as interpreted by the philosemites—was to act out of love and care. Encouraging Jews to convert to Christianity was considered to be an act of compassion, saving Jews from suffering and guiding them to their true destiny.[16]

The problematic issues surrounding Christian efforts to convert Jews are innumerable, but ironically, one of these problems defeats the philosemitic impulse. Assuming that the philosemitic view ascribes at least some religious components to Jewish identity and does not view Jewishness as an exclusively ethnic category, the intention to convert Jews would then ultimately leave the philosemite with no object of adoration, for the Jewish object of philosemitism would be no longer Jewish but Christian. Quite simply, a "successful" mission would convert a Jew to a Christian, thereby erasing the object of philosemitic adoration.[17]

CONCLUSION

To what extent, then, is philosemitism essentially a practice of conceiving of Jews as a symbol of everything that is different from the norm, of everything that cannot be fit into a category of the known? Jean-Paul Sartre wrote, "If the Jew did not exist, the anti-Semite would invent him."[18] It is worth asking whether this claim could also rightfully be made of philosemitism—that is, "If the Jew did not exist, the philosemite would invent him." If philosemitism reinforces the otherness of Jews based on the exaltation of their supposed distinctiveness, perhaps then a mythical, idealized Jew would be invented (if none existed) to fit this role. If antisemitism is a scapegoating of Jews, in which fears and hatred of the other—or of anything or anyone different from oneself—are placed on the figure of the Jew, then we must ask if philosemitism functions in a similar way but is marked by adulation rather than hatred.

Is philosemitism, then, simply the same old wolf in a new set of sheep's clothing? To be able to conclusively answer this question, philosemitism would have to be a clearly defined phenomenon with enough homogeneity across its many manifestations to allow such a judgment to be made. This is particularly difficult to gauge in our contemporary time, without the benefit of hindsight. The major scholarly studies of philosemitism, such as those by Stern, Levenson, Rubinstein, Edelstein, and Karp and Sutcliffe, rarely address contexts beyond the immediate postwar period.[19] The conclusions reached by scholarship on philosemitic movements from earlier historical contexts do not always apply to philosemitism in contemporary contexts, and contemporary forms of philosemitism have received little scholarly attention, with the exception of research on the philosemitic aspects of Christian Zionism.[20]

Unlike antisemitism, which is a destructive impulse based on hatred, the value or harm of philosemitism depends on its context and specific form. As Frank Stern observes, "One cannot simply analyze philosemitic content and meanings in the sense of value orientations, analogous to the analysis of antisemitism. . . . The way in which place and function change have an impact on the relevance of philosemitism; i.e., philosemitism is a highly 'contextualized' social phenomenon."[21]

In the specific iteration of philosemitism that this book investigates, a distinct system of factors is at play. As Christians and as Westerners in Israel, the subjects of this study are doubly "other." They are not Jewish, they are not Palestinian, and they are not from the Middle East; they compose a minority within a minority on the outskirts of the society in which they live. They are not the dominant group looking at the foreign other; they themselves are the outsiders. They *are* the other. This context is vastly different than that of pre- or postwar Europe, and the philosemitism that results, regardless of how it is evaluated, is certainly more than simply allosemitism with a positive tone.

Although many efforts in Christian-Jewish dialogue today aim for the normalization of Jews, rejecting portrayals of Jews as distinctly different from other people, the phenomenon explored here exhibits an ambivalent relationship with normalization. On the one hand, arising from Western efforts in Christian-Jewish dialogue and reconciliation, it inherits the contemporary emphasis placed on normalized perceptions of Jews, rejecting all earlier stereotypes that portrayed Jews as inherently different from other people. Furthermore, set in the context of Israel, it sees Jews as the demographic majority and Judaism as the cultural norm. And yet on the other hand, many of the voices shared in the following chapters also express glorified or idealized notions of the Jewish people, reflecting a religiously shaped worldview that sees Jews as set apart from all others. This new Judeocentric Catholic phenomenon thus swings between a socially conscious desire for normalization informed by secular cultural ideals and a philosemitism based on a biblically inspired vision of the uniqueness of the Jewish people.

CHAPTER 3

Christian Constructions of the Jew

THE MYTHOLOGIZATION OF THE JEWISH PEOPLE

"They support the hope for the world," Sr. Marie Yeshua says, sitting beneath the tall trees of the monastery garden. Sheltered within the high stone walls of the monastery, in the garden the sounds of the city are muffled, and pine needles and palm fronds whisper and rustle in the breeze. But outside, Jerusalem roars with heat and noise, cars honking and radios blaring and voices raised in argument under the dusty haze of the city. "The Jewish people are like a laboratory with all the hope of the world."

In the hills to the west of Jerusalem, Fr. Jacques's face is alight with energy as he sits by the lavender beds in the garden of his monastery. "Living with Jews sort of breaks your own culture—it opens it. In a way, it makes it burst out, and then you have all the pieces of the puzzle, and you are then free to recompose the puzzle." He leans forward, eagerly searching for the precise words. "This is the way the existence of Israel is working in the world."

On a quiet street in Rehavia, a residential neighborhood in central Jerusalem, Sr. Carmen looks out of her kitchen window. "Living here is providential because I breathe the same air that the Jewish people breathe."

These are lofty visions of the Jewish people. They portray the Jewish people as a laboratory for the cultivation of hope, sustaining the hope of all the world; they are a force that breaks through the embedded patterns of life, causing a reawakening in those whose worldview has been shattered and rebuilt through the encounter with them; they are the blessed ones whose presence infuses the very air with grace. These glorified portrayals beg a question: To whom, precisely, do these visions of the Jewish people refer?

This chapter investigates Christian constructions of the notion of the Jewish people, asking to whom or what the phrase "the Jewish people" refers when viewed through Christian lenses and shaped by the Christian imagination. It asks if the concept of the Jewish people in Christian understanding is seen as a relic of the biblical past and as a nearly mythological concept. It also examines the extent to which the notion of the Jewish people becomes, through Christian eyes, a biblically shaped projection of Christian self-understanding in relation to Judaism, reflecting a specifically Christian vision of salvation history.

THE NOTION OF THE JEWISH PEOPLE

The concept of the Jewish people is not easily defined, but across its many definitions, it is generally understood to involve the categories of both religion and nationality or peoplehood. By this understanding, common to the Jewish people across its many geographically, culturally, and religiously diverse expressions are shared religious traditions and values and a notion of the unity of the Jewish people. Unlike most of the so-called world religions, Judaism has an ethnic component as well as the collection of beliefs and rituals that generally defines a religion. The concept of the Jewish people, therefore, is integral to Judaism, and it incorporates this ethnic dimension into what are more traditionally considered to be religious dimensions, such as belief and ritual.

The challenges of defining the concept of the Jewish people can be expressed as two questions, each referring to a different aspect of the challenge: the first asks "Who is a Jew?" and the second asks "Who are the Jewish people?" When the question concerns individual Jewish identity, the issue has both genealogical and religious components. These include issues of maternal heritage, biological descent, conversion, apostasy, and the tension between the halachic determination of a Jew and the Israeli legal understanding.[1] Although the halachic definition of a Jew is clearly demarcated, there are still many debates about the parameters of Jewish identity. Many factors complicate the determination of Jewish identity, including people born to religiously mixed families, Jewish converts to other religions, converts to Judaism, secularism and assimilation, adoption, and a host of other factors. In short, determining Jewish identity and the concept of the Jewish people in today's world is anything but clear.[2]

However, the central question at stake in this chapter is not "Who is a Jew?"; rather, the question raised here asks "To whom does the notion of the Jewish people as a collectivity refer?" "The Jewish people" is not the same as the plural of a Jewish person, and it is a reflection of the particular nature of Judaism as a peoplehood.

The concept of the Jewish people has not escaped critique, questioning, and challenges for revision. It was controversially deconstructed in Shlomo Sand's *The Invention of the Jewish People*, which attempts to disprove the notion that there is any truth to a historical Jewish people. His book has been widely discredited, yet the intentionally incendiary publication remains popular. In contrast to claims such as Sand's, however, the majority of scholars of Judaism are adamant about the centrality of the concept of the Jewish people to Judaism. As Adin Steinsaltz claims, "Jewish peoplehood is always central. It comes before the Jewish nation or the Jewish state. We live in modern times, but our peoplehood is still essential, primitive. We never ceased to be a clan or tribe."[3]

To explain the centrality of this peoplehood to Jewish tradition, Meir Soloveichik rhetorically asks, "Why, in Judaism, *must* the political be bound up with the religious? Why cannot one observe the commandments of the Torah without associating oneself with a particular people? Why did God elect a nation, rather than a universal movement?"[4] He answers these questions by describing the familial nature of Judaism as "a blood community: a Jew is not only the coreligionist, or the fellow citizen, of all other Jews, he is their sibling. The nation that God chose is a physical family, and Jews are joined first and foremost by their common descent from Abraham and Sarah. The election of Abraham was a carnal election, and the resultant bonds of blood link Jews eternally, demanding that they do everything in their power to perpetuate their family."[5] For Jacob Neusner, the significance of the Jewish people as a whole is greater than the sum of its parts. He asserts, "The Jewish people is my homeland." Continuing, he clarifies, "This is not a social datum nor a political assertion. It is an affirmation of Jewish peoplehood. We Jews form a unique entity, neither wholly a nation, though part of us constitute a nation, nor wholly a religion, though part of us share a common faith, and all of us derive from that faith."[6]

THE JEWISH PEOPLE THROUGH A CHRISTIAN BIBLICAL FRAME

From a Christian perspective, the notion of the Jewish people is often understood in the biblical sense—that is, as the chosen people whose narrative is told in the Hebrew Bible and continued in the New Testament. When the concept of the Jewish people is understood by Christians in this biblical sense, a definitive historical parameter is established, reaching only as far as the years that the biblical narrative encompasses—namely, only to the Jewish people prior to and up until the time of Jesus. This includes the time range of ancient Judaism up through Second Temple Judaism and leaves out two thousand years of rabbinic Judaism.

When this biblical historical parameter is used, the representation of Judaism and the Jewish people ends precisely with the end of the life of Jesus and the beginning of early Christianity. This means that when "the Jewish people" is understood from a Christian biblical perspective, it is seen in relation to Jesus: first as a precursor to the birth of Jesus and then as a people who encountered—and, crucially, rejected—the person Christianity recognizes as the messiah. Thus the Christian biblical view sees the history of the Jewish people to come to a quick end with their rejection of Jesus as the messiah.

In the biblical narrative, this Jewish encounter with the messiah is portrayed as collective—that is, Jesus came first to the Jews, and not just to the Jews who happened to live in the Galilee and Jerusalem at that time but to the Jews as a whole. With this encounter, from the perspective of Christian history, the Jewish people were faced with the choice of accepting or rejecting the messiah. The distinction that has often been lost in centuries of interpretations of the New Testament, however, is that nearly all the people featured in the New Testament were Jews; it is a Jewish story of Jewish people doing Jewish things. The places in the biblical text where the authors of the New

Testament chose to identify people as Jews, however, are primarily in the cases of those who did not believe that Jesus was the messiah, particularly in the Gospels. The first people to begin following Jesus and preaching about him were also Jews, but the biblical text does not generally identify them as such. In this way, the New Testament usage of the term "Jew" became an accusatory label; although nearly every character and biblical author was a Jew, the identification of Jewishness was often reserved for those who did not believe in Jesus.

In short, if the concept of the Jewish people is understood as a biblical concept from a Christian perspective, then the Jewish people are understood not on their own terms but in relation to Jesus and to Christianity, reduced and instrumentalized as part of the Christian historical narrative. In this process, the notion of the Jewish people is seen through the colored lenses of a distinctly Christocentric worldview. Through these lenses, the Jewish people are framed as a relic of antiquity, a wayward people who failed to recognize the messiah, and as a peoplehood whose existence is closer to myth than to mundane reality.

In many cases, Christians use the biblical term "Israel" to refer to the Jewish people, which casts the Jewish people as characters in the biblical narrative. In addition, the use of the term "Israel" to refer to the Jewish people is a particularly loaded statement today, and has been since 1948, for it intentionally transfers the meaning away from the contemporary State of Israel, placing it back in a biblical frame. In many cases, this Christian usage of "Israel" is also accompanied by the choice to refer to the State of Israel as the "Holy Land." This results in an intentional elision of the existence of the State of Israel, subsuming it within the Christian concept of the Holy Land. While many Christians claim that this choice of terminology is intended to bypass political issues, favoring a "universal" religious concept, the result is the linguistic erasure of the nation. When these terms are used this way, the Jewish people are placed in a biblical framework, and at the same time, the State of Israel is replaced by a Christian concept, for the term the "Holy Land" is primarily used in Christian contexts despite the ancient Jewish origin of the concept of the sanctity of the land.

All of this contributes to a mythologization of Jews and Judaism, intentionally viewing the Jewish people through the lens of a biblical category divorced from the contemporary context. This is reminiscent of Edward Said's notion of Orientalism, but in this iteration, it is Jews who are portrayed as the exoticized other.[7] However, rather ironically, in Christian thought Jews and Judaism are rarely portrayed as *fully* other or as entirely distinct from Christianity; to the contrary, they are often portrayed as just one aspect of a sweeping Christian narrative.

SEEING THROUGH A CHRISTIAN WORLDVIEW

We return now to the central questions: Who are the Jewish people in the Christian imagination and through Christian interpretation? Is the concept of the Jewish people in Christian understanding seen as a kind of myth developed in the biblical narrative and existing today as a relic? Through Christian eyes, are the Jewish people interpreted through a Christian vision of salvation history, and in this way, are the Jewish people seen primarily as a reflection of Christian self-understanding? An immediate answer must conclude that yes, these representations—or misrepresentations, from a Jewish perspective—have historically occurred and continue to occur. Yet more recent progress indicates that Christians are finally moving away, slowly but surely, from these patterns.

The answers to these questions are multifaceted. On one hand, the concept of the Jewish people, as interpreted by the Christians in this study, is not primarily an abstraction or a myth, nor a projection of Christian self-understanding. Rather, it is informed by a deep understanding of Jews and Judaism developed over years of living in Israel and studying Judaism. However, while it is not *primarily* any of these, it does contain aspects of these tropes, and it reflects the influence of a comprehensive Christian religious worldview. In this way, the conclusion is twofold: these perceptions are both remarkably freed from the entrenched Christian vision of Jews as a nearly mythical biblical people and shaped to some extent by this very same influence.

If this Judeocentric Catholic phenomenon were developed elsewhere, in a place that was primarily Christian, it might be reasonable to conclude that a love for the Jewish people might be directed toward an idealized abstraction of Jews drawn from the biblical narrative. However, the phenomenon explored in this study is contextually grounded in Israel, where the subjects are immersed in Israeli life, even those who live in enclosed monasteries. For one who lives in Israel, accustomed to regular interactions and immersion into Jewish Israeli culture, the Jewish people cannot be seen as an abstraction. Even for one who lives in a monastery, daily life in Israel does not allow an abstracted idea of the Jewish people to persist without being altered or broken open by the very human reality all around. As expressed by Sr. Pilar, one of the nuns whose reflections are shared in the following pages, "When you live abroad, when you live in Europe and I suppose in America, it's the same: you have the Palestinians and the Jews. But here, they are not the Palestinians and the Jews; they are Yohanan, Sara, Yosef, Muhammad. They are people that you know. . . . They are not Jews and Palestinians; they are normal people with a face, with a history, with a family, with kids. It's totally another thing; it's not abstract. [They're] real, concrete people."

The majority of those whose views are shared in this book say that their perspectives on the Jewish people were developed in Israel and not trans-planted unchanged from other contexts. Even those who came to Israel inspired by their love for Judaism found that it grew deeper and more nuanced after years of living in the country. Yet despite the contextual nature of this phenomenon, which suggests an understanding of the Jewish people that was developed and concretized in contemporary Jewish life, a certain degree of the myth seems to still remain. For a Christian whose life is shaped by religious vows and the practice of Christian faith, a Christian worldview is inherent. Christian faith is not merely a belief set or a series practices; it also incorporates a comprehensive worldview that interprets the shape and meaning of life, from creation to the eschaton, based on the Christian narrative of salvation history. It follows that a Christian love for the Jewish people, even if this includes the Christian's friends and neighbors, is also a love for an idea, or a mythical concept shaped by the biblical narrative.

The notion of the Jewish people, when interpreted through Christian eyes, inevitably involves a reframing, viewing Jews through the lenses of Christian theology. Even with the best of intentions, perceptions of Jews as "other" inevitably recast Jewishness in a Christian frame that is far removed from Jewish self-understanding. Interpreting the other through the categories of one's own experience and understanding is a fundamental hermeneutical problem intrinsic to all encounters between the self and other. However, although this process is an inevitable part of interpreting the other, it is not to be equated with the distortions of Jews seen in antisem-itism and some extreme forms of philosemitism. Reflexive interpretations of the other are unavoidable; distortions and stereotyped characterizations are not.

Through this inevitable interpretative process, the distinctiveness of the Jewish people can at times be flattened, consuming and annihilating Jewish difference within a Christian vision. "The Jew" remains an image constructed of myth and characterized by otherness. And yet it is no longer the centuries-old image portrayed by the well-worn tropes of antisemitism, marked by notions of deicide and negative stereotypes such as carnality and greed. In the wake of the Holocaust and after the theological reforms of the mid-twentieth century, the Christian imagination is now more likely to construct "the Jew" as a noble victim and as a member of God's chosen people, persecuted and at the same time endowed with spiritual gifts. The image has been drastically revised, its symbols turned around, and yet the process of typological construction continues.

And so what or who, then, are the Jewish people seen through Judeo-centric Christian lenses? They are seen as both abstract and concrete, both biblical and contemporary, both mythical and a part of the messy reality of everyday life.

CHAPTER 4

Christian Responses to Israel

CHRISTIAN POPULATIONS IN ISRAEL AND THE PALESTINIAN TERRITORIES

This new form of Judeocentric Catholicism is situated within the complex and unique socioreligious context of Israel, in which Christian-Jewish relations take on distinct forms. Of the many forms of Christian engagement with Judaism and the Jewish people in Israel and the Palestinian territories, a few polarized paradigms are dominant. These paradigms tend to apply theological interpretations of the land, people, and biblical narrative to political contexts, linking theological agendas with support for political movements. This is seen in pro-Palestinian theological movements on one end and in largely evangelical pro-Israel movements on the other end. The Judeocentric phenomenon explored here, while closer to the latter than the former, does not entirely align with the views of either of these poles. However, to situate it within its cultural and religious context, this chapter examines these polarized movements, addressing issues of nationalism, cultural affiliation, and solidarity. Thus it provides a necessary contextual backdrop to the Judeocentric Catholic phenomenon by examining very different forms of Christian responses to Jews, Judaism, and the State of Israel that coexist alongside this lesser-known phenomenon.

Although Christians comprise a religious majority in worldwide statistics, within Israel and the Palestinian territories, they compose less than 2 percent of the overall population.[1] In the State of Israel, Christians are a small religious minority within a Jewish majority, and in the Palestinian territories, Christians are a minority within a Muslim majority. In Israel, the power dynamic between Christians and Jews is now the opposite of what it had been for many centuries in Europe, with Judaism serving as the dominant religious tradition in culture and politics. This marks a drastic reversal of power relations, and prior to the establishment of the State of Israel in 1948, Jewish sovereignty in Israel had never existed contemporaneously with the Christian religion.

However, most Christians in Israel and the Palestinian territories do not experience this as a role reversal in the same way as European Christians would, for most of the local Christian populations have roots not in Europe but in the Middle East. Since the introduction of Islam in the seventh century, Middle Eastern Christians have not shared the position of Christians in the West, who have historically been the religious majority in relation to a Jewish minority. Rather, for centuries Christians in the Middle East have been a part of a religious demographic reminiscent of the current one and have lived as minority communities in the midst of primarily Muslim societies.

The Christian communities of Israel and the Palestinian territories are composed primarily of Arab Christians native to the land, who often self-identify as Palestinian. The term "Palestinian Christian" is generally used to refer to all Christian people native to the land, including those who today are either Arab Christians with Israeli citizenship or Christian residents of the Palestinian territories.[2] The terms "local Christians" or "indigenous Christians" are also often used, emphasizing the embeddedness and historicity of this population in the region.[3] In recent years, there has also been a dramatic increase in non-Arab lay Christians in the area, primarily composed of migrants seeking employment in Israel.

However, in addition to these local communities, there are also many Christian populations from around the world who have established a long-standing presence in Jerusalem. The Armenian community is a notable example, having maintained a presence in Jerusalem since the fifth century. A number of international Catholic and Orthodox religious orders have also been established in Jerusalem and the surrounding area for many years, and

although they practice celibacy and therefore have not established a genealogical heritage in the land, many have maintained an ongoing presence, such
as the Franciscans, who have held the office of the Custody of the Holy Land
since the thirteenth century. Israel and the Palestinian territories are also
home to a sizable population of Christian clergy, nuns, and monks from all
areas of the world who come to live and work within Christian communities
that are primarily centered in Jerusalem as well as the Christian pilgrimage
cities of Bethlehem and Nazareth.

PALESTINIAN CHRISTIAN THEOLOGIES AND CHRISTIAN-JEWISH RELATIONS

In Israel, religious relations between Palestinian Christians and Jews are
inextricably linked with national affiliations and characterized by conflict.
The position of Palestinian Christians in Israel is described succinctly in the
document "Reflections on the Presence of the Church in the Holy Land,"
released by the Latin Patriarchate of Jerusalem in 2003: "Our contemporary
context is unique: we are the only Local Church that encounters the Jewish
people in a State that is defined as Jewish and where the Jews are the dominant and empowered majority, a reality that dates from 1948. Furthermore,
the ongoing conflict between the State of Israel and the Arab world, and in
particular between Israelis and Palestinians, means that the national identity
of the majority of our faithful is locked in conflict with the national identity
of the majority of the Jews."[4] David Neuhaus, the former patriarchal vicar
for Hebrew Speaking Catholics in Israel, describes the situation in more
direct terms, pointing to the highly charged perspectives of Jews common
in Palestinian contexts: "A degree of animosity toward Jews is common
among Arab Christians in Israel. . . . Jews are not generally perceived as the
victims of centuries of marginalization and even persecution but rather as
the face of a problematic political reality, the State of Israel, with the added
complexity of the continuing occupation of Palestinian lands."[5]
    In a list of significant factors that contribute to the distinctiveness of
Christian-Jewish relations in Israel, as well as in the Middle East in general,
Neuhaus first cites the non-European, non-Christian context of Israeli culture and the reversal of power relations it entails. The impact of this context
becomes particularly evident when viewed in contrast to Christian-Jewish

dialogue in the West, which usually addresses historical relations in situations in which Christians are the dominant population—culturally, religiously, and politically. While in European contexts the Holocaust often serves as the central event focusing Christian-Jewish dialogue, in Israel and the Palestinian territories, the Israeli-Palestinian conflict is at the center of dialogue between local Christians and Jews.[6] Another factor influencing the state of Jewish-Christian relations and dialogue is the fact that for many local Christians in Israel and the Palestinian territories, interreligious dialogue with Muslims, rather than Jews, is seen as a priority, as Palestinian Christians are linguistically and culturally a part of the same community as Palestinian Muslims.[7] Intensifying the strain between Palestinian Christians and Israeli Jews is the fact that many Palestinian Christians, living among Muslims, rarely encounter Jews. This is the case throughout the Palestinian territories, where Jews are generally not seen at all except as soldiers or as residents of Israeli settlements in highly charged contexts that are not conducive to dialogue. Finally, Neuhaus points to the unique role that the Bible takes on in relations between Israeli Jews and Palestinian Christians. Although the Hebrew Bible serves as a shared scriptural text between Christians and Jews, in Israel and the Palestinian territories, this shared heritage rarely serves as a basis for mutual understanding. In this context, readings of the Bible are often complicated by the use of biblical interpretation in political ideologies, particularly regarding the political application of the passages on the promise of the land to the Jewish people, which many Palestinian Christians feel have been used to alienate them from their homeland.[8]

The unique social and theological context of Palestinian Christians in Israel and the Palestinian territories has led to the formulation of a specifically Palestinian Christian theological movement spearheaded by theologians such as Naim Ateek, Mitri Raheb, and Yohanna Katanacho and expressed in events such as a biennial Christ at the Checkpoint conference hosted by Bethlehem Bible College.[9] The Palestinian social context has also given rise to a sympathetic theological movement arising out of a Western context, which sees itself as expressing solidarity with Palestinian Christians. Both the local Palestinian and Western theological movements have developed interpretations of Christian social justice teachings that focus on political activism in support of Palestinian rights. These theologies see Palestinian Christians as the "living stones" of Jesus and emblematic of the marginalized and oppressed. This movement creates theologies of liberation that are highly politicized, often framing Palestinians and Israeli Jews as victims and aggressors, respectively.[10] As Fr. Jamal Khader, rector of the Latin Patriarchate seminary in Beit Jala, expresses it, "For the Palestinians, Jews are now the Zionists of the State of Israel who occupied our land and control our lives with a military occupation."[11] These theologies often reflect the current political tensions in statements that portray Israelis—and by suggestion, Jews—as the enemy. This results in claims that, while perhaps intended primarily as anti-Zionist declarations, often slide into anti-Jewish rhetoric.

Pro-Palestinian Christian theologians have often accused European and American traditions of Jewish-Christian dialogue of favoring Zionist perspectives and, in extension, of being complicit in the oppression of Palestinians. For example, Michael Prior asserts that Christian-Jewish dialogue reflects "vested political interests, a certain myopia with respect to historical facts, and a lack of moral engagement with realities" and is, in essence, a "monologue in two voices."[12] Following a similar argument, Rosemary Radford Reuther claims that Christian post-Holocaust theology leads to a "guilt and repentance argument" and "demands repentance in the form of unstinting support for Israel." Adopting a totalizing line of argumentation, she continues, "The repentance argument typically takes the form of a devastating rebuttal of any effort by Christians who are aware of injustice to the Palestinians and seek to criticize Israel."[13] These statements reflect the unfortunate polarization of interreligious relations and views of attempts at reconciliation, and most participants in Jewish-Christian dialogue and post-Holocaust theologians would firmly disavow the accusations made by Prior and Reuther.

This perspective is also evident in the Kairos Document, an ecumenical document released in 2009 by the movement Kairos Palestine, signed by the heads of the major local churches of the Holy Land and authored by a commission of Palestinian Christian theologians.[14] The Kairos Document presents the political struggle of Palestinians in a theological perspective, offering religious readings on both religious and secular issues related to the conflict. The document criticizes "certain theologians in the West" who "try to attach a biblical and theological legitimacy to the infringement of our rights," referring to the biblical narratives of the land promise and to theologies that implicitly or explicitly support Zionism through the interpretations of these verses. In an impassioned tone, the document continues, "Thus, the promises, according to their interpretation, have become a menace to our very existence. The 'good news' in the Gospel itself has become 'a harbinger of death' for us."[15]

The distinction between the State of Israel and the Jewish people is a challenging point in relations between Palestinian Christians and Jews. While the authors of the Kairos Document make efforts to not confuse three distinct categories—the religion of Judaism, the Jewish people, and the State of Israel—these categories are closely related, and despite their efforts to keep them distinct, the categories blend in this document. For example, the document criticizes Israeli political action through the use of the theological categories of "evil" and "sin": "The aggression against the Palestinian people which is the Israeli occupation, is an evil that must be resisted. It is an evil and a sin that must be resisted and removed."[16] By using theological categories to describe political contexts, the language elides the distinction between the political and religious and, in this case, between the State of Israel and the Jewish people.

The murkiness of the distinction among the Jewish people, the religion of Judaism, and the State of Israel is also seen in the work of the Palestinian theologian Mitri Raheb, who claims, "As Palestinians, we have nothing against Jews for being Jews. But we do have something against them insofar as they are an alien occupation force in the West Bank and Gaza who suppress us and occupy our land against our will."[17] Although Raheb frames this statement as an assertion of the distinction he draws between Jewish people and the State of Israel, in effect, he then collapses the distinction. Elsewhere in this passage, Raheb attempts to disavow antisemitism, stating that it is a "racist ideology," but in his decision to refer to the occupying force as "Jews" rather than as the Israeli military, he effectively eliminates the distinction between anti-Zionism and anti-Judaism.

The merging of anti-Zionist views with anti-Jewish views, whether intentional or not, often occurs in the context of the Israeli-Palestinian conflict when "Israeli" is confused with "Jewish" and vice versa. Another example of this allusion is found in a statement entitled "The Year of Painful Memories," published by Kairos Palestine in 2017 on the occasion of the fiftieth anniversary of the Six-Day War.[18] The statement is a letter in five parts, and each part is addressed to a different audience: "1) To ourselves, we as Palestinians say . . . 2) To the extreme right-wing Israelis who reject peace, we say . . . 3) To Christians we say . . . 4) To the Muslims we say . . . 5) To the international community we say . . ." The document's choice of categories is telling. It addresses its own

Palestinian community, the international community, and the three Abrahamic religions that share the land. However, in place of what would be an address to Jews if the categories were consistent, there is only an address to so-called peace-rejecting Israeli extremists, in effect replacing the concept of Jews as members of one of the three Abrahamic faiths with this characterization.

Many Palestinian Christian views of Jews evidence an intentional distancing from any association with the long history of Christian antisemitism, which they identify as a specifically European legacy. As a result, most of the Palestinian Christian population denies any sense of communal responsibility not only for the Holocaust but also for the legacy of Christian antisemitism in general.[19] Given that reflections on the Holocaust often serve as the historical focal point of Christian-Jewish dialogue in the West, the insistence of Palestinian Christian communities on their nonculpability for the history of Christian anti-Judaism marks a major distinction between Christian-Jewish relations in Western and Middle Eastern contexts. For many Palestinian Christians, the Holocaust is remembered not as a tragedy in which the church as a whole was implicated in any way but rather as a tragedy whose roots lie in another culture. While the document "Reflections on the Presence of the Church in the Holy Land" by former Latin Patriarch Michel Sabbah concedes that "with the entire Church, we regret the attitudes of contempt, the conflicts and the hostility that have marked the history of Jewish-Christian relations," the General Pastoral Plan, released only two years earlier and also under the oversight of Sabbah, reiterates the insistence on a lack of responsibility for the Holocaust. The latter document recognizes the tragedy of the Holocaust but immediately reminds the reader that "the people of our countries were not party to this."[20]

Reflecting this view, Khader remarks, "As horrible as the Holocaust was, it is not part of our history as Palestinians; we suffered indirectly from the consequences, as victims of the victims of the Holocaust."[21] Khader expresses a significant perspective held by many Palestinian Christians: not only do they refuse any communal accountability as Christians for the Holocaust, but they also feel that they have been victimized by its aftermath. His claim to be a part of the "victims of the victims" recasts the Jewish survivors of the Holocaust as perpetrators. Perspectives such as these indicate the extent to which Christian-Jewish relations in Israel and the Palestinian territories are fraught on religious and political levels, for the fundamental collective memories of each religious community have been recast by the other; where each community understands itself as an innocent victim, the other can see it as the perpetrator.

CHRISTIAN ZIONISM AND CHRISTIAN-JEWISH RELATIONS

Within the spectrum of Christian forms of engagement with Jews and Judaism in Israel and the Palestinian territories, Christian Zionist theologies occupy a position that is nearly opposite to that of pro-Palestinian Christian theologies. Each movement has developed distinct theological views arising from essentially opposing interpretations of political situations, and each holds a unique perspective and approach to Christian-Jewish relations. While Palestinian Christian theologies are developed in the midst of a political conflict that is linked to religious and ethnic identities, Christian Zionist perspectives can arise from a number of social contexts but are primarily associated with evangelical Protestants from the United States, whose theologies are mapped onto pro-Israeli political views.

Today, the term "Christian Zionism" generally refers to evangelical support for the State of Israel, involving views that are informed by literal interpretations of biblical literature. However, in earlier iterations, prior to 1948, the term referred to any form of Christian support for the notion of a Jewish state in Palestine.[22] The phenomenon today encompasses a wide range of views, and the Christian perspectives that can be classified as Christian Zionist join together in a few organizations that cross denominational lines, such as the International Christian Embassy of Jerusalem (ICEJ).

Most expressions of Christian Zionism fall within the spectrum of evangelical Protestant Christianity. Evangelicalism tends toward fundamentalist and literalist interpretations, understanding the Bible to be inerrant and revelatory for the contemporary world, prophesying and revealing its truths in current and future events.[23] Christian Zionists may be distinguished from other evangelicals by their interpretations of the State of Israel and the Jewish people. They ascribe a vigorous theological significance to both— specifically to the "ingathering" of Jews to the land of Israel. Most Christian Zionists see the return of the Jewish people to the land to be a significant part of a Christian eschatological vision and consequently express staunch political support for the State of Israel.

Christian Zionism is often portrayed by its critics as being "prophecy-focused, rather obsessed with Armageddon, essentially political, somehow vaguely sinister, and more or less synonymous with premillennial dispensationalism."[24] These representations paint it with broad strokes, portraying it as a cultlike movement preoccupied with apocalyptic prophecies. While some of these traits are indeed exemplified by many Christian Zionists, the movement as a whole is not uniform in regard to these issues. Some scholars argue that the emphasis on premillennial dispensationalism is exaggerated, suggesting that the movement is less wedded to a specific vision of dramatic end-time events than many suspect it is, and the ICEJ has officially distanced itself from dispensationalism, claiming its teaching to be erroneous.[25] Faydra Shapiro argues that this apocalyptic emphasis is indeed exaggerated, as reflected by the data from her fieldwork, in which her informants explain their Christian Zionism based on a broader range of beliefs than the specific end-time prophecies of dispensationalism.[26]

The Christian Zionist adoration of Jews, however, generally does not extend to the religion of Judaism. It sees Jews as God's chosen people and a blessing to the world and yet as imperfect and incomplete in their faith. Through Christian Zionist eyes, as long as Jews remain Jews, they remain ultimately imperfect. Yaakov Ariel notes that despite "unprecedented devotion toward the Jews as God's chosen people," and despite sizable support to assist Jewish communities and individual Jews, Christian Zionists remain critical of Judaism as a religion. The only acceptable purpose of the existence of Judaism today, according to many Christian Zionists, Ariel explains, is to help pave the way for the return of Jesus: "For the most part, evangelicals have rejected Jewish religious liturgy, piety, and biblical exegesis, except as a means to keep the Jews oriented toward the eventual arrival of the messiah, and they have remained confident that the Jews will eventually come to recognize Jesus as their Lord and savior."[27] In this way, the continuity between the Jewish people and the Jewish religion is severed in much Christian Zionist thought, which favors the former while seeing the latter as imperfect at best—as a misguided religion that fails to follow God's will.[28] Nevertheless, biblical Judaism holds a special status in much Christian Zionist thought. Whereas rabbinic Judaism is generally portrayed as flawed, the ancient Judaism presented in the Hebrew Bible is seen as the ideal of Jewish life.[29] Yet even this idealization of ancient Judaism is ultimately an expression of the superiority of Christianity, for it is based on the notion that this is the kind of Judaism that Jesus practiced.

Unlike developments in many liberal Christian denominations that have led to theologies that respect the ongoing covenantal validity of Judaism, the Christian Zionist insistence that Judaism as a religion is flawed and incomplete can be generally categorized as supersessionism. It is based on the notion that Christianity superseded Judaism and presents the final truth that Judaism failed to reach, consequently invalidating earlier Jewish teaching. However, supersessionism, in most Christian Zionist thinking, is a grave error, as it is responsible for antisemitism. As Shapiro observes, most Christian Zionists do not understand their own beliefs to be supersessionist. Rather, she claims, "Christian Zionism sets itself up as the lonely, stalwart defender of the Jews as God's eternal chosen people, in contrast to those other 'Christians' who would see Jews replaced with the church as the new Israel and heir to God's promises."[30]

One of the basic beliefs common across the range of expressions of Christian Zionism is that Jesus is the messiah and savior of all and that failure to believe in Jesus as the messiah is a sin. The perfection of a Jew, along this line of thought, is a Jew who believes in Jesus, and thus the desire for Jewish conversion to belief in Jesus remains implicit in most Christian Zionist thought.[31] This is the case across the spectrum of Christian Zionism, and it is even more pronounced in those whose faith is heavily eschatological, focusing on the return of Jesus and the conversion of Jews.[32]

In many cases, support of Zionism and the evangelism of Jews are linked together in Christian Zionist thought and practice. Often the same people are engaged in both activities simultaneously, and these two undertakings are inseparable for some organizations, such as the American Messianic Fellowship and the Friends of Israel.[33] This is surprisingly unproblematic for some Jewish communities interested in receiving support from Christian Zionists. Indeed, the most enthusiastic Jewish supporters of Christian Zionist activities in Israel tend to be members of the nationalist-religious movement, and in their support of Christian Zionism, they might either not fully perceive the Christian Zionist interest in evangelism or willfully ignore it.[34] However, some Christian Zionist organizations, most notably the ICEJ, explicitly state that they do not engage in any missionary activities in Israel even though they still hold to the belief that the recognition of Jesus as the messiah is necessary for all people, including Jews. The choice to abstain from missionary activity in Israel is likely a public relations decision more than an expression of religious conviction or respect for Judaism, for such organizations would be unlikely to be welcomed in Israel if they engaged openly in evangelization. Many do not see the attempt to convert Jews in Israel as their personal responsibility based on the idea that "it is ultimately unnecessary since the Jews will in any case realize that Jesus is the Messiah at some point in the eschatological future."[35]

Despite the Christian Zionist critique of Judaism as a religion, the movement has engaged in countless social and political activities intended to assist Jews, marking a radical change from earlier Christian oppression and condemnation of Jews. Ariel lists just some of the "paradoxes and anomalies" that mark this complicated relationship, noting that they have "consistently expressed hopes for the redemption of the Jews" while they have also shown "concern over the well-being of the Jews and have at times tried to protect communities of Jews from persecution." Many Christian Zionists, he notes, "have devoted years of their lives to evangelizing Jews, considering their work to be a sign of goodwill and dedication," and "have lent their support throughout the last century to Jewish public causes, such as facilitating Jews' emigration from countries in which they had been persecuted."[36] In short, the relationship of Christian Zionism to Jews and Judaism is complicated and paradoxical, and Christian Zionists are often as passionately dedicated to assisting and serving the Jewish people as they are to the desire for Jewish conversion.

The Judeocentric Catholic phenomenon explored in this book is notably different than the philosemitism expressed in Christian Zionism. A brief summary of the many differences sees that whereas Christian Zionism is evangelical and theologically fundamentalist, this phenomenon is Catholic and more theologically progressive, particularly regarding methods of biblical interpretation and soteriology. Second, Christian Zionism is characterized by explicit support for the State of Israel; in contrast, while many in the phenomenon explored here express a sense of connection to and solidarity with the Jewish people, it is not equated with an uncritical allegiance to the State of Israel. Third, Christian Zionism's support of Israel is motivated by the expectation of the fulfillment of end-time prophecies, which include the conversion of Jews to Christianity. In contrast, those involved in the phenomenon at the center of this book avoid linking eschatological expectation to political situations and reject the historical tradition of the Christian desire for Jewish conversion to Christianity, maintaining instead that Judaism's ongoing validity is unquestioned as a religion and a people in an unbroken covenant.

MESSIANIC JUDAISM

Yet another form of Christian relationship with Jews and Judaism in Israel arises in the context of Jews who have developed a belief in Jesus. These Jewish believers do not always formally convert to a Christian denomination, nor do they in all cases consider themselves to be Christian. While some convert to established Christian denominations, others choose to be identified as Messianic Jews, a religious movement that incorporates aspects of Jewish tradition into an evangelical Christian faith.

Although there have been instances of Jewish conversion to Christianity for centuries and in many different contexts, Messianic Judaism is different from Jewish conversion to mainline Christianity and maintains a distinctively Jewish identity through a variety of practices carried over from Judaism.[37] Messianic Judaism is closely aligned with evangelical Christianity and shares the basic beliefs of evangelicalism, such as belief in biblical authority, the divinity of Jesus, the Trinity, eternal life, the threat of damnation, and the imperative to evangelize. It generally embraces evangelical ways of reading the Bible, tending toward literalism, and also shares the emphasis on being born again through an experience of personal conversion. What sets it apart from evangelicals is primarily the desire to maintain elements of Jewish tradition and identity.[38] The degree to which Messianic Jewish congregations maintain aspects of Jewish tradition varies greatly and can include the wearing of a *tallit* and *kippah* and the celebration of Jewish holidays such as Passover, Sukkot, and Yom Kippur. These traditions are altered and adapted to serve liturgical celebrations aimed at the worship of Jesus.

However, Messianic congregations are also home to many non-Jews who are drawn to the sense of continuity with Judaism, and in some congregations, these non-Jews are in the majority. In these cases, the element of Jewish identity is no longer widely shared, and the central element separating these congregations from evangelical Christian Zionism is often simply the inclusion of aspects of Jewish tradition into the liturgy. Ariel's description of Messianic Judaism highlights the blurred lines between the movement and evangelical Zionist Christianity in general:

> In essence, Messianic congregations serve as meeting spaces for Jews and non-Jews holding to a conservative Protestant faith as well as to the idea of the role of Jews and Israel in God's plans for humanity. Messianic Jews, like conservative evangelicals in general, subscribe to conservative social and political views, seeing themselves as patriotic Americans or Israelis. Messianic Jews support Israel, along similar understanding as those of many premillennialist evangelicals. Their relation to Israel serves to re-affirm their Jewish identity at the same time that it carries the theological perceptions and political agenda of the evangelical camp.[39]

Messianic Judaism is widely rejected as a legitimate form of Judaism, and the four major denominations of Judaism—Orthodox, Conservative, Reconstructionist, and Reform—are in agreement that Messianic Jews may not properly be considered Jewish, holding that belief in Jesus is incompatible with Judaism. Despite this conclusion, Messianic Jews assert that they are not Christians but Jews who remain Jewish while believing in Jesus and worshiping with Messianic Jewish congregations.[40] There is, in short, no agreement between Messianic Judaism and the major mainline denominations of Judaism regarding the identity and status of Jewish believers in Jesus, and the movement continues to hover between Christian and Jewish traditions and identity while remaining aligned with the basic views and traits of evangelical Christian Zionism.

CONCLUSION

This discussion of various modes of Christian engagement with Israel demonstrates the complex issues surrounding the encounters of Christians and Jews in this conflicted land, where religious, ethnic, and national identities are linked. Theological and political issues intertwine in these perspectives, resulting in a range of Christian movements whose political affiliations are difficult to disentangle from their theological views. The post-Holocaust Judeocentric Catholicism explored in this book is situated within this sociopolitical context, and yet in its origin, expression, and motivation, it is substantially different from the movements discussed in this chapter. The differences between this phenomenon and pro-Palestinian theologies are clear, although many within the Judeocentric phenomenon are deeply sympathetic to the struggles of Palestinians. The phenomenon explored in this book is also notably different than the philosemitism expressed in Christian Zionism. First, whereas Christian Zionism is evangelical and theologically fundamentalist, this phenomenon is Catholic and more theologically progressive, particularly regarding methods of biblical interpretation and soteriology. Second, Christian Zionism is characterized by explicit support for the State of Israel; in contrast, while many in the phenomenon explored here express a sense of connection to and solidarity with the Jewish people, it is not equated with an uncritical allegiance to the State of Israel. Third, Christian Zionism's support of Israel is motivated by the expectation of the fulfillment of end-time prophecies, which include the conversion of Jews to Christianity. Those involved in the phenomenon explored here, however, avoid linking eschatological expectation to political situations and reject the historical tradition of the Christian desire for Jewish conversion to Christianity, maintaining instead that Judaism's ongoing validity is unquestioned as a religion and a people in an unbroken covenant.

Those who contribute to this Judeocentric phenomenon are outsiders: they are not Palestinian, they have not been connected to the land through generations, and they are not personally impacted by the political conflict to the degree that many Palestinians are. Nor are they Israeli citizens despite decades of living in Israel. Although they are outsiders, in certain regards they have also become insiders; they have lived in Israel for decades and intend to stay for life, and they have established friendships and a network of relationships with local Israelis and Palestinians. They remain outsiders but are also immersed within Israeli life in yet another illustration of life on the border.

PART 2

A Judeocentric Catholicism

It seems hardly possible that the person whom I had first met at a monastery six months earlier was the same person I met on the street on that spring day. It had been winter when I first met Sr. Talia, and we sat in a chilly, shadowed room in her monastery and spoke for about an hour. She was cordial but guarded and asked that I publish neither her name nor the name of her monastery. A pseudonym of her choice is used here. When we met the first time, I had requested to interview her for a different research project, and as we spoke, I began to sense that my questions were only peripheral to her central interests. When our conversation was drawing to a close, I asked if there was anything that was on her mind after our conversation that she'd like to share. She gazed intently at me, and her eyes began to light up as she said, "I also think there's something very, very important and interesting to understand now. It is the new relationship between the Catholic Church and Judaism that began during the sixties, during the Second Vatican Council, in the declaration *Nostra Aetate*, and all this kind of work that is building on it. I think it is an incredibly deep insight. It's really fascinating. I think the question of the relationship between Christianity and Judaism . . . it is—eternity is not enough to understand." She concluded, "What a mystery! And I think it is one of the keys of my vocation, just to think about it."

After meeting Sr. Talia and many others who shared her strong inclination toward contemplating the relationship between Christianity and Judaism, I began to see the need for research exploring this phenomenon closely. It was with this new focus that I contacted her again, six months later, and requested another meeting. I explained that this time I'd like to talk to her specifically about her interest in Judaism and in the relationship between Christianity and Judaism.

She responded readily to my request to speak to her about this topic, which is so central to her spiritual life, and said that she would be delighted to meet with me. On a bright and warm morning in late summer, we met not far from Damascus Gate in the neighborhood of Musrara. When I approached her, she gave me a strong, impulsive hug, and there was no trace of the reserved and wary attitude that she had kept during our first meeting. She led me to a café on a terrace shaded with flowers and palms, and we sat with coffee. As we turned to the topic of Christian-Jewish relations, her expression opened and filled with light, and as she continued to speak, the words flowed from her without pause, tumbling like a rushing stream.

Sr. Talia's eyes sparkled with excitement. "We Christians, we have a word to describe it," she began when I asked her to tell me about her love of Judaism. "But I know that this word is not very well received in Judaism," she continued. "We call it the mystery of Israel."[1] She acknowledged then that this phrase can be easily misunderstood if it is interpreted as referring to something secretive or even senseless. She clarified, "But you have to understand that it is a mystery in the Christian definition of the word. We speak about the mystery of Incarnation, for example. Or the mystery of resurrection." Her eyes brightened even more, and her words fell faster. "It is like an ocean. You enter this ocean, and you can just have a drop of it. You cannot understand it with your intelligence; it is bigger than your intelligence. And I think my approach to Judaism is like that—it's such a mystery. It's a mystery!" She explained that this mystery is something she experiences everyday living in Israel, and she feels that it is ineffable and yet also completely mundane: "You can be dizzy with it if you think of it. And at the same time, it's so matter-of-fact. You see the ladies with the kids, and we are here drinking coffee, and there is nothing more simple than that. And we are talking about incredible things."

She told the story of her conversion to Christianity, which she attributes, paradoxically, to her encounter with Judaism in Israel. She was in her twenties, and an atheist, and had traveled to Jerusalem as a tourist. After some time in Jerusalem, however, her religious skepticism began to disintegrate as she found herself deeply spiritually moved. She described an experience observing Jewish prayer that left a profound effect on her: "The first witness for me that maybe there was somebody upstairs was the

Jewish people praying at the Western Wall. I knew the story, I knew what happened to them, and for me it was very strange to see them praying after such a story." She said that she couldn't understand how a people who had suffered through the Holocaust could believe in God. "This," she declared, "was my first opening to God." She felt the stirrings of Christian faith but had been inspired to it through observing the Jewish faith. She became involved with a Messianic Jewish community and continued to develop faith in this Jewish-Christian context. Only three months after arriving in Israel as an atheist, she was baptized in the Messianic congregation. "I have a love, a very specific love for the Jewish people," she said. "I received my faith from Judaism."

After this conversion experience, she returned home to France, and in that context, her conversion took two more dramatic steps: she converted again, this time to Catholicism, and then made the radical decision to become a nun. She entered a monastic congregation in France and returned to Israel twenty years later at the invitation of the superior of her monastic community. She had longed to be in Israel during those decades that she was away, but she did not want to make the trip on her own volition; she was determined to wait until the time was right and until the moment that she was invited to go by her superior. During these twenty years, she said that every year she prayed "next year in Jerusalem," echoing the plea of the Passover Haggadah. And now, after twelve years of living in Israel, she still feels continually fueled by it: "I know that just being in Jerusalem I can see that there is so much life, so much joy; I receive so much here."

Pointing to the gold band she wears on her left hand, she reflected, "If I could sum it up, it is in just one word—and this word is written in my ring, the ring I received for my vows." She and the other sisters in her congregation receive a ring when they take their final vows, symbolic of a spiritual marriage, and she explained that each sister chooses a phrase to be engraved inside of it. Many chose the name of Jesus or biblical passages. But inside her ring there is only a single word, "Israel," written in Hebrew. Reflecting on her choice, she wondered, "What is Israel? Is it a country, is it a people? Is it an idea, is it a religion? I do not have a clue. I don't know! But this is the way I'm connected. This is why I'm here; I will tell you I am here for that."

Radiant and invigorated by speaking about something so close to her heart, she spoke about the Eucharist, explaining how she understands the practice of taking communion every day to connect her to the Jewish people:

"I receive the body of Jesus every day; I receive his flesh. I receive the body of Israel. And without the faithfulness of the Jewish people up to Jesus, I would not be able to have him, my love, my reason for living, my life." She believes that this connection is also physical, and continued, "The body of Jesus is a Jewish body. I believe in the Incarnation. I believe that he was God, in his flesh and in his blood, and I am receiving this in my flesh." People flowed in and out of the café, but she seemed unconcerned with having such an intense and controversial conversation in public. It was as if we were on an island at our little table.

Our meeting fell on the Catholic holy day of the Feast of the Exaltation of the Holy Cross. Pondering the spiritual meaning of this day, she said that her understanding of the relationship between Christianity and Judaism, what she calls the "mystery of Israel," is "in solidarity with what we are celebrating today: the cross of Jesus, the holy cross, something that is painful. On the one hand, [the cross] is painful, and on the other hand, it is something that has to do with joy, with glory. It is very difficult to explain." In the Feast of the Exaltation of the Holy Cross, she saw a dichotomy of pain and joy, and she said that this dichotomy is part of her spiritual vocation. She spoke of feeling herself to be perched on a narrow line between the two apparent contradictories and torn between two states of being in a few different senses. She explained that she sees this conjunction of pain and joy when she contemplates the painful memory of the injustices that Christians have perpetrated against Jews throughout history, and at the same time, she experiences the joy of living in Israel with the Jewish people. She also feels torn between wanting to share her experience of faith and yet recognizing the need to refrain from doing so to avoid offense. She feels inspired by her love for the Jewish people to communicate the faith that is at the center of her life and brings her joy, and yet she knows that she must not out of respect for Judaism. She told me that this is the symbolic theme of her life, begun when she was born at midnight on the night of Good Friday, poised on the line between death and resurrection, as she understands it.

The café in which we spoke was also poised on a historically tense line. We were on the Green Line, or Armistice Line, drawn in 1949 to mark what was then the border between Israel and Jordan. Today, the line is invisible, and fifty years have passed since Israel gained control of the land east of the line, but it still separates two cultures and peoples in one city, where Jewish West Jerusalem meets Arab East Jerusalem. As we discussed this, noting that we were sitting on yet another narrow line between two different realities, she nodded vigorously, agreeing that this is part of the mystery that she contemplates in prayer.

Citing a line from Zechariah, she said, "Truly, one who touches you touches the apple of my eye," explaining that she feels fiercely protective of the Jewish people.[2] But laughing, she added, "Of course, I know they are normal people; they are my friends. But this is what I feel. And if you think of it," she continued, "it is a huge mystery." She laughed then with a light, musical laughter. "I feel like a little bird that is just chirping," she said. "This is my vocation. I don't say it because I consider myself small; I am an adult, I am grown up, I know. But it's just like if you have this incredible mystery in front of you. You don't know what to do, so you have to just chirp, chirp, chirp!"

CHAPTER 5

The "Mystery of Israel"

Common to many of the first-person narratives shared and analyzed in this book is one word that arises time and again: "mystery." In the contexts in which it is used here, it bears a weight and meaning distinct from its common usage. In these passages, it is linked with theological notions of divine mystery—specifically with the concept of the "mystery of Israel," a rather opaque phrase derived from the Letter to the Romans. Two monks used the phrase "listening to the mystery of Israel" to describe the purpose of their life in a monastery in Israel, while Sr. Talia returned to the phrase multiple times, saying that she understands the "mystery of Israel" to be "in solidarity" with the "mystery of the cross." The mission statement of the first community of Hebrew-speaking Catholics in Israel lists among its goals the aim "to ensure among the faithful a solid Christian spirit sensitive to 'the mystery of Israel.'"[1]

The phrase is drawn from an oft-cited passage in the eleventh chapter of Paul's Letter to the Romans, which addresses Gentile Christians concerning the nascent Christian movement's origin as a Jewish sect. St. Paul writes of a "mystery" regarding the Jewish refusal to accept Jesus as the messiah, and this passage has given rise to the phrase "mystery of Israel." It was written during the early years of Christianity, when Christianity had not yet formed into a distinct religion but was still a sect within Judaism, into which Paul and other Jewish missionaries struggled to find ways to incorporate Gentiles. In this passage, Paul speaks to a Gentile audience about what he sees as the paradox of God's election of the Jews as the chosen people in relation to their "stumbling"—that is, their refusal to believe that Jesus is the long-awaited messiah: "So that you may not claim to be wiser than you are, brothers and sisters, I want you to understand this mystery: a hardening has come upon part of Israel, until the full number of the Gentiles has come in" (Rom. 11:25).

Rather than surveying the multiple and diverse interpretations of this passage, our concern here is the way that the idea of the "mystery of Israel" has been internalized in the spirituality of the voices heard in this book and instrumentalized in the development of their own Catholic theologies of Judaism. Although the layers of meaning and association suggested by the phrase are different for each person who chooses to interpret it, in the narratives of those shared in this book, a common strand of interpretation is evident. In these contemporary interpretations, notions that Jewish unbelief in Jesus is a "stumbling" or sin are gone, and all that remains is a question without an answer—a mystery regarding the relationship between Christianity and Judaism.

Sr. Marie Yeshua, a nun of the Poor Clare Sisters, uses this phrase when she speaks about the life-transforming spiritual experience she had as a young woman during her first visit to Israel, before she had decided to become a nun. Her narrative bears many similarities to Sr. Talia's, as they both experienced a profound spiritual transformation when they came to Israel for the first time and when they visited the Western Wall, which inspired a deep love for Judaism in them. As Sr. Marie Yeshua looks back on her first visit to the Western Wall those many years ago, she reflects, "For me it was very, very powerful to see the Jewish people with the power of life. . . . I received it like a gift because it's like a veil that you take off. I understood in one second the mystery of Israel." Explaining more of what she understood about the concept of the "mystery of Israel," she continued, "It's a gift that these people and we are one body. It's the same tree and the same revelation. We are in a different level, but it's the same dynamism, same light." She recalls that she had begun weeping at that moment of revelation, and a woman who had accompanied her began to pray for her. Sr. Marie Yeshua says that this woman opened the Bible to a random page and began reading, and it turned out to be the passage from Paul's Letter to the Romans—precisely the verses about the olive tree that lead up to the line about the mystery of Israel. When she heard these words read to her, Sr. Marie Yeshua says that she experienced a powerful insight. "I listened like it was the first time," she remembers. "It was very, very deep, and it was one week after I came to Israel, and I think it was a gift." For Sr. Marie Yeshua, the concept of the "mystery of Israel" is truly mystical; she experiences it as an ineffable reality, perceptible through spiritual experience, and this mystery fuels her spiritual life.

Sr. Anne Catherine, a religious sister originally from France, relates that a similar interest and inclination had been present since early in her life. Her interest in Judaism and Christian-Jewish relations led her to become a religious sister with the Congregation Notre Dame de Sion, commonly known as the Sisters of Sion. The Sisters of Sion are recognized in Israel and in many places around the globe for their work in Christian-Jewish relations, and they oversee educational programs aimed at teaching Christians about Judaism.[2] Sr. Anne Catherine has been living in Israel for forty-five years and works with the guesthouse at the Sisters of Sion monastery in Ein Kerem, which receives many Jewish Israeli guests from the surrounding area who are interested in seeing the monastery and learning something about Christian traditions and monastic life. She finds that the eagerness of the Israeli guests to visit the monastery and engage in conversation provides an opportunity for interreligious dialogue and learning. "For me," she explains, "interreligious dialogue with Jews is not trying to change the other but to change myself. And to welcome from the other what can enrich my own faith. To receive from the other what can enrich my own faith and widen my idea of God. . . . God is much beyond what I think he is." She describes her engagement in Jewish-Christian dialogue as a part of her daily life: "I don't *participate*; I live in it, from morning to evening, because most of our guests are Jews. When I go on the tram, in the village, wherever, my life is Jewish-Christian dialogue."

Sr. Pilar, also a Sister of Sion, says she felt a particular love for the Jewish people very early in her life, even in childhood. In her recollection, at the age of five, she became inflamed at what she had been taught in school about Judaism and shouted at the teacher. As she tells it, "The sister who was preparing us said to me that God loved the Jewish people, but after they were nasty, God didn't love them anymore. I stood up and said, 'No, if God is like that, then I don't want him!' For me, God is faithful—to the Jewish people and to us." She later chose to become a nun: "My decision to enter religious life was for the love of the Jewish people. That is why I joined the congregation of Our Lady of Sion. Because in my heart, if God is God, God is faithful, and if God is faithful, God is faithful to his people, which he has chosen. God doesn't change his mind." This conviction, she explains, led her to choose to become a nun, and she speaks of the struggle she had in finding a congregation that would be receptive to her sense of being called to "the love of the Jewish people." When she discovered the Sisters of Sion, she knew she had found her home.

The Sisters of Sion has an institutional dedication to Jewish-Christian relations, but not all of its members entered the congregation intentionally to contemplate the "mystery of Israel" or to work to further Jewish-Christian understanding. Many gradually developed an interest in Judaism initially inspired by the congregation's work in Christian-Jewish relations, which eventually became personalized and interiorized in them over the years. Such is the case with Sr. Carmen, originally from Malta, who has been living in Jerusalem for fifty years. She first lived in East Jerusalem, which was then within Jordanian territory, and later in Israeli West Jerusalem. Although she entered the congregation as a young woman without a specific interest in Judaism, her work as a Sister of Sion changed that, and today her dedication to Judaism and the Jewish people serves as the focal point of her religious vocation. She reflects, "I didn't come to Sion for this, and yet I am led. . . . It's God's call. That's what I love, and that's what gives me strength." Finding words to express her deep dedication to the Jewish people, she notes that while some people are called to live a spiritual life by taking care of the poor or the sick, she feels that her call is different. "I think I've been called to share in God's love for everyone," she says, "but specifically the Jewish people."

Although the Sisters of Sion is unique in its explicit dedication to Christian-Jewish relations, it is certainly not the only Catholic religious congregation or community in Israel with a special interest in Judaism and Christian-Jewish relations. None are as wholly committed in their official mission statements to this goal as the Sisters of Sion, but a number of other communities make efforts to work toward Christian-Jewish dialogue and reconciliation and to battle against the remnants of anti-Judaism that can still be found in many Christian communities.[3]

One such community is the Benedictine monastery in Abu Gosh, a village west of Jerusalem. The monastery encircles a church built by the Crusaders, who believed it to be the site of the historical Emmaus, and since the late 1970s, a Benedictine community has maintained a monastic community there and cared for the church.[4] Upon the foundation of the Benedictine monastery on this site, Fr. Jean-Baptiste Gourion, a Jewish convert to Catholicism, was chosen to lead the community as its abbot.[5] From its earliest days, under Gourion's direction, the monastery developed a focus on the Jewish roots of Christianity and contemporary Jewish life in Israel. Fr. Olivier, a monk at Abu Gosh, recalls the original intention of the founding of the monastery at Abu Gosh: "When we were sent here in 1976, when the first monks were sent here, the father abbot in Bec in Normandy said, 'You have to be a heartfelt, cordial presence in the roots of our faith, in the land of our roots, but also in the people of our roots.'" Elaborating on the troubled anti-Judaic history that Christianity carries, which necessitates an intention such as this, Fr. Olivier explains, "Substitution theology . . . has caused so much damage, so . . . we have to be only a presence. It's not to make noise but [to be] a presence of prayer, for listening to the mystery of Israel." He made sure to clarify, however, that the intention of community is to pray not exclusively for the Jewish people but for all people, including the local Muslim population, which comprises the majority in the Arab village of Abu Gosh. As Fr. Olivier recalls, the abbot insisted that the monastic community should be a presence of prayer "without any exception"—that is, without excluding any populations or religions.

As Sr. Michaela, who has been living at the Abu Gosh monastery for thirty-four years, describes, "This community was founded from our community in France with this optic of a presence of prayer and reconciliation with the Jewish people, which is unusual for a Catholic community in Israel. There aren't many others like that." The French monastic community that founded the Abu Gosh community, the Bec-Hellouin Abbey, had expressed an "openness to the Jewish people" since the 1930s, as Sr. Michaela explains, and had moved against the grain of Catholic thought at that time in their desire for reconciliation and dialogue. However, she feels that in the early years, when Abbot Jean-Baptiste Gourion was still living, the monastery had a much more defined communal dedication to Judaism, and in her experience, it has become less central over the years. Despite this shift, the monastery continues to express a dedication to Christian-Jewish reconciliation and to interreligious relations with all their neighbors, which they aim to practice through a spirit of prayer and presence.

In addition to these cases of institutional and communal dedication to Christian-Jewish relations and the study of Judaism, there are also individuals in other congregations in Israel who express a powerful personal interest and engagement in these areas even though they are not part of the shared goals of their community. Sr. Marie Yeshua is one such person, remaining privately dedicated to the examination of the "mystery of Israel" while living in a small community of contemplative nuns who do not share this dedication, few of whom maintain connections with the Jewish milieu in which they are located. She lives hidden behind high monastery walls, but in the thirty-two years that have passed since she arrived in Jerusalem, Sr. Marie Yeshua's love for and sense of spiritual connection with the Jewish people has grown extremely strong. While she continues to live a quiet hidden life of prayer within the monastic cloister, she speaks Hebrew, studies Judaism, and maintains close friendships with Jewish Israelis.

Across the city, at the Yad Vashem Holocaust Museum and Memorial, Sr. Gemma del Duca works with educators whom she has brought from the United States to Israel to learn about Holocaust education. Sr. Gemma developed a love for Judaism and the Jewish people on her own as a member of the Sisters of Charity, a religious congregation without any particular engagement with Judaism or Christian-Jewish relations. She put this feeling into practice when she founded the Catholic Institute for Holocaust Studies, an organization that trains Catholic educators in Holocaust studies.[6] In one of our many meetings, she remarked that she had been in Israel for exactly forty years that month, and playing with the biblical narrative of wandering for forty years on the way to the Promised Land, she laughed and said, "Forty years of wandering *in* the Promised Land!" Sr. Gemma's congregation is based in the United States, and yet she came to Israel alone and has remained there living mostly apart from her congregation. The dedication that she has to the Jewish people, and to working toward Christian-Jewish reconciliation through directing the Catholic Institute for Holocaust Studies, is one that grew within her during her decades in Israel, while the other members of her congregation remained in the United States, working in other fields. She lives in Jerusalem in a community house of sisters from a different congregation, the Sisters of St. Joseph of the Apparition. Yet aside from living in a Catholic religious house, she lives very much as many Israelis do: she speaks Hebrew fluently, she maintains close friendships with Jewish Israelis, and she attends a synagogue almost every Saturday.

To the east of Jerusalem's city center, Br. Yohanan Elihai lives in a small and comfortable apartment. Br. Yohanan is yet another person who has made remarkable strides in Jewish-Christian reconciliation on his own, independently motivated to it while remaining a member of the Little Brothers of Jesus, a religious congregation that does not share his passion. He has lived in Israel since 1956 and bears the striking distinction of being the first priest in history to celebrate a Catholic mass in Hebrew by special permission from the Church. Now after over sixty years of living of Israel, he lives on his own on the edge of West Jerusalem, by the Green Line that separates Israel from the West Bank. Sitting in his living room, he admits, "I love the Jewish people more than anyone else." He goes on to explain that this love has arisen due to both circumstance and religious tradition: through the simple circumstance of living among Jews for many decades and through the historical relationship between Christianity and Judaism. He makes these two reasons clear: "One, I love them more than any other people. Like those who are in Peru love the Indians more than any people.... That's the first reason. If I had chosen to live with the Palestinian people, I would say that I love them fully. But I am here. The second reason is that they are our elder brothers, and they are special."

Each of these people, and many more whose voices will be heard in the following pages, are drawn to the contemplation of the "mystery of Israel" as they understand it. They have interpreted this biblically inspired concept in light of their own experiences and their own theologies; they have personalized and internalized the concept and have given it a central place in their lives. The term "mystery of Israel" has become a richly associative symbol to them, suggesting something that is ultimately ineffable and yet intimately related to their own faith. While the phrase suggests a way of framing Judaism through a Christian perspective and a way of perceiving Jews as "other," these voices also interpret it as a way of seeing the Jewish "other" as one who is deeply related to themselves.

PORTRAIT: SR. MARIE YESHUA

The circuitous path to meeting Sr. Marie Yeshua began when I walked into a pharmacy on Yafo Street in Jerusalem and saw a nun wearing a Carmelite habit comfortably settled into a chair at the front of the store, chatting with the man working at the counter and watching the afternoon pass by on Jerusalem's main shopping street. She introduced herself as Sr. Francine and explained that she lived in a home for retired nuns and monks in East Jerusalem.[7] We spoke for a few minutes, and I explained my research and asked if she would like to participate. She was excited by the prospect of meeting for an interview, and we scheduled a date.

In her verbal directions to her home, which included neither a street name nor numbered address, she told me to catch a bus and take it "all the way," get out by a gas station whose name she did not know, and look for a gate that was either blue or green—she couldn't remember which. I thought it was quite unlikely that I would find her home with these directions, and so the day before the meeting, I began scouring maps of East Jerusalem to see if I could locate this unnamed place with no address. As I was struggling with the maps, the phone rang. It was Sr. Francine, announcing that she had changed our plans. She'd arranged for us to meet in the company of a third person, a friend of hers who lives in a monastery on Hebron Road. She suggested that we meet at the bus station by Damascus Gate, and together we would travel to her friend's monastery. She insisted that it was very important for my work that I meet this friend of hers.

The bus station was densely crowded, but it was not difficult to spot the elderly nun in a habit. We pushed through crowds to the taxi stand and began to negotiate with a long series of drivers. Sr. Francine negotiated boldly and finally reached an agreement with a driver. We got into the car. The driver promptly drove the wrong way, and we found ourselves in stand-still traffic, heading in the wrong direction.

We eventually reached the monastery, and as I stepped out of the taxi, I was surprised to find myself beside a tall stone wall stretching the length of a block that I had walked past many times and yet had never recognized as the exterior of a monastery. Only a very small sign by the gate set into the stone wall indicated that this was a monastery of the Poor Clare sisters. The gate swung open after we rang the bell, and once inside, we entered an oasis of evergreen trees. When the gate closed behind us, we found ourselves immersed in a quietude so peaceful that it seemed that the busy main thoroughfare and the chaos of the city outside had only been imaginary.

We were met by Sr. Marie Yeshua, a tall, lean woman with calm, clear eyes and a strikingly intense presence. She offered me a firm handshake and led us into a sitting room on the edge of the garden. Sr. Francine was eager for me to listen to Sr. Marie Yeshua, and so she sat quietly with us, content to have brought us together.

It immediately became clear that contemplating the relationship between Christianity and Judaism is at the heart of Sr. Marie Yeshua's spiritual life. She had brought a slim book with her, a copy of a recent Vatican document, "The Gifts and Calling of God Are Irrevocable: A Reflection on Theological Questions Pertaining to Catholic-Jewish Relations on the Occasion of the 50th Anniversary of *Nostra Aetate* (No. 4)." Lifting it and placing it directly in front of her, she placed her hands on it and declared definitively, "All that we are living inside in prayer is here. All." She continued, "I feel as though my work is finished with this document." She clarified that of course her work is never finished, but "all that is written here is in the heart of the church. It's fifty years of struggle and of suffering." She said she was driven by the contemplation of the "mystery of Israel" and continued, "In the church, in the parish, this mystery has not been received—only by very few people."

Sr. Marie Yeshua arrived in Jerusalem for the first time in 1984 after becoming involved with an ecumenical Christian group from France that was planning a pilgrimage to Israel to ask for forgiveness for the Christian history of violence against Jews. She decided to travel by herself, on foot. She was able to walk from France all the way to Rome, and with the eventual help of moving vehicles, she made it from Rome to Jerusalem. In Jerusalem, she found herself deeply spiritually moved, as recounted in the previous chapter. She came to the conclusion that she was called to be a contemplative nun in Jerusalem and decided to enter the Poor Clare monastery—to live in Israel as a nun for the rest of her life. Today, although she lives within the monastery walls, she has learned to speak Hebrew and maintains active relationships with many in the city around her.

A deep mysticism characterizes many of Sr. Marie Yeshua's reflections, and her vividly alert presence is matched by the intensity of her spiritual expressions. Speaking of her mystical love for the Jewish people, she said, "I think it's a gift. It's like to receive faith, to receive the love for his own people. It's a gift when you discover the beauty of the Jewish people and the richness. . . . It's impossible not to love them." She uses the word "love" to describe her feeling, but it's not only affective; she also believes that the Jewish people hold an important spiritual role in the world. "They support the hope for the world," she explained. "In the body of the Jewish people, you have all the nations. . . . All the nations are in this little people. It's a microcosm. And around the Jewish people, you have the Muslims, the Christians. Jerusalem is like a laboratory."

Sr. Marie Yeshua believes that the Jewish people are "the vector of unity of all the nations," and she said that this can be seen in Jerusalem today. Although her outlook is very mystical, she placed this vision of the Jewish people and Jerusalem firmly within the present-day city, with all of its political conflicts: "It's a contradiction because this country is always in struggle and war, but it flourishes very much—with the economy and many things. You can see and you can experience the blessing of the Lord on this country and on this people. It's a mystery." She continued, "We live also with misunderstanding and with solitude. But, like a balance, you can feel the experience of the protection of God, the presence of God for his people." Reflecting on the energy in Jerusalem, she observed, "When you are here, when you meet people, when you live with the people, you receive a lot of life. The dynamism of life is very strong." She recognizes that this dynamism is not something that many people outside of Israel are able to sense or understand, and she noted, "From outside, people can see a lot of struggle and obscurity, but from inside, it's a lot of life and dynamism and hope. Very big hope."

The mysticism that Sr. Marie Yeshua expresses is oriented toward the prophetic and toward the eschatological future. She doesn't claim to have any notion of when the envisioned time of redemption might arrive, but she feels that she can sense its proximity: "The end of time can be a hundred years, twenty years, a thousand years—I don't know. But the end of time is a special time of waiting. *Geulah sh'lemah* [total redemption] for the Jews, and for us it is the coming back in the glory of the Lord, and to be on our guard, and to be awake in prayer. But the Jewish people in this country flourishing is a sign for all the world that the *geulah* is very near."

In the eschatological vision that Sr. Marie Yeshua holds, the Jewish people play a crucial role, and in this way, her theological views bear similarities to many Christian Zionist theologies. However, unlike many other Christians, she does not hope that Jews will develop faith in Jesus. When she says "Jews have a role to play in the history of redemption, and it's not finished," she adds firmly, to clarify any misunderstanding, that they have this role "as Jews"—that is, as observant Jews and not as converts to Christianity. She is adamantly against any attempts to persuade Jews to believe in Jesus and believes that Jews must remain Jewish.

The Jewish messianic hope that is so vividly expressed in Jerusalem serves as a source of inspiration for her. Describing the sounds that spill out onto the street, she said, "We can hear all around us, at the synagogue, *beit ha-knesset*, at Chabad—'*Mashiach achshav, mashiach achshav!*' [Messiah now, messiah now!] They are waiting with ardor and fire for the coming of the *mashiach.*" She finds this messianic expectation to serve as an awakening call to Christians and explained, "It helps us also to be awakened, and to await, for the coming back in glory of the *mashiach.*"

Sr. Maria Yeshua believes that Christians and Jews are moving "in one body" toward the eschatological future, but she recognizes and respects the two very distinct visions of this future, Jewish and Christian. She sees this difference as a paradox, and she admits that it's a struggle for her to reconcile this paradox. She allows the distinction to be maintained as a point of irresolution, and it serves as a source of mystery in her contemplation. "It's a different point of view," she continued. "Different levels, but we're on the same way. It is a contradiction. But in prayer, we can live this in peace—and with joy and with hope. But it's a struggle, a very hard struggle."

CHAPTER 6

Precedents and Predecessors

BUILDING THE FOUNDATIONS

The post-Holocaust Judeocentric Catholicism explored here follows in the footsteps of a number of predecessors in Christian-Jewish relations who set the groundwork for this phenomenon in the mid-twentieth century in Israel. The visions and goals of these predecessors, all of whom lived through the Second World War, were shaped by the Holocaust and by the establishment of the State of Israel in 1948. The majority, quite noticeably, are of Jewish heritage, and each of these Jewish Catholics felt personally driven to immigrate to Israel, where they struggled to maintain Jewish identities while living as Catholic monks and nuns. Some have become fairly well known for their work in Christian-Jewish relations as well as for their participation in other issues of public interest, as the following pages detail, but others remain unknown outside of a small circle.[1]

One of these influential figures is Fr. Bruno Hussar, who was born in Egypt in 1911 to a Jewish family. He attended a university in Paris, and in that setting, he converted to Catholicism. In his memoir, he writes of his conversion to Catholicism in the early to mid-1930s as a gradual process that he initially resisted, not wanting to be swayed by Christian belief. He was troubled by persistent spiritual questions and found himself intrigued and moved by certain aspects of Christianity, but for some time he refused to speak to a priest about these thoughts, for he was "afraid of being won over and deceived."[2] He eventually overcame this hesitation and engaged in many long conversations with a priest whom he trusted. He still resisted the possibility of conversion and a few times resolved to never return to the priest, but in the summer of 1935, he had a profound spiritual experience while alone in the forest, which he recognizes as the moment of his incontrovertible assent to Christian faith, and in December of the same year, he was baptized. He wanted to enter religious life immediately, but his widowed mother needed financial assistance, and he chose to delay his vocation to work to support her. A few years later, the war broke out, and he recalls that "under German occupation I became much more deeply aware of my Jewishness."[3] He remained in Paris until it became clear that his life was at risk and then fled to the unoccupied southern part of France with assistance from the resistance.[4] After the war was ended, and when his mother was financially secure, he entered the Dominican order and was ordained in 1950.

In 1953, Hussar was sent to live in Israel by the Dominican provincial, who felt that the Jewish convert to Catholicism would be well suited to serve as the founder of a Dominican center for Jewish studies, along the lines of their center for Islamic studies in Cairo. This plan came to fruition in 1959 with the opening of the Isaiah House in West Jerusalem, on the Israeli side of Jerusalem, which was then separated by the border between Israel and Jordan. The decision to locate the Isaiah House in West Jerusalem set the center apart from many of the other Catholic religious communities that, like the Latin Patriarchate, were located in Jordanian East Jerusalem, which served local Arab Christians. The choice to establish the institute in West Jerusalem reflected the goal of creating a center where Catholics could contemplate the theological relationship between Christianity and Judaism, living within a Jewish milieu.[5] In 1983, over two decades after its founding, Hussar described the role of the Isaiah House as "not only a centre for biblical research and the study of the theological and historical aspects of Judeo-Christian relations" but also "a link between the Church on the one hand and Judaism and the State of Israel on the other." Hussar noted that by the early 1980s, the Isaiah House had "become an integral part of the country," and three of its brothers had become Israeli citizens.[6] Explaining the role of the institute in Israel in a 1997 interview, Fr. Marcel Dubois used the analogy of an old French house, with an interior garden side and an exterior court side: "If you consider the garden side, the interior life of the community, we were founded as a centre for Jewish studies and reflection on the link between the Old and New Testaments, between Israel and the Church, Judaism and Christianity. . . . [A] second purpose was from the beginning to be a Christian presence among the Jews, and for this reason the inclination of our vocation led us to request Israeli citizenship."[7]

When the Second Vatican Council was in session, Hussar was invited by Cardinal Augustin Bea to participate as an expert in the Conciliar Commission of the Secretariat for Christian Unity, and in this position, he contributed to drafting the material that eventually became *Nostra Aetate*. While in Rome, Hussar also spoke with a number of Council Fathers, urging them to consider the importance of the text and also explaining to them what he saw as the serious errors in the second version of the document.[8] His work was successful, and the second version was eventually discarded, making way for the much improved final document.[9]

In the following decade, Hussar began envisioning establishing a community in Israel where Jews, Christians, and Muslims could live together in peace in a place dedicated to interreligious harmony in the midst of the generally religiously segregated environment. After a long period of planning, this dream was realized in the form of an Israeli-Palestinian joint village founded by Hussar in 1970. The village was given the dual name Neve Shalom / Wahat Al-Salam, or "oasis of peace" in Hebrew and Arabic, respectively. After considering many different locations for this village, Hussar and his collaborators eventually leased land from Latrun Monastery, approximately halfway between Jerusalem and Tel Aviv, located precisely on the Green Line, which until 1967, just three years earlier, had marked the border between Israel and Jordan. The community of Neve Shalom / Wahat Al-Salam, although small, thrived, and by the mid-1980s, it consisted of approximately seventy members, half of whom were Jews and half of whom were Muslim and Christian Palestinians.[10] Hussar passed away in 1996, and of his many contributions to interreligious and intercultural relations, he is associated today primarily with the still active community of Neve Shalom / Wahat Al-Salam.

Another of the well-known figures who lived at the Isaiah House with Fr. Bruno was Fr. Marcel-Jacques Dubois, a theologian who taught at Hebrew University. Dubois was born in 1920 in France and entered the Dominican order at the age of eighteen. During the Second World War, he was one of a group of Dominicans who hid Jewish children in Catholic institutions in France, and he became attuned during this time to the existential struggle of the Jewish people. This also shaped his attitude toward the State of Israel when it was founded in 1948, an event that he considered "profoundly improbable and nearly sublime."[11] Dubois was sent to Israel by his religious superiors in 1964 and obtained a post in the philosophy department of Hebrew University.[12] He developed fluency in Hebrew, immersed himself in Israeli life, and became a well-known intellectual through his teaching at Hebrew University and through his theological publications on Christian-Jewish relations.

In 1974, Dubois was appointed to the Vatican's Commission of the Holy See for Religious Relations with the Jews, and during that same year, he also became a citizen of Israel at the special request of Teddy Kollek, the mayor of Jerusalem.[13] Over the next decades, until his death in 2007, Dubois maintained an active presence in Jerusalem through his work in Catholic-Jewish reconciliation and was also involved in efforts to increase Arab-Jewish understanding as a path to peace.[14]

The St. James Association, also called the Work of St. James, was another foundation that proved to be instrumental in the formation of a Catholic community in Israel oriented toward Catholic-Jewish relations and toward a Catholic spirituality that drew more directly from Jewish roots and tradition. It was founded in December 1954 by the Latin Patriarchal Vicar for Israel, Msgr. Antonio Vergani, and a small group of Hebrew-speaking Catholics to serve the increasing number of Catholics who were arriving in Israel in the years after the Second World War.[15] Unlike the local Arab Catholics who were members of Palestinian communities that had been living in the land for centuries, these newcomers arrived primarily from Europe as refugees or immigrants, many from mixed Jewish and Christian families. The St. James Association served as a community for these Catholics and provided a place where they could feel at home practicing their Catholic faith in a Hebrew-speaking congregation, which had become their common language after immigrating to Israel.[16]

In February 1956, the first mass at the newly opened St. James Center in Jaffa was celebrated by Bruno Hussar. This mass was in Latin, as was required of all Catholic masses at this time, a decade before the reforms of the Second Vatican Council allowed for mass to be said in the vernacular. However, only one month later, a remarkable landmark in the St. James Association occurred: a mass was given in the Hebrew language for the first time. This mass was celebrated in Haifa in March 1956 in the Syrian Catholic rite by Br. Yohanan Elihai, a Little Brother of Jesus.[17]

In 1957, the St. James Association received permission from Pope Pius XII to celebrate large portions of the Latin rite of the mass in Hebrew.[18] This is particularly remarkable given that this was still almost a decade before the Second Vatican Council permitted the celebration of mass in the vernacular. However, Hebrew was not only the newly established vernacular of the young State of Israel; it was also the language of the Hebrew Bible, and so it served as the linguistic foundation of scripture.

Br. Yohanan Elihai had just turned ninety years old when he welcomed me into his apartment in a modest but comfortable building in Talpiot, a barren industrial zone on the outskirts of Jerusalem. His energy and sharp intellect showed no signs of decreasing despite his age, and for an hour and a half Br. Yohanan told me stories about his life, his work in Christian-Jewish reconciliation, and his remarkable work in publishing dictionaries and textbooks of Palestinian colloquial Arabic.

After the US Army drove the Nazis out of France in 1944, Br. Yohanan traveled to Paris from his home near Versailles to join in the celebrations. He was only eighteen years old then, and as he walked along the street, he saw posters hung from the windows of the United States Embassy with photographs from the concentration camps. He was shocked and horrified, and those images changed the direction of his life. As we sat at his table, he spoke of that moment of recognition—when he realized that the anti-Jewish teachings he had heard while growing up in a French Catholic community were connected to these horrifying images. "I knew the way of thinking," he recalled, "and I felt that I must do something to reverse that thinking."

This experience led him eventually to move to Israel, where he has now been living for sixty years. Reflecting on this same moment in an earlier interview with an Israeli journalist, Br. Yohanan observed, "That shock is what brought me here." After learning about what had happened during the war, he felt that "the Holocaust made me want to live with this people and share its experiences in Israel. The new life you've created here is the answer: The Germans were unable to annihilate you."[19]

Br. Yohanan entered the French Army, and in 1946 he was sent to Lebanon, where he was stationed as a French teacher in a local school. There, he wanted to learn Arabic the way it was spoken colloquially but learned that no such dictionary had been compiled at that point, so he began studying on his own, with the plan of writing his own dictionary one day. Inspired by the life of Charles de Foucauld, who lived as a monk in North Africa, he joined the Little Brothers of Jesus. As a monk, he requested to be sent to Israel, following the deep conviction that had struck him when he had learned about the Holocaust. His superior sent him to Damascus for one year instead, where he learned the Syrian Arabic dialect, and then finally in 1956 he was allowed to go to Israel. Only three years after he arrived in Israel, Br. Yohanan received Israeli citizenship, taking the name Yohanan Elihai. Yohanan is the Hebrew version of his given name, Jean, and he chose the surname Elihai, which means "God lives." As he recalled, he was the only Catholic religious at that time who requested Israeli citizenship; Bruno Hussar received citizenship after him.

It was immediately upon his arrival in Israel in March 1956 that Br. Yohanan celebrated the very first Hebrew-language Catholic mass in Israel in the Syrian rite. As we spoke about that groundbreaking liturgical celebration, I asked him if, at that time, he had thought of Hebrew as a biblical language and as the language of the roots of Christianity, or as the language of the Jewish people in the State of Israel. Without hesitation, he replied that he thought of it primarily as the latter. His response was surprising, for even today, fifty years after *Nostra Aetate*, from most Christian perspectives, Hebrew is valued predominantly as a biblical language rather than as the contemporary language spoken in Israel.

After almost a decade of living within a Jewish population, in 1965 Br. Yohanan was sent to the Galilee to live among an Arabic-speaking population, and there, hearing a dialect of Arabic that he'd never encountered in an Arabic textbook, he began working on a dictionary of colloquial Palestinian Arabic.[20] In the following years, he wrote a series of textbooks to teach colloquial Palestinian Arabic to Hebrew-speaking Israelis, and more recently, he compiled yet another dictionary of Palestinian Arabic.[21] Br. Yohanan has left a lasting mark in Israeli society through his extensive publications on the Arabic language, and many Israelis who have studied Arabic in an effort to better understand their neighbors have used Br. Yohanan's dictionaries and textbooks. As a Catholic brother belonging to the humble and unassuming order of the Little Brothers of Jesus, Br. Yohanan was making waves in linguistics, but in addition, he was making a major contribution

to Israeli-Palestinian relations, drawing the two communities into communication. Although he came to Israel sixty years ago driven by the desire
to live among the Jewish people and to work toward Christian-Jewish reconciliation, he has made great strides in bringing Israelis and Palestinians
together through language.

Throughout the years, Br. Yohanan remained dedicated to Christian-Jewish reconciliation, particularly within the Catholic Church, and he has also
written a short book on the history of Christian anti-Judaism, *Juifs et chrétiens: D'hier à demain* (Jews and Christians: From yesterday to tomorrow).[22]
Today, in the foyer of the Sts. Simeon and Anne Church, the center for the
St. James Vicariate for Hebrew Speaking Catholics in Jerusalem, copies of
this small book are available for free, translated into a number of languages,
printed from a home printer, and stapled by hand.

In the 1970s, Br. Yohanan collaborated with a number of scholars of
various Christian denominations on the translation of the New Testament
into Modern Hebrew. He had previously participated in translations of
portions of the New Testament into Hebrew for use in the liturgies of the
St. James Association. These were intended for the use of Hebrew-speaking
Catholics in Israel and not for a Jewish audience; however, in the process of
translating the New Testament in its entirety into Hebrew, he worked with
a group that included Messianic Jews and Protestants, and he worried that
this new project might be used to try to persuade Israeli Jews to convert
to Christianity. Recalling the process of being invited to participate in this
project, he said, "I heard that the Protestants wanted to publish the entire
New Testament in Hebrew in a new translation, etc. And they asked if we
were ready.... And I said: 'Wait a second; I didn't come here to participate
in something like this. Later on, they will distribute it. This is not my intention.'"[23] He chose to participate, however, to ensure that the translation was
as correct as possible and free of misrepresentations.

Among the scholars involved in this project was another Catholic, the
Dominican friar Fr. Gabriel Grossman, who was yet another contributor
to work in Christian-Jewish relations and learning in Israel. Grossman was
born in Germany in 1931 to a Jewish father and a Christian mother, and his
family survived the war together by fleeing and living in hiding. After the
war, he entered the Dominican order in Lyons. He came to Israel in 1967 and
lived at the Isaiah House with Marcel Dubois and Bruno Hussar. Grossman
studied Jewish thought at Hebrew University and became such a dedicated

scholar that the other friars often called him "the rabbi."[24] Grossman also translated a number of other texts into Hebrew, including the monastic rule of the Benedictine order, the Rule of Saint Benedict.

This translation was done at the request of Fr. Isaac Jacob, a Benedictine monk who had established a small religious community in Tel Gamliel. Jacob was born in the United States in 1929, also to a Jewish father and a Catholic mother. He became a Benedictine monk in 1951 after entering St. Vincent Archabbey in Latrobe, Pennsylvania. He arrived in Israel in 1970, inspired by the renewal of Catholic thought on Judaism after the Second Vatican Council and also by what he believed to be the theological significance of the return of the Jewish people to the land of Israel. In 1975 he founded a small community in Tel Gamliel, near the town of Beit Shemesh, with the intention of establishing a Benedictine community that would share a spiritual life centered on the Rule of St. Benedict and a spirituality attuned to the significance of Judaism and the land of Israel to Christian faith.[25]

In a paper laying out this spiritual outlook, Jacob discusses reading the Rule of St. Benedict in the context of Israel. He felt that the rule could be interpreted as "a Christian *halakhah*" and "an apt instrument for a Christian community enabling that community to exist in Israel in a theological way that is attuned to Judaism."[26] Applying Jewish thought and literary categories to the Rule of St. Benedict, he writes that his community at Tel Gamliel found that the rule functions as a *midrash halakhah* because it "strives to create a 'way' to walk in the commandments, which is to walk in the word of the Lord. The Hebrew word for *to walk* comes from the verb *holek*, and the way of walking is *halakhah*."[27] Although he was never able to establish a Benedictine priory at Tel Gamliel, he lived there for two decades until his death in 1995, in a kibbutz-like environment with both laypeople and religious who together shared a spiritual life following this line of theological thought.[28]

Another important contributor to early efforts in Christian-Jewish relations in Israel is Sr. Charlotte Klein, a Sister of Sion. Klein is the only woman discussed in this brief overview of predecessors, and this reflects the public attention and opportunities offered to men in the mid-century Catholic context rather than any lack of involvement of women in this area. Klein was born in Germany in 1915 to an Orthodox Jewish family. After experiencing increasing oppression and acts of violence against Jews in their community after the Nazi regime came to power, Klein and her family left Germany and made aliyah, immigrating to Palestine. The details of her conversion

to Catholicism and her choice to become a nun were not preserved in published writing; all that is publicly known of this chapter in her life is that
she became a Christian at some point after making aliyah and entered the
Sisters of Sion in Jerusalem. After this transformation, she became deeply
dedicated to studying the teachings of contempt against Judaism embedded in Christianity. Her study of this topic was before its time, preceding
the Catholic Church's public recognition of these issues. She remained in
Jerusalem through the establishment of the State of Israel and eventually
moved to London in 1955 to pursue a PhD. She continued with a career
in the study of antisemitism and Christian-Jewish relations, teaching at
universities in England, Germany, and the United States, and founded the
Study Centre for Christian-Jewish Relations in London in 1962 in a move
that was groundbreaking prior to the Second Vatican Council.[29] Klein passed
away in 1985, leaving a legacy of work in Christian-Jewish understanding
and reconciliation.

BR. DANIEL

The Carmelite monk known as Br. Daniel—who became well known in
Israel in 1962, when his request for citizenship was taken to the Israeli High
Court—was born into a Jewish family as Oswald Rufeisen in Poland in 1929.
His biography reveals a chain of events as unlikely as they are heroic and
tragic. Both of his parents were killed at Auschwitz, but Rufeisen managed
to flee Poland before he was transported to the camps. He found himself
in Vilna, where he joined the Akiva Youth Movement and trained as a
shoemaker. He was arrested by local police who were collaborating with
the Germans and was taken to prison and questioned. His life was spared
because he was categorized as a "necessary Jew" due to his skill as a shoemaker. He was kept alive to work as a slave laborer but soon was captured
again in a roundup of all the Jews when the Nazis arrived to "liquidate" the
Vilna ghetto. He managed to escape in the midst of the chaos, slipping away
and finding a hidden space in a basement. There, he shed his identification
papers and the armband that identified him as a Jew and vowed to try to
survive from that point forward by hiding his Jewish identity.[30]

After this escape, Rufeisen began to identify himself as a Polish citizen of
German origin, a claim strengthened by his fluency in the German language

and by his physical characteristics, which did not fit the Nazi stereotypes of Jews. With these traits, he made a bold move: he was offered a job as a translator for the German military police, who believed that he was a Polish citizen of German descent, and with much fear, he accepted.[31] From 1941 to 1942, he served as a translator for the Nazis in the Belorussian town of Mir. He wore an SS uniform, carried an SS identity card, and was given access to all areas, including the Jewish ghetto. Working for the Nazis while hiding his Jewish identity was an excruciating position to be in, although it kept him alive. There were times when he was required to translate execution orders and then stand by and watch the executions of Jews.[32] However, his complicity in these acts kept him in his position, and in this role, Rufeisen soon accomplished a heroic act.

In utmost secrecy, he managed to make his Jewish identity known to a few Jews in the Mir ghetto. When he received the insider knowledge that the ghetto was scheduled to be liquidated, he warned the inhabitants and arranged for them to escape. He supplied the ghetto resistance fighters with guns and ammunition from the Nazi supplies, and with this assistance, over three hundred Jews fled the ghetto immediately before it was liquidated. Those who did not escape, fearing that Rufeisen's warning was a trap, were all killed.[33]

Rufeisen's assistance in the ghetto revolt was discovered, and when he was arrested and questioned, he admitted to his actions. When asked for the reason, he agreed to confess but requested that he be allowed to kill himself directly afterward. He then revealed that he was a Jew. However, the officer who questioned him had worked closely with him in his position as a translator and had grown fond of him. The officer suggestively told Rufeisen that it would not be necessary for him to kill himself, and that evening Rufeisen discovered a lapse in security, likely arranged by the officer. In this way, he escaped death yet again.[34]

After finding nowhere else to hide after this turn of events, Rufeisen begged for shelter in a Carmelite convent located on the grounds of the Nazi headquarters where he had worked. The nuns knew full well that he was an escaped convict, but they offered him shelter, and from his hiding place in the hayloft, he was able to look down on the Nazis striding through the courtyard below.[35] Within a few weeks of hiding in the convent, he experienced a spiritual conversion and was baptized three weeks after arriving there.[36] He remained in hiding in the convent for over a year, and after escaping while dressed as a nun, he had another long series of adventures and close calls, including fighting against the Nazis with the Jewish resistance group known as the Bielski partisans.[37] In 1945, he entered a Carmelite monastery in Kraków—this time not to stay in hiding but to become a monk.

After making many requests to immigrate to Israel, Rufeisen arrived there in 1959, now with the name Br. Daniel, a name chosen for his miraculous escapes, like Daniel in the lion's den. He lived at Stella Maris, the Carmelite monastery in Haifa, and began monastic life in Israel with the intention of ministering to Catholics of Jewish origin. Recalling the thoughts that had struck him during his conversion process, he reflected, "I became convinced that perhaps I have some special function to perform in this church, maybe to improve, to fix the relation between the Jews and the Christians."[38] Br. Daniel envisioned a distinct community of Jewish Christians within the Catholic Church, resembling the early church in Jerusalem.[39] However, he was adamant that he did not seek converts; he worked to bring together those who were already Christian within the State of Israel.

At Stella Maris, however, Br. Daniel was not the only Jewish convert to Catholicism. Fr. Elias Friedman, a South African Jew who had converted to Catholicism during the Second World War while serving in the South African Army, was a monk in the same monastery. Friedman entered the Carmelite order after his conversion and arrived in Israel in 1954. Like Br. Daniel, Friedman was also interested in ministering to Jewish Christians, but his aim was very different. Friedman sought a distinctively Jewish community within the Catholic Church, but unlike Br. Daniel and all the others whose stories are told in this chapter, each of whom rejected all forms of proselytization, Friedman wanted to create a community that would be more appealing to potential Jewish converts.[40]

Br. Daniel stayed away from these motives, as he did not support any efforts to convert Jews, and meanwhile, he became well known as an activist in his struggle to become an Israeli citizen. Part of the life he envisioned for himself and for other Jewish converts to Christianity within Israel involved the ability to receive Israeli citizenship under the Law of Return, established after the Second World War with the intention of allowing all Jews the opportunity to seek safe haven and citizenship in Israel. Soon after moving to Israel, Br. Daniel requested citizenship through this provision, but his request was denied. He continued to fight for citizenship, and in 1962, his case came before the Israeli High Court. This was only two months after the conclusion of the Eichmann trial, during the period of its appeal, and the two cases were heard by the court at the same time. Due to Br. Daniel's work in saving the Jews of the Mir ghetto, he had become well known in Israel, and in the public eye, the two cases became somewhat related.[41] However, despite his heroic actions during the war and despite his Jewish birth, he lost the case due to his conversion to Catholicism.

Br. Daniel fought intensely to set a precedent for other Jewish converts to Christianity, and the case brought the question of how one determines Jewish identity to the forefront of public discourse. In the end, quite ironically, the court's decision to refuse him citizenship based on the Law of Return reflected a rationale resembling Christian thought on religious identity—namely, that one's religious belief overrides one's identity by birth. Br. Daniel eventually became a citizen through naturalization in 1964. He continued to live at the monastery in Haifa until his death in 1998 and was also engaged in many charitable projects outside of the monastery, which he supported by working as a tour guide, all the while continuing to maintain close ties with many Catholics of Jewish heritage.[42]

When I first met with Sr. Anne Catherine at the Sisters of Sion convent in Ein Kerem, she had been living in Israel for forty-five years. After arriving in Jerusalem as a young Sister of Sion, she studied at Hebrew University and eventually became a scholar of Jewish studies. Although she is retired now, she maintains an active schedule and still teaches at Bethlehem University, where she gives classes on Judaism to Palestinian Christians and Muslims preparing to become tour guides. She considers this work to be part of her efforts in interreligious dialogue and peacemaking and also works with a local peace program that brings Jewish and Palestinians teenagers together.

Sr. Anne Catherine is a petite French woman with bright dark eyes, and when she and I began speaking, she was very cordial, although a bit reserved. She did not know much about me or how her interview would contribute to the aims of my research, and she answered my questions with a mixture of gracious hospitality and caution. When I returned to meet with her a second time, after she began to learn more about the nature of my own research in Christian-Jewish relations, a noticeable change occurred in her demeanor. She became more warm and present, and her eyes shone with a brighter intensity.

Enlivened by this new turn in our relationship, her responses rapidly became intensely theological, and she returned time and again to the concept of Jews as the chosen people. In her interpretation, this biblical concept serves as an example of a theological paradox; through God's choice of the Jewish people, she believes, the paradox of God's universalism and particularism is illustrated. She explained, "God is much more concrete than we are. He cannot say 'I love all the people' if he doesn't show that he loves specific people."

To illustrate this, she shared a rabbinic interpretation of the election narrative: "There is a very old Jewish tradition that explains this very well—why the choice of the land, why the choice of the people. And they say through the choice of this land, God chose all the lands. So the choice of God is what we don't know how to do. It's inclusive." She proposes that this shows that God's intent was to choose all people by choosing a particular people. And yet the particular choice, she believes, is not erased by the universal implications. She emphasized, "But inside there is the concrete choice, which has never been denied."

Elaborating on the paradoxical relationship between the particular and universal in this biblical narrative, she explained, "You cannot have universalism true and complete without particularism. . . . Universalism without particularism would be vague." Conversely, she continued, "And you cannot have particularism without universalism—it is restrictive." Applying this reading to a specifically Christian concept, Sr. Anne Catherine then reflected on the interplay of the particular and universal within the theological concept of the Incarnation: "The Incarnation is between particularism and universalism. It's the extreme of the particular. In becoming a human being, God made a choice. He could not be everywhere, so he incarnated in this specific people, in a specific country, in a specific family, in a specific time. It's the extreme of the particular, and that's why it can have an extreme universal message." This is a rather complex theoretical understanding of the theology of the Incarnation, but Sr. Anne Catherine insists that it is not abstract at all, but quite concrete. The Incarnation occurred within a particular human body, and it is, in her words, "less vague than we are."

Sr. Anne Catherine is well aware of the tensions and complications connected to the biblical concept of the chosen people and the chosen land when it is applied in political contexts. If any specifically religious concepts can be attributed to the complex mixture of factors behind the Israeli-Palestinian conflict today, then the theology of the chosen people and chosen land is most implicated in this struggle. Sr. Anne Catherine acknowledges this and yet insists on not abandoning or glossing over this biblical narrative. Rather, she feels that a deeper understanding of the narrative shows that the central message is not division or exclusivism but rather the equal love of all people and all places through a particular choice. She encounters the tensions around this narrative often, particularly in her work with Palestinians, and she is unafraid to discuss the theology openly. Recalling some of these conversations, she said, "My Palestinian friends ask me, 'Why are these people chosen?' . . . I say to them, 'God is not exclusive. God knows how to choose without excluding. So he knows how to love without excluding.'"

She continued, "We learn from God how to love without excluding the other. . . . He wanted to show with a specific people what it is to love. So we do the same. How do we love all humankind? We love especially *these* people, and through that, we are drawn to love others and to help them also." Sr. Anne Catherine sees this as part of a greater spiritual process of working within the divine plan. As she described it, "We try to enter the plan of God, the project of God, who chose a people in order to reach all humankind. So we absorb that, and we develop it within our spiritual life, and we share it with other Christians."

This affects the way that she teaches the Christian students and pilgrims who visit Jerusalem, as she strives to communicate this complex network of beliefs. Describing these encounters, she said, "I teach [Christian] people from abroad, and they believe that *we* have the truth, the Christians, *we* have the truth, and everything began with the New Testament, and the Old Testament is the past, and all kinds of things like that, and we don't believe that. And so we have to communicate the love of the Bible, the love of the Jewish people, from whom we have still to learn."

For Sr. Anne Catherine, the concept of the Jews as God's chosen people opens countless theological doors. It serves as a template for understanding how love can be both particular and universal and, by extension, how the narrative of the election of the Jewish people is not exclusionary but extends toward all people. From this, she has developed a theology of interreligious relations, specifically of the relationship of Judaism to all other religions. She boldly discusses this even in the conflicted contexts of Israeli-Palestinian relations and defends a theology that both maintains the belief in the concept of the chosen people and extends it to all people.

CHAPTER 7

A Mission Reversed

The Sisters of Sion

THE FOUNDING OF THE CONGREGATION OF OUR LADY OF SION

During the mid-twentieth century, a revolution began in a congregation of nuns that would eventually make a major impact in Jewish-Catholic relations in Israel. The Congregation Notre Dame de Sion had been founded in the 1840s with the purpose of praying for the conversion of Jews, but one hundred years later, the congregation turned in an entirely different direction. In the wake of the Holocaust, as the congregation struggled to make sense of what it had witnessed during the war, it began to realize that it could not continue to pray for the conversion of Jews. In the 1950s, a decade before the Catholic Church began to revise its teaching on Judaism, the Sisters of Sion began a shift that would soon entirely reverse their mission. Over the following decade, changes were instigated across all branches of the international congregation, resulting in a dramatic shift in its relationship to Judaism and Jews. Today, the three commitments of the congregation are represented by an image of three interlinked rings with a dove at the center with the following phrases within the three rings: "Church," "Jewish people," and "A world of justice, peace and love."[1] The following pages trace this transformation and explore the events and influences that motivated it.

Theodore Ratisbonne, a French Jew who had converted to Catholicism, founded the Congregation of Our Lady of Sion in 1847 with the assistance of his brother, Alphonse. Theodore was baptized in 1827, and recalling his conversion, he later wrote, "I believed that I was called to spread the knowledge of Jesus Christ among the blind children of Israel." After Alphonse also converted to Catholicism fifteen years later, in 1842, the two brothers worked together with the aim of evangelizing Jews and founded the congregation. The goal of working toward the conversion of Jews was made explicit in these early years, and each woman wishing to become a sister in the congregation would recite the following vow: "I undertake to employ all my zeal for the conversion of the Jewish people, to devote my time, my efforts, my sufferings, my prayers, my whole life to obtain their salvation through the knowledge of the Gospel."[2] However, despite this clear intention, the members of the congregation did not engage in active proselytization. Although Theodore Ratisbonne was eager for Jewish conversions, he made it clear that the sisters were forbidden from proselytizing explicitly; the desire for conversion was to be expressed only in prayer.[3]

A letter written by Theodore in 1844 to a Jewish woman by the name of Hélène demonstrates the extent to which he was determined to abstain from coercing Jews to convert to Christianity despite his clear desire for Jewish conversion: "And, since according to your declaration, you wish to remain a good Jewess, I leave you every liberty to follow the law of Moses, as practised by our fathers in the Holy Land. Moreover, I will take you to the synagogue each Saturday. . . . I could even remind you of all the old traditions, so much forgotten in our family; and thanks to these souvenirs, you could become an excellent Jewess." However, in the following lines, Theodore expresses a classically supersessionist view, implying that Christianity is the perfection of Judaism. He continues, "And then, my dear Hélène, we shall not be far from one another and we shall find ourselves more in agreement than you think, for the Christian is nothing else than an excellent Jew, and the Gospel calls them true Israelites."[4]

While the desire for the conversion of Jews was central to the prayer intentions of the congregation, outside of prayer, there was very little in their activities that related to Jews or Judaism. The main work of the congregation was in education, and they ran schools, often for boarders. These schools not only were for Catholic students but also welcomed Jews, Muslims, and Christians of all denominations.[5] Yet despite this educational focus and the institutional injunction to refrain from proselytization, the conversionary intentions did not always remain within private prayer, and in 1905, members of the congregation founded a group called the Association of Prayer for Israel (API). The API sought Jewish conversion through prayer groups, lectures, and conversation, and from its first centers in Jerusalem and Paris, it quickly spread internationally and attracted participation from many outside of the congregation.[6]

IMPETUS FOR CHANGE

In the 1950s, the Sisters of Sion began what would become a radical change in their mission. A process of review and revision of the aims of the congregation was under way, and by the time they were completed, the congregation had called for a complete stop to praying for the conversion of Jews. A number of factors throughout the first half of the twentieth century contributed to this change, and among this complex mixture of influences, the Holocaust stands out as perhaps the primary instigation for change. Many sisters in the congregation had harbored Jews during the war, and across the congregation, all were stunned by what they witnessed throughout the war and in its aftermath. Theologian Mary C. Boys lists two other important causes in addition to the impact of witnessing the Holocaust: (1) the theological ferment that was already occurring in the Catholic Church in the years leading up to the Second Vatican Council and (2) the presence of the congregation in Israel and their interaction with Jewish neighbors and communities after the establishment of Israel in 1948.[7]

Charlotte Klein, a Sister of Sion, offers a different enunciation of the various factors that contributed to this transformation in the congregation's thinking and practice. She first cites the changes in exegetical studies of the first half of the twentieth century, noting that these new ways of interpreting scripture, informed by modern scholarship, delegitimize the deicide charge that Christians historically levied against Jews. Second, she writes that the history of violence against Jews, particularly during the Holocaust, makes conversion efforts inappropriate, for "it is the Christians who need conversion and who should ask Jews to forgive them for 2000 years of often theologically inspired persecutions."[8] She next highlights the congregation's recognition that "dialogue and conversion are mutually exclusive" and argues that if the congregation is to engage in open interreligious dialogue and learning, there can be no intention for conversion. Klein also discusses the congregation's eventual recognition of Jewish self-understanding regarding conversion to Christianity and draws attention to the importance of the theological conviction that the Jewish people are in an unbroken covenant with God and possess "all that is necessary for a living faith."[9] Finally, Klein offers the theological proposal that Christian claims about Jesus may be too absolute and argues that Christians should make efforts to reformulate Christology to take into account the validity of other religions.

Celia Deutsch, another Sister of Sion, discusses four factors contributing to the congregation's mission change. She begins by citing the influence of the philosemitic movements of the early twentieth century. Although these philosemitic groups and movements, such as the API and others, generally maintained hope for Jewish conversion, they were also dedicated to fighting antisemitism, and they drew attention in Christian circles, particularly within Notre Dame de Sion, to the need for revision of Christian understandings of Judaism. The second factor Deutsch considers is *ressourcement*, the midcentury Catholic theological turn to the early sources of Christian tradition, including a renewed emphasis on scriptural scholarship.[10] This *ressourcement* led to new insights into the Jewish roots of Christianity as well as a revision of interpretations of scriptural passages about Judaism, which Klein also cites. Echoing both Boys and Klein, Deutsch points to the experiences of members of the congregation during the war, both in their witness of Jewish experiences and in their efforts in resistance, including harboring many Jews.[11]

The fourth factor that Deutsch examines is the Finaly Affair, which revolved around two Hungarian Jewish children who had been placed under the care of the Sisters of Sion in Grenoble during the war, who then sent them to a city daycare center. Their parents were killed, and when relatives arrived to claim the children after the war, the center that had taken care of the boys refused to surrender them and then baptized them. A court case followed, and eventually the Sisters of Sion intervened and helped hide the children. The majority of the Sisters of Sion had been unaware that the relatives had appeared to claim the children and that they had not been involved in baptizing the children, which was against church policy. The affair scandalized the congregation.[12] The complicity of some members of the congregation made it even more shocking, fueling self-examination and institutional change.

Following the scandal, Mother Marie-Felix, then the superior general of the congregation, reflected, "We do not know the Jews."[13] With these words, she expressed the sentiment behind many of the changes that the Sisters of Sion instigated in the decades following the Second World War. Having witnessed the incomprehensible tragedy of the Holocaust, members of the congregation began to question the extent to which they truly understood Jews and Judaism. In addition, in the wake of the Holocaust, the contribution of Christian theology to antisemitism became all too clear. In recognizing the complicity of Christian tradition in the history of violence, and in realizing their own lack of understanding, the congregation set out to try to "know the Jews" more deeply and to revise its own teachings and practices.

One of the ways this was achieved was through living among Jewish communities. In the early years of the congregation, most members had very little contact with Jews apart from teaching Jewish children in the schools they ran, and many had never even met a Jew.[14] Beginning in the early twentieth century, a group within the congregation, the Ancelles, began living within Jewish communities. The Ancelles were originally an independent group that joined the congregation in 1936. They dressed in secular clothes and lived within Jewish neighborhoods first in Palestine and then in Europe. Like other groups within the Sisters of Sion, they never proselytized directly, but prior to the congregation's mission change, Jewish conversion was a central prayer intention of the group, and the congregation urged them to transmit Christian ideas within Jewish intellectual circles.[15] Since the nineteenth century, the congregation had kept centers in Jerusalem and the village of Ein Kerem, but with the establishment of the State of Israel in 1948, Ein Kerem became a primarily Jewish town. From this point on, the sisters in Ein Kerem "knew Jews as neighbors, not as an abstraction."[16]

This was also in the immediate aftermath of the war, and the congregation was just beginning to process what it had experienced and learned during the conflict. As Deutsch observes, "The journey from 'loving the Jews' to witnessing genocide and risking their lives to hide people brought many of the sisters to a new level of understanding their vocation."[17] This was a source of a shocking awakening that inspired a serious examination and rethinking of theological views of Judaism as well. As the general councilor Sr. Marie-Dominique later reflected, "We would discover that, while we were asking God to forgive the Jews their infidelity, they were dying in the extermination camps, victims precisely of their fidelity."[18]

A RADICAL REVERSAL

While the eventual outcome of the transformation was drastic, the changes were gradual, and the first stages of the process were still mired in supersessionism. An example of this is seen in the General Chapter of 1951, which, while suggesting some revisions, also reiterated that one of the main missions of the congregation was the sanctification of Israel and returned to the theology of the wandering Jews, stating that Jews have wandered the earth since rejecting Jesus. These statements reveal a combination of philosemitism and anti-Judaism, as made clear by the document's assertion that the "mystery of Israel" is double: "On the one hand, grandeur and sanctity; on the other, lowliness and sin."[19] Progress was in the works, however, and in 1962, the General Council wrote a letter suggesting that all work and prayer for the conversion of Jews be abolished. It recommended that the sisters should turn their energies toward working to counter antisemitism and engaging in the study of Judaism.[20]

Yet changes in practice seemed to be easier to accomplish than changes in theology, and even after this letter, the congregation still had a long way to go in their theological interpretation of Judaism.[21] Nevertheless, changes were occurring, and a 1964 letter from the superior general concerning the API stated, "The Church is becoming conscious of the religious values existing among all believers, non-Catholics and even non-Christians; she particularly recognises and respects the faith of the Jews; this faith can lead them to salvation. . . . Consequently, we shall no longer recite any prayers for the 'conversion' of the Jews."[22] With this, the work of the API was halted with the injunction that the sisters in the organization must either transform the API or abolish it.

Surprisingly, despite their conversionary motives, the work of groups such as API also contributed to laying the groundwork for changes that eventually led to Nostra Aetate and to the radical transformation in the Catholic Church's theologies about Judaism. As Deutsch observes, these groups developed networks of friendships that helped make these changes possible, and the discussions that took place in these networks also influenced theologians outside of the congregation.[23] The Sisters of Sion also became directly involved in the Second Vatican Council, working with bishops internationally to help formulate a new understanding of Judaism.[24] A few sisters collaborated on drafting material that eventually became Nostra

Aetate, and after its promulgation in 1965, they remained instrumental in its implementation.[25] The contribution of the Sisters of Sion to the theological revisions of the Second Vatican Council is remarkable in multiple ways: first, they came into this work from an unlikely position, as a congregation whose early history was plagued with prayers for the conversion of Jews; second, they were groundbreaking in initiating the radical reversal of their mission prior to the institutional change in the Catholic Church; and third, as a women's congregation, they were instrumental in a council in which only men were allowed formal participation.

These changes continued throughout the following decades. Every Sister of Sion was educated in elements of Jewish studies and Christian-Jewish relations, and in 1970, the congregation decided that 10 percent of all the sisters should specialize in Christian-Jewish relations. Today, each sister lives in Israel for a period of time early in her vocation, and many return to live and work in Israel again later. The Sisters of Sion have developed a number of educational programs focusing on Jewish-Christian reconciliation, interreligious dialogue, Israeli-Palestinian relations, and Jewish studies for Christian students.

In Jerusalem, the Bat Kol Institute has been offering courses in Jewish studies to Christian students for over thirty years.[26] The institute was founded in 1983 by Sr. Maureena Fritz, a Sister of Sion, who still serves as its director as of this writing. The institute defines itself as "Christians studying the Word of God within its Jewish milieu, using Jewish sources." The majority of the professors are Jewish, specialists in rabbinic literature and in contemporary Judaism, and the students are taught not only the fundamentals of Judaism but also ways of reading midrash and the Talmud. Although it is a Christian faith–based program aimed at allowing students to "encounter anew the God of Israel whose identity is not frozen in the pages of the Tanach" so that their "understanding of God deepens and further encounter with God is facilitated," Sr. Maureena is adamant that this approach to the study of Jewish texts must never Christianize Judaism by imposing Christian readings on Jewish texts and traditions.[27] She encourages her students to leave behind their previous assumptions and to be open to Jewish ways of understanding.

The Sisters of Sion have developed another educational institute in Jerusalem, the Centre for Biblical Formation, which is also intended to educate Christians about Judaism in the context of Israel. Maureen Cusick, the program's director, explains that the program "is based on three main pillars. So we have an encounter with text, an encounter with the people, and an encounter with the land." She clarifies, "That means biblical studies, meeting Israelis and Palestinians, and archaeological studies of areas matching the text that is studied." She explains that the main thrust of the program is to guide students to more fully understand the roots of their own Christian faith through studying Jewish history and traditions in Israel. In her words, the program aims to "enable people to understand, from the destruction of the temple into Pharisaic Judaism into present-day Judaism, that they remain Jews, and Jesus remains a Jew. People find that quite hard to understand, even educated people." She adds, "We Christians have been so well taught badly. We've been badly well taught. It's quite difficult to eradicate. And so a lot of our work is undoing some of the rubbish we've been brought up with."[28]

The transformation that occurred within the Sisters of Sion in the decades following the Second World War shows how this group of sisters navigated a new path in a religious tradition steeped in a heritage of anti-Judaism and, through an ongoing struggle with embedded traditions, eventually completely changed their mission in order to combat antisemitism and religious anti-Judaism and to strengthen Christian-Jewish relations. The current constitution of the congregation, released in 1984, expresses an attitude toward Judaism that is far removed from the original view of the congregation. Summarizing the mission of the congregation today, the document states, "We are called to witness by our life to God's faithful love for the Jewish people. This call implies that our apostolic life is characterized by a three-fold commitment: to the Church, to the Jewish people and to a world of justice, peace and love."[29]

PORTRAIT: SR. CARMEN

In Israel, Sr. Carmen goes by the Hebrew name Karmela. Not Sr. Karmela, but simply Karmela. Upon meeting her, one is given no indication that she is anything but a Jewish Israeli. She wears no cross outside of her clothes or any other visible sign of her Christian faith, and with her fluent Hebrew, she blends seamlessly into the Jewish Israeli milieu. She's a talkative woman, originally from Malta, who first moved to Jerusalem in the early 1960s. She lived then in Ecce Homo, the Sisters of Sion convent in the Old City, which was under Jordanian control at the time. She was there during the Six-Day War and has remained living in Israel ever since.

When I met with Sr. Carmen for the first time, she welcomed me into her home, a modest apartment directly across from the house where the president of Israel lives. The location was extraordinarily significant for Sr. Carmen, who is an ardent supporter of Israel. And yet, when choosing a new apartment in Jerusalem, which she has done many times over the fifty years that she has lived in the city, she has always avoided living in homes that were owned by Arab families before 1948 and seized during the war because she does not want to be complicit in what she understands to be a tragedy and an injustice.

By the time of our second visit, a year later, she had moved into a new apartment on HaLamed He Street in West Jerusalem. She told me the details of searching for the apartment and said she was thrilled to be living on that particular street because its name relates to the founding of the State of Israel.[30] Again she welcomed me into her home, and even in the privacy of her own apartment, she was discreet about visual displays of her Catholic faith, with no crosses and no devotional pictures visible from where I sat in the living room.

Sr. Carmen loves living among her Jewish Israeli neighbors. "Living here is providential," she said, "because I breathe the same air that the Jewish people breathe." She tries her best to not disrupt the religious observance of her neighbors, and on Shabbat, she makes sure not to run any machines that might make a noise and risk causing offense to her neighbors. She holds a degree in Jewish studies from Hebrew University, and she explains that she chose this field because she "wanted to learn . . . what makes the Jewish people tick." Although she considered studying the Talmud to reach this goal, she settled on Jewish history because, in her words, "It embodies the Jewish people—as who they are. I think it's a mystery in itself. It's very difficult to put words to it."

Sr. Carmen regularly prays for the Jewish people, but unlike many of the other voices heard in this study, her prayer has a political bent. She explained, "The people I have at the forefront [are] the leadership, that the leadership would be inspired by God according to his or her conception of what is the best state for the people to live fully their life the way they see fit." She continued, "That's why I'm here. I'm here to pray for all of them, for Netanyahu, for Rivlin, for all of them, for the Knesset . . . so I pray for the leadership in Israel, and the people, because the leadership is not separated from the people."

When Sr. Carmen prays for Jews, furthermore, she does not pray in the name of Jesus. She prays only in the name of God, beginning her prayer in the way that many Jewish prayers begin: "ha kadosh baruch hu" (the holy one, blessed be he). She even prays using Jewish liturgical texts, such as the *Amidah*, which is recited three times a day in Jewish liturgical practice. Sr. Carmen says that she prays the benediction of the *Amidah* referred to as the *binah*, specifically for the leadership of Israel.

During our first meeting, she explained that she felt that the location of her apartment, directly across from the president's house, was a part of God's plan. She said, "The fact that I have an apartment here is very accidental, but it's not accidental; it's in God's plan. Why would he bring me just next door to the president?" From her balcony, she could look down on the palm trees of the president's estate, and she pointed out, "When he has events, I hear them from the kitchen. When I want to *see* them, I turn on the television." I joked with her that she'd been placed there because the president needs a nun to pray for him, and before she moved in, he didn't have that office filled. She laughed, but then she added more seriously, "I am more and more affirmed that that is my role living here."

When I asked her if she draws a distinction between loving the Jewish people and loving the State of Israel, she replied emphatically, "No, how can you divide that? How can you dissect that? If you dissect, they are not whole anymore." For Sr. Carmen, this wholeness encompasses the history of the Jewish people all the way to the biblical roots, and inherent in this history is the role of the land of Israel. She continued, "When we look at the Jewish people today, we cannot look at them as isolated from what their history has been. . . . If I made partitions, I would be violating what my call is. . . . And I don't think it's true to the choice that God made with the Jewish people." She concluded, "If you love somebody, you love them whole, as they are."

Even after over fifty years of living in Israel, and despite her strong affiliation with the State of Israel, the land of Israel, the Jewish religion, and the Jewish people, Sr. Carmen still feels like a stranger in the land. "I am a *ger*, and I'm happy to be a *ger*," she explained, using the biblical Hebrew word for "foreigner." This is not easy for her, she said, but she feels that it is part of her religious call: "It's hard. If you ask me for something difficult, that's the hard thing. Living here fifty years, and you'll find you are always a foreigner. I've lived through all the wars, through the positive and negative, and yet I've never belonged. That is the hard part. But that's what I'm called to."

Despite all her efforts to blend into Jewish Israeli society and her remarkable half-century of life and service in Israel, she remains an outsider—a Catholic nun living as a *ger* in a land that she loves and to which she cannot fully belong.

CHAPTER 8

A Christian Aliyah?

LIVING IN THE HOLY LAND

In the Christian tradition, the land of Israel is seen as the Holy Land. The determination of the boundaries of the Holy Land is dependent on interpretation and is not contained entirely by the contemporary boundaries of Israel; nevertheless, the key sites in the Christian conception of the Holy Land reside today within Israel and the West Bank. The notion of the sacredness of the biblical land of Israel has its roots in the Hebrew Bible, in which the land of Israel was given by God to the Jewish people, and this tradition was later reinforced and developed in rabbinic literature, which emphasizes the great religious significance of living in the land.[1] As Christianity arose out of the context of Second Temple Judaism, it also developed traditions of the sacredness of the land originating in these Jewish traditions, but in its specifically Christian enunciation, the concept took a very different shape.

As Christian thought developed, the belief that the biblically promised land is sacred and distinct gradually became prefaced not on the promise of the land in the Hebrew Bible but rather on the New Testament narrative of the life of Jesus. This resulted in a Christian understanding of the Holy Land as the place where Jesus was born, lived, and preached, and Jerusalem as the city where he was crucified and resurrected.[2] As the Christian concept of the Holy Land developed, it began to shift in emphasis away from the physical land and toward an eschatological vision of which the actual land was only a symbol. The notion of the heavenly Jerusalem took root in the Christian imagination, personified in an apocalyptic vision in the New Testament as a bride descending from heaven.³ These Christian ideas of a heavenly or symbolic Jerusalem were utilized to disparage Jewish traditions of Jerusalem as the sacred city in the sacred land. Early Christian thought, seeking to distance itself from Judaism and to strengthen its supersessionist claims, held that just as the heavenly Jerusalem had abrogated the earthly Jerusalem, so too had Christianity abrogated Judaism. The anti-Judaic roots of this spiritualized Christian vision of Jerusalem and the Holy Land as a whole have by now receded below the surface of much Christian thought about the Holy Land. This history of the development of Holy Land piety has been largely forgotten, and few Christians today associate Christian understandings of the Holy Land with anti-Jewish theologies; nevertheless, whether acknowledged or not, this history is implicit in the Christian vision of the Holy Land.

Br. Tiago, a member of the Brothers of Sion, the men's branch of the Congregation of Our Lady of Sion, expresses that living in the Holy Land is deeply spiritually important to him. However, demonstrating his sensitivity to Jewish tradition and to the current sociopolitical context, he clarifies that he prefers to not use the term the "Holy Land" when referring to Israel, as many Christians do. He explains that he does not want his language to ignore the political reality on the ground, and he prefers to refer to land within the current borders of Israel as "Israel." Br. Tiago, like many others in this study, is making a linguistic choice that pushes back against a tendency exhibited by many Christians to use the term "Holy Land" in an effort to avoid the use of the term "Israel" and to view the land only from a supposedly neutral theological viewpoint. However, neutrality is rarely achieved; while in most cases, the use of the term "Holy Land" is simply habitual, following in the tradition of much Christian language, in other cases, it becomes an intentionally political statement. Either way, the choice to avoid using the title "Israel" effects a verbal erasure of the State of Israel, reframing it as the Christian Holy Land.

Br. Tiago feels that the use of the title "Israel" is also important for Christian theological reasons. He explains, "If we forget what Israel is in a theological sense, we don't have Christianity, we don't have Jesus." Here he makes a connection between the use of "Israel" to designate the political state and its use to designate the Jewish people as represented in biblical literature. Br. Tiago finds that living in Israel is significant not only for the insight it gives him into biblical history but also because the spirituality of his congregation is based in Jerusalem, as evidenced by the "Sion" in the congregation's name. He clarifies that the spiritual connection to Jerusalem is not experienced simply by living there; rather, he feels that it necessitates an interior receptivity: "It's not only living in the sense of being, but to be present to the expression. We need to feed ourselves from this place; otherwise, we cannot even be called the brothers of the Congregation of Sion, and there would be no sense at all."

The suggestion that the land of Israel might hold serious theological significance for Christians beyond the ambivalent traditions of Holy Land piety is something that a number of the voices heard in this book have contemplated. Sr. Gemma, the founder of the Catholic Institute for Holocaust Studies, feels a deep sense of attachment to the people and land of Israel, where she has lived for forty years. She begins, "I've been here, and lived here, and loved people here, and experienced so much of what goes on here—the pain as well as the joy. So you get attached—you can't help it, it's very normal—with any country that you go to." Although she notes that living in any country for so long would likely lead to feelings of attachment and solidarity, she feels that in Israel, the religious significance of the land causes her attachment to become more intense. She continues, "But in a way, this is special because it comes out of our sacred text. There's such a strong relationship there that it's very difficult not to be sometimes defensive of Israel—and certainly very attached."

In an interpretative move that goes against the grain of the supersessionist roots of Holy Land piety, Sr. Gemma believes that the Jewish religious concept of the land and the contemporary Jewish return to the land also have significance to Christian spirituality. Expressing a unique theological interpretation that diverges substantially from many other Christian claims, she reflects, "The return of the Jews to this land has a deeply spiritual significance for the Jewish people, that's true, but at the same time, it has significance for the Church, for Christians too." She disavows a connection with Christian Zionist theology, which often enunciates a similar claim, and clarifies, "Now, I'm definitely not with the fundamentalist Christians, who have their particular position, but I do feel that there is a source of holiness here that we need to understand and to plumb and to experience." She recognizes that few Catholics feel the way she does and observes that "we don't have that taste [for the land] . . . but if you are here for a while, and if you're open to it, you do acquire a way of looking at things." This "way of looking at things," in her experience, involves a recognition of the sacredness of the land according to Jewish traditions rather than Jesus-centered Christian traditions.

Sr. Gemma's views were developed in part through her close relationship with Fr. Isaac Jacob, the Benedictine monk who founded a community in Tel Gamliel based on the spirituality of the Rule of St. Benedict, and inspired by Jewish biblical and rabbinic traditions. In his preface to the translation of the rule into Hebrew, which Sr. Gemma had worked on, Fr. Jacob asks, "Does the reemergence of Jewish sovereignty in the Land of Israel portend theological significance?"[4] The document raises multiple implications of this query but does not conclusively answer it, suggesting that the community at Tel Gamliel would continue to ponder the question. Fr. Jacob saw this question to be of pressing concern to his community and wrote, "A School of the Lord's Service in Israel has a special obligation to probe the theological and religious implications for understanding the Word of God because of Return to the Land" and must "focus on the theological implications of dwelling and settlement in the Land," for he believed that "the Land of Israel is a *locus theologicus*, a vantage point for perceiving theological issues."[5] Fr. Jacob felt that this theological focus on the land might serve as a way for Christians to better understand their relationship with Judaism and with Islam: "With its return theologically to Israel and the Middle East, the Church will sense more keenly its relationship with Judaism and Islam, and the other monotheistic communities in the Lord where it was born."[6]

These theological interpretations are far from common within mainstream Catholic thought.[7] However, the notion that the Jewish presence in the land of Israel might be significant for Christians as well can also be found among more public and authoritative voices within the Church hierarchy. Archbishop Pierbattista Pizzaballa, currently the Apostolic Administrator of the Latin Patriarchate of Jerusalem, reflected on this in an interview I held with him in September 2015, when he served as the Custos of the Holy Land, the title given to the head of the Franciscan Custody of the Holy Land. In both positions, Pizzaballa was one of the most authoritative voices, if not the definitive authority, of the Catholic Church in the Holy Land.[8] Addressing what he sees as an overspiritualization or abstraction of the land within most Christian notions of the Holy Land, he commented, "Our understanding of the land now as holy is purely spiritual. For the Jews, it is spiritual of course, but not only. In Judaism, there is a very strong connection between faith, people, and land; it's really concrete. And we Christians spiritualize it." He laughed and added regretfully, "Maybe, too spiritualized!" He continued, "This is also my question, I am wondering. God is saying something. I don't think that the people of Israel who live in Israel are just a causality, are just an accident." Pizzaballa refrains from making any definitive statements about the spiritual meaning of the land to Christians or about the Jewish presence in Israel, but he suggests that both might be theologically significant to Christianity.

SOLIDARITY AND AMBIVALENCE

Israel represents a tangled nest of concerns and interests for many Christians, and these issues are quite different across distinct Christian groups. For Palestinian Christians, issues of social justice, land rights, and political independence rise to the forefront. For many Christian Zionists and Messianic believers, eschatological messianic expectations involving the return of Jesus are paired with political Zionist interests. But for the Catholics discussed in this book, the issues are less clear cut and less polarized. While most insist that theological views should remain distinct from political interests, they nevertheless find themselves immersed in political issues, for in Israel, religion and politics cannot be easily separated, and the distinction between the two often blurs.

After many years of living in Israel, the participants in this study say that they have learned to identify intimately with Israel; the land, the history, the culture, the political struggles, and the sense of communal belonging have become part of their lives and worldviews. They speak of a sense of solidarity and emotional attachment that arises through living in Israel and identifying with the Israeli experience. The relationships they have developed over the years have fostered a more intimate sense of identification with existential Israeli concerns and a deeper understanding of the motivation behind Zionist sentiments; at the same time, for many, these relationships have also led to a better understanding of Palestinian perspectives and a more personal concern for Palestinian issues. Each is strengthened through the variety of relationships that each person develops, and many speak of ultimately feeling torn.

This can be seen in Sr. Carmen's narrative when she reflects on her nearly thirty years of teaching in schools for Palestinian girls. Her ardent Zionism is not prefaced on any sense of antagonism with Palestinians, and she speaks of what she feels is a very real and deep love for both Palestinians and Israeli Jews. Sr. Carmen taught first in a school for Christian Palestinian girls beginning in 1965, when she was living and teaching in present-day East Jerusalem, which was then a part of Jordan. Following this, from 1971 to 1993, she taught Muslim Palestinian girls in a municipal school in East Jerusalem. She taught in these schools through some of the worst moments of the Israeli-Palestinian conflict: in the first school, she taught before and after the Six-Day War, and in the second school, she taught through the First Intifada. While she says that she sincerely loved her Palestinian students, she also carried the same deep love for the Jewish people then that she has today. She recalls, "I was loyal to Palestinians and to Israel at the same time. Never did I allow myself to love one at the expense of the other. For me, that's the biggest strength that I carry with me, and I hope that I will always be faithful."

Sr. Maureen Cusick, a Sister of Sion, expresses her own intention to always retain her equanimity and openness to both Israeli and Palestinian perspectives. She lives at Ecce Homo, the Sisters of Sion convent located in the Muslim quarter of the Old City, which is considered part of Palestinian East Jerusalem. She admits, "It's quite stressful in Jerusalem, with all the feelings of being here in the middle of East Jerusalem with Palestinians and people taking a stance, pro-Palestinian or pro-Israeli." She finds it particularly challenging to live in the midst of a tumultuous and politically charged Palestinian area given her work in Christian-Jewish relations. She reflects, "As a Sister of Sion, that's a quite hard one to walk. It's quite hard. But we have to; we have to find a way to be honest, to see what is just and what are the fears on the side of the Israelis, what are the fears on the side of the Palestinians, what are the injustices on the side of the Israelis, and what are the injustices [on the side of the Palestinians]. It's very complex." Sr. Maureen directs the Centre for Biblical Formation, an institute for Christian students in Jerusalem, and speaking of how she strives to imbue students with a necessary stance of humility and ambivalence regarding the conflict, she says, "When we have students, we try to be very careful that they don't go home with a one-sided picture. Most of the time, we say, 'Look, you have to be able, when you go back, to say "I don't really know. This is what I've seen; this is what I've experienced.""'"

Fr. David Neuhaus, who served as the patriarchal vicar of the St. James Vicariate for Hebrew Speaking Catholics from 2009 until 2017, reflects on his experience of feeling compassion for those on both sides of the Israeli-Palestinian conflict. He avoids discourse about taking sides, and rather than speaking of a middle position, he prefers to speak of a position of empathy: "I don't think it's the middle. I think a place of empathy that goes out in order to empathetically understand what could be two sides of a conflict—even though even presenting the conflict as having two sides is already too schematic." He uses the image of being torn, which he feels better describes a truly empathetic position: "It's a place of being open, and openness means to be torn. 'Middle' sounds like you're not here and you're not there, whereas I think the truly empathetic person is both here and there."

This is precisely the phrase that Sr. Rebecca, a Sister of Sion who lives as a hermit near Jerusalem, uses to express her conflicted feelings: "Seeing the injustice that is a reality here—much of which, but definitely not all, but much of which comes from the Israeli side—I often feel torn apart."[9] She speaks of feeling solidarity with the Jewish people but clarifies that this feeling is complicated and challenged by the political reality of the Israeli-Palestinian conflict: "In the meantime, because of this injustice and the government, the word 'solidarity' has become a little difficult for me, and what has come into the foreground is much more that it's simply out of love for this people."

Sr. Rebecca explains this feeling of solidarity or love through relating a saying of St. Therese of the Child Jesus: "[St. Therese said,] 'My place is at the table for sinners,' meaning not because I'm so generous that I choose to sit with the sinners but meaning that I too am a sinner. And so now, when I talk about solidarity and love, that includes my feeling torn apart by the things that happen here—certainly not my solidarity with the injustice that is done but my solidarity with the people, because I too am a sinner." The love and solidarity she feels are not diminished by her recognition of political injustices, for she identifies her own sins with those of others and places herself at that metaphorical table. She believes that the love she feels is neither affiliated with any particular political movement nor challenged by political conflicts.

The sense of solidarity through conflict that Sr. Rebecca expresses is complex, and she remains cognizant of suffering on many sides. A similar sense is expressed by Sr. Pilar, also a Sister of Sion. When Sr. Pilar speaks about the friendships she has developed with Israelis, she playfully jokes, "I know that sometimes they are a big pain in the neck, but I love them, like a mother loves her child even if it is a pain in the neck. . . . I really love them. They're a pain in the neck, but I love them!" However, when Sr. Pilar speaks about her feeling of solidarity with the Jewish people and Israel, she takes a much more serious tone. "Do you know when I became really in solidarity with the Jewish people?" she asks. "At the most difficult moment."

She speaks of how she felt when she heard about the 1982 massacre at Sabra and Shatila, two refugee camps in Lebanon. This massacre, which shocked the world, was committed with the complicity and strategic assistance of Israel. Her eyes burning with feeling, she says, "It was the first time that in my heart I stopped saying, 'God, what have they done?' Instead, I said, 'God, what have we done?'" She continues, "Since that moment, my solidarity is total. . . . I know all the things that are happening; I'm not blind. I love Israel, but I love the real one, with all the injustices." In this profound admission, Sr. Pilar identifies the moment of greatest horror and shame as the moment when her solidarity became clear. Her solidarity, she realized, was not because of the virtues of Israel; rather, like the love one develops for a person, it was a love that encompassed everything—the sins and injustices as well as the strengths and acts of compassion.

Sr. Michaela, a Benedictine nun, feels a similar sense of being torn in her love for Israel and the Jewish people. She reflects, "I have friends in Bethlehem who live behind the wall and have their water cut off for three weeks in the summer, and they really suffer. And I don't have a solution for that." Speaking of one family in the West Bank with whom she is particularly close, she relates, "Khalil told me that his father left him the olive grove. . . . There were three hundred trees, and now there are only three left. The wall cut them off, and they cut them down, and that was that. I said, 'Wow, how do you feel about that?' And Khalil said, 'The Lord gives, and the Lord takes away. Blessed be the name of the Lord.'" Sr. Michaela is deeply moved by the injustices that her Palestinian friends in the West Bank suffer, and yet she still maintains, "It doesn't diminish my love for the land [of Israel] and the Jewish people. It has opened me [to] the reality of the other people who live here." She concludes, "Carrying this love does not negate the other." To try to understand her own sense of a special love for the Jewish people that does not preclude a love for other peoples, she ponders the biblical narrative of Abraham's two sons, Ishmael and Isaac: "I'm sure that Abraham loved both children equally. And I think God loved both children equally even though Isaac was the child willed by God. So maybe there's something in that symbolism—that my call for Israel is this call of God, but at the same time there are another people, and I love them too."

Fr. Marcel Dubois, the Dominican involved in the Isaiah House, felt intensely torn during his many decades in Israel, and his allegiances shifted with time. Early on, he was highly influenced by the pro-Zionist philosophy of Maritain, and he remained in West Jerusalem, on the Israeli side of the city, through the wars of the 1960s, 1970s, and 1980s and maintained his political support of Israel. However, this changed with the Second Intifada, after which he left West Jerusalem and moved to a nearby Arab village in a "very Israeli trajectory of discontent and an inchoate feeling that Israel had deviated from the path of righteousness."[10]

Fr. Michael McGarry, the former rector of the Tantur Ecumenical Institute in Jerusalem, conscientiously refuses to take sides. He notes that political affiliation has worked its way into many Christian modes of engagement with Israel, and he argues that this is a weakness. He observes, "For some, siding wholeheartedly and unquestionably with current Israeli (political) policies is the litmus test of whether we Christians have truly overcome the centuries of antisemitism that have plagued Christian communities. Others, more sympathetic to a Palestinian perspective on the past sixty years, will wonder whether we have succumbed to the logic that those who passionately work for Christian-Jewish understanding, as we do, must, therefore, be willing to ignore Palestinian suffering and cries of injustice." He concludes, "I wish to go beyond either-or-propositions. In my experience, too many on all sides say, in effect, 'If you wish to be my friend, you must hate the people I hate.'"[11]

According to McGarry's telling, when Msgr. Richard Mathes, the former rector of the Notre Dame of Jerusalem Center, left Jerusalem in the early 2000s, Mathes said, "When I first came to Jerusalem, my sympathies were with the Israelis and I was angry with the Palestinians. The more I worked in Jerusalem and the more I saw in the land, my sympathies shifted to the

Palestinians and I was angry with the Israelis. When I left, my heart wept for both of them."[12]

Like Mathes, many in this study have experienced a "heart that weeps for both of them." They have found ways to live in this position, feeling compassion for those on all sides of the conflict and also feeling a particular sense of solidarity with the Jewish people and with Israel. They feel torn, and let themselves remain torn, while maintaining that they are outsiders in the land and must not insert themselves into the conflict through activism. Fr. Jacques, a contemplative Benedictine, echoes this sentiment when he says that according to Psalm 109, "Everybody on this land is a *ger*, a foreigner. This is very important. Even the pious Jew in the psalms considers himself as invited by the Lord—a foreigner, not the owner."[13] So in his experience, to live as a monk in a land torn by conflict, he and his community must maintain a stance of spiritual openness and alertness, as if remaining awake all through the night in a vigil. He concludes, "Being vigilant is the only possible answer or attitude, at least for us monks and Christians in this land. We are not the owners of this land."

Fr. Olivier is an energetic, stocky man with rosy cheeks and an intense, direct manner. He served in the military in France before becoming a Benedictine monk at the Bec-Hellouin Abbey. When the abbey began a foundation in Abu Gosh in 1977, he was one of the first monks to arrive, joining the others in their shared purpose of contemplating the "mystery of Israel," as he understands it, and he has now lived at Abu Gosh for forty years. Fr. Olivier is involved in educational programs for members of the Israel Defense Forces, and he holds the rare distinction of being one of the only monks or nuns in Israel to be granted Israeli citizenship.

Growing up France, Fr. Olivier had little knowledge of Israel, but he recalls being very moved by an experience he had when he was thirteen years old while watching the film *The Exodus*. He explained, "I was very moved. Something that was new for me was to discover that people wanted to live according to an ideal. They had no choice; it was after the war. They wanted to found a state here. It seems that I always kept this feeling in my heart. And I can tell you today that this is one of the reasons I am here today." When he entered the monastery as a young man, he found that as he studied Christian scripture and history, he began learning more about Judaism as well. He identifies this as one of two main factors that led him to his feelings for Israel and for the Jewish people. He had "the religious contact with Israel by faith but also a contact with Zionism."

Many nuns and monks have desired to become citizens of Israel, but in most cases, it is impossible. Although Israeli citizenship is available through the Law of Return to any Jewish person, it excludes a person who openly

practices a religion other than Judaism, as seen in the well-known case of
Br. Daniel Rufeisen. However, Fr. Olivier is not of Jewish descent and was
granted citizenship for his dedication and service to Israel. He recalled, "It
was a dream [to become a citizen]. I remember that I spoke about this to
a good friend of mine, who was at that time in charge of the education of
the army in Jerusalem. It was in 1989, and I told him, 'Yuval, I would like to
share with you one of my dreams. I would like to be an Israeli citizen.' But I
thought at the same time it was completely impossible." However, it proved
to be possible, although Fr. Olivier was never entirely certain what allowed
this exception to be granted. He pondered, "When I look back, I think there
was a window open in the ministry of the interior. . . . [They asked,] 'Please,
tell me why do you want the citizenship?' I told him, 'My destiny is here.'"

Fr. Olivier has developed close ties with members of the Israeli Defense
Forces, and he regularly meets with soldiers to teach them about Christianity
in the context of Israel. Telling the story of one recent encounter, he recalled,
"A few months ago, I had a visit with a group for military preparation. There
were fifty boys, and maybe twenty were with a *kippah* [yarmulke]. The leader
of the group . . . hugged me, and asked me, 'Olivier, did you learn the verse
of the psalm that we sang last year with the boys as a group in the church
together?'" The previous year, they sang a Hebrew song based on the fourth
verse of Psalm 23, the English translation of which is "Even though I walk
through the darkest valley, I fear no evil, for you are with me." Fr. Olivier
paused to sing the verse and then continued, "We sang it together, and it
was a kind of prayer together. And afterward, the leader asked me, 'All these
boys standing before you are going to the army, so could you bless them?'"
It is highly unusual for the leader of an Israeli army group to ask a Catholic
monk to bless them; indeed, it's very rare for a monk to be asked to bless
any group of Jews. However, the leader of this group trusted Fr. Olivier to
respect their Jewish traditions, and Fr. Olivier responded in kind: "I didn't
do anything forbidden to them—no sign of the cross. They are Jews, all [of]
them, and many of them with *kippahs*. My prayer was ' *ha kadosh baruch hu*;
bless them, bless their families.'"

Religious Identity After the Holocaust

CHAPTER 9

Navigating Jewish-
Christian Identity

INTRODUCTION

Part 3 of this book follows the negotiation of Christian and Jewish identity and formulations of the border, often blurred, between Christianity and Judaism. This border takes different shapes in the experience of the people whose stories are heard here, as each navigates his or her own unique path along this terrain. They struggle with the negotiation of complex social and religious components of identity, which in many cases are accompanied by a fluid exchange of religious belief and identification. These chapters consider the experiences along this border by Jewish converts to Christianity, many of whom are Holocaust survivors who converted in the throes of trauma during the war, entered monastic life, and later immigrated to Israel. The chapters analyze these conversion narratives and personal histories, exploring the impact of Holocaust trauma on the conversions and tracing the converts' subsequent negotiations of religious identity.

Jewish conversion to Christianity is a highly sensitive topic, particularly from Jewish perspectives, and the narratives of conversion discussed here can be read in very different ways. From Christian perspectives, Jewish converts to Christianity can be seen as continuing in the path of the first followers of Jesus in the early Christian community, who were Jewish believers in Jesus. Through this lens, they can also be read as stories of finding hope, truth, and peace through faith. But from Jewish perspectives, conversion is apostasy and is often seen as an offense to Jewish tradition and the Jewish people. The notion of a Jewish Christian can be seen as yet another Christian attempt to adopt and abrogate Judaism. Like all hermeneutical issues, it depends on the lenses through which one reads and the affiliations and concerns reflected through those lenses.

CONVERSION AND APOSTASY

A striking number of those whose narratives are told in this book are of Jewish heritage, particularly among the predecessors discussed in chapter 6, who set the groundwork for this Judeocentric Catholic phenomenon. Some are Jews who converted to Catholicism, and others are of mixed Jewish and Christian families, and yet each of them immigrated to Israel driven by a sense of Jewish identity and by the understanding of Israel as the Jewish homeland. Their views and experiences present a different sort of Catholic engagement with Judaism and Israel, one that cannot easily be termed philosemitism, for it is their own sense of Jewish identity, rather than the Jewish "other," that motivates their work in Christian-Jewish relations.

The converts whose stories are told here insist that they have remained Jewish even after converting to Catholicism and eventually entering vowed religious life as nuns and monks. In their experiences, they feel that their Jewish identity and Christian faith are not in conflict. In making this assertion, they follow a long history of debates on the determination of Jewish identity and on the often indeterminate margins between Jewish and Christian identity. Debates over Jewish and Christian identity began during the development of early Christianity as a Jewish religious moment within both Jewish and Gentile communities. These debates continued in different forms throughout history in contexts such as the determination of Jewish identity in instances of forced conversion as well as voluntary conversion. Related struggles can also be found in cases of Christian conversion to Judaism, such as the contemporary discussion about the legitimacy of conversions conducted by non-Orthodox rabbis.

Despite the long-standing debates on Jewish identity and Christian faith, the issue of determining Jewish identity in the case of conversion to other religions is clearly delineated in halachic thought. According to halacha, a person born as a Jew can never cease to be a Jew, regardless of his or her religious beliefs. Even a Jew who formally adopts another religion and renounces his or her Jewish faith remains a Jew. A Jew who adopts another religion becomes an apostate, but significantly, a *Jewish* apostate. Pointing to the familial nature of Judaism, Meir Soloveichik observes, "It is precisely because Jewishness is familial that anyone born a Jew can never undo his Jewishness, no matter his beliefs. A Christian who does not believe in Christian dogma is no longer considered a Christian; but a Jewish apostate remains a Jew, and his return to the faith of his fathers is eagerly awaited by his brothers."[1] A Jewish convert to Christianity, then, remains a Jew even though he or she has left behind the Jewish religion.[2] What has been left behind is not Jewishness but Judaism.

Located on the other end of the spectrum of interpretations of what constitutes Jewish identity is a radically progressive definition offered by the Israeli novelist Amos Oz:

> A Jew, in my unhalachic opinion, is someone who *chooses* to share the fate of other Jews, or who is *condemned* to do so. Moreover: to be a Jew almost always means to relate mentally to the Jewish past, whether the relation is one of pride or gloom or both together, whether it consists of shame or rebellion or pride or nostalgia. Moreover: to be a Jew almost always means to relate to the Jewish present, whether the relation is one of fear or confidence, pride in the achievement of Jews or shame for their actions, an urge to deflect them from their path or a compulsion to join them.[3]

This definition, as Oz admits, is very far from the halachic definition, and yet it reflects a position held by many along the margins of Jewish identity.

A number of different criteria can be used to determine Jewish identity. As Daniel Cohn-Sherbok observes, these include "1) the religious definition of Jewishness; i.e. being Torah observant; 2) the social and cultural definition: identifying with and being committed to the Jewish people; 3) the nationalist definition: living in Israel or supporting Zionism."[4] These are far from the authoritative guidelines for determining Jewish identity, but similar views are shared by many non-Orthodox Jews today. By these parameters, the converts whose stories are told here would be considered Jewish according to the last two categories, although not the first.

Judaism places a very strong emphasis on the preservation of Jewish tradition, and this notion of preservation is characterized by separation, drawing a clear and impassable boundary around Jewish tradition. Indeed, the development of Jewish tradition has been shaped in part by this goal, making an art of resisting assimilation for the sake of the survival of the Jewish community. This reflects the biblical concept of election, in which the Jewish people are chosen and set apart. As a rabbinic dictum enjoins, it is necessary to "make a fence around the Torah" and to preserve Jewish tradition by keeping its boundaries distinct (Pirkei Avot 1:1).

THE CASE OF EDITH STEIN

One of the most well-known twentieth-century Jewish converts to Catholicism was the philosopher Edith Stein, who converted to Catholicism, became a Carmelite nun, and was killed in the Holocaust. She has been used as a symbol by the Church for Catholic-Jewish reconciliation, much to the chagrin of many who find that her status as a Jewish convert to Christianity—in other words, an apostate from a halachic perspective—is not well suited to such a role.

Edith Stein was born in Breslau, Germany, in 1891 to an observant Jewish family. At the age of thirteen, however, she lost her faith in God, abandoned Jewish religious observance, and remained adamantly secular into adulthood.[5] She received a doctorate in philosophy in 1916 while studying with Edmund Husserl and earned the distinction of being the second woman in Germany to receive a PhD in philosophy.[6] For the following nearly two decades, she built a successful career as a philosopher, teaching at the University of Freiburg. Her life took a radical turn in 1922, when, at the age of thirty, she converted to Catholicism, shocking many in her decidedly secular milieu. In 1933, as antisemitism was intensifying in Germany, she entered the Carmelite order and began life as Sr. Teresa Benedicta of the Cross. Her writings during the following decade indicate that she had an intimation of her fate and was well aware that she would not be protected in the monastery. In August 1942, Edith Stein and her sister Rosa were arrested from the Echt Carmel monastery and deported to Auschwitz, where they were killed in the gas chambers of Birkenau.[7]

In October 1998, the Catholic Church canonized Edith Stein as St. Teresa Benedicta of the Cross, and the following year, Pope John Paul II declared her the copatroness of Europe. The Catholic Church sees Stein as a martyr and a witness to the Catholic faith and also as a witness to the horrors of the Holocaust and has utilized her as a symbol of Christian-Jewish dialogue. In his letter proclaiming her the copatronesses of Europe, Pope John Paul II speaks of "her witness as an innocent victim" and writes, "We also recognize in it the pledge of a renewed encounter between Jews and Christians." Suggesting that her role as a copatroness would increase awareness of the Holocaust and consequently lead to an overcoming of discrimination, he continues, "Today's proclamation of Edith Stein as a Co-Patroness of Europe is intended to raise on this Continent a banner of respect, tolerance and acceptance which invites all men and women to understand and appreciate each other, transcending their ethnic, cultural and religious differences in order to form a truly fraternal society."[8]

The use of Edith Stein as a symbol of Christian-Jewish reconciliation was already well established by the time of her appointment as the copatroness of Europe in 1998, as evidenced by a statement from the National Conference of Catholic Bishops on the occasion of her beatification in 1987. The statement declares her beatification to be "a unique occasion for joint Catholic-Jewish reflection and reconciliation. In honoring Edith Stein, the Church wishes to honor all the six million Jewish victims of the Holocaust." It continues, "Catholic veneration [of Edith Stein] will necessarily contribute to a continuing and deepened examination of the conscience regarding sins of commission and omission perpetrated by Christians against Jews during the dark years of World War II."[9] However, to many, particularly those outside of the Catholic Church, it remains unclear why the veneration of a Jewish convert to Catholicism would be a more effective examination of conscience regarding Christian violence against Jews than the veneration of any other Jew who was killed in the Holocaust.

Stein's role as a symbol of Catholic-Jewish reconciliation has met with varied yet largely critical Jewish responses. The choice has been seen by many Jews as not only ineffectual but also offensive. David Novak takes this stance, arguing, "Edith Stein accepted what Christians have always had to say to Jews, namely, that Christianity solves the problems of Judaism better than Judaism does because Christianity provides the savior to whom Jews have always looked. She therefore did not consider herself a runaway from Judaism (however rudimentary her own Judaism was) but rather a Jew whose Judaism brought her into the Church. Her logic was clearly supersessionist."[10] Here, Novak finds that Stein's continued identification with the

Jewish people is precisely the problem. Judith Banki adds, "Though perhaps not deliberate, there is an inescapable triumphalism implicit in using the name/example of a person who has abandoned your community of faith for another's purposes of reconciliation."[11]

The writings that Stein left behind indicate that she did indeed follow the standard Catholic view of Judaism during her time—namely, that salvation was attainable only through belief in Jesus and that the Jewish "failure" to believe is a sin. This is indicated in her last will and testament, written on June 9, 1939, in which she says, "I pray to the Lord that he may accept my living and dying . . . as an atonement for the Jewish people's unbelief and so that the Lord may be accepted by his own and that his reign may come in glory, that Germany may be saved and that there be peace in the world."[12] The supersessionist theology expressed in this passage was certainly not unique to Stein, as it is typical of Catholic thought up until very recently.[13] We can only surmise how Stein's theologies may have changed had she lived only a few decades more and witnessed the changes that the Church underwent during Vatican II. Although Stein's theological perspectives of Judaism may have been a sign of the theological atmosphere during her time more than a sign of her most deeply held convictions, the Church's choice to utilize her as a model of Jewish-Catholic reconciliation exhibits a blindness to the sensitive issues that Stein's life ignites.

A "CATHOLIC ISRAELITE"

A similarly supersessionist theology is seen in Elias Friedman, another Jewish convert to Catholicism of the same era, who, like Stein, also became a Carmelite. Friedman was introduced in chapter 6 as a monk residing with Br. Daniel Rufeisen in the same monastery in Haifa, and although Friedman was active in the movement of Hebrew-speaking Catholics that arose in the late 1950s in Israel in conjunction with the St. James Association, his theology was unapologetically supersessionist.

Friedman was born into an observant Jewish family in Cape Town, South Africa, in 1916. According to his memoir "Branch, Re-ingrafted into the Olive Tree of Israel," he became agnostic after his bar mitzvah.[14] When he was in his twenties, he began to believe again in the existence of God, but in his memoir of his conversion, he describes his faith at this time as dry and incomplete. He writes that even after coming to this faith in God, "unfortunately, the God whom I discovered remained for me the solution to a harassing intellectual problem and no more. My heart remained closed, and I could not bring myself to pray" (20). He makes this observation in an essay written for a Catholic readership, and his dismay at his unsatisfactory faith seems to allude to the fact that his faith at that time was not yet Christian—that is, it was still Jewish—and therefore incomplete.

During the Second World War, Friedman was employed as a medical doctor at a military hospital in South Africa, and it was during this time that he experienced a conversion to Christianity. Although this experience likely caused him at least some degree of anxiety, as it complicated his Jewish identity, he writes about it in peaceful, rather facile terms. He recalls that while working as a doctor, one day he experienced "a state of inner darkness and confusion" and lay down on his bed. At this point, he writes, "It seemed that a thin ray of light from far and high penetrated my inner darkness. . . . When I rose, a new light shone in my eyes and I perceived that a way of salvation had been opened to me" (21).

Although Friedman does not write about his Jewish identity as a point of contention in his conversion, he does explain how his newfound faith in Jesus relates to the "Jewish problem." As a teenager, he had been active in a Zionist youth movement and had been concerned about the need for a Jewish homeland and about the threats of antisemitism. In the midst of his conversion a decade later, he saw faith in Jesus as a solution to these problems. Dwelling on that conversion moment, he writes, "How could the Jewish problem be explained? The answer came in a shaft of light: Jesus Christ" (21).

Moreover, he explains that the struggles of the Jewish people appeared then to him not as an argument against conversion, as many would conclude, but precisely as an argument *for* Christian faith: "The historical reality of the fate of Israel appeared to me so strong an argument for the divinity of Jesus Christ that all difficulties which my agnostic past and scientific formation could have raised against the possibility of miracles and prophecy, fell away." He then explains this surprising conclusion with a theological rationale that exemplifies classical supersessionism and explicit Christian anti-Judaism: "The people of Israel had been exiled from its land to languish in a shocking dispersion for two thousand years, because it had not believed. The punishment fitted the crime" (22).

Friedman was baptized in 1943 and immediately began writing a book entitled *The Redemption of Israel*, eventually published in 1947. In it, he developed a Zionist philosophy based on Christian theology, which prophesied that with the establishment of a Jewish homeland in Palestine, "the Christian era in the history of Israel was imminent" ("Branch, Re-ingrafted," 25). Offering what seems to be a Catholic version of evangelical Christian Zionist eschatology, he claimed that "the drama of the Jews offered the key to a Catholic interpretation of the events of our time until the end of the world and the Second Coming of Christ" (25).

Driven by his Zionism, which was now backed with Christian eschatological expectation, Friedman immigrated to Israel in 1954 after entering the Carmelite order and becoming ordained. He lived at the Stella Maris monastery in Haifa, the site of the original Mt. Carmel, of which the Carmelite order bears the name (28–29). Early in his process of conversion, he had begun to believe that the "Jewish problem" could be solved only by Jewish belief in Jesus, and in an effort to make mass conversion feasible while preserving a distinctively Jewish element, he envisioned creating a distinct community of Jewish Christians (22).

Inspired by this original impulse, after more than two decades in Israel, he founded the International Association of Catholic Israelites in 1979 (29).[15] Now under the name the Association of Hebrew Catholics, the aim of the organization today, according to its website, is "to preserve the identity and heritage of Catholics of Jewish origin within the Church, to enable them to serve the Lord and all people within the mystery of their irrevocable calling."[16] The Association of Hebrew Catholics is unaffiliated with the St. James Vicariate for Hebrew Speaking Catholics in Israel, the contemporary development of the St. James Association, which distinguishes itself as a community of Hebrew-speaking Catholics, which is quite different than the concept of "Hebrew Catholics."

Friedman's supersessionism is notably different than the theological views explored in this book, and the inclusion of his narrative here demonstrates the diversity of perspectives evident in this Judeocentric phenomenon in Israel. His story provides a case study of a Jewish convert to Catholicism who immigrated to Israel to live as a monk, but with a substantially different outlook than the others profiled here. Based on his writings, he seemed to believe that he was concerned for the Jewish people and that his hope for conversion expressed what he viewed as the best possible outcome for Jews.[17]

In this, he chose the path of pre–Vatican II Catholic supersessionism, which he continued to hold even after the theological reforms in the Church, as his conversion memoir of 1987 reveals.

Friedman's views are unacceptable by the current standards of thought in Catholic-Jewish relations, but this was the norm in Catholicism before Vatican II. Although he was involved in the circle of Catholics in Israel who were interested in building bridges between Christianity and Judaism, unlike the others involved in these initiatives, the supersessionism of midcentury Catholicism did not seem to cause any conflict of interest for Friedman, and he readily kept it after others had long abandoned it. The other early figures in this phenomenon have not produced any written materials so clearly condemning Jews to the "sin" of disbelief in Jesus. However, assuming that they may have entertained similar theological views at earlier points in time, given the theological consensus of the Church prior to Vatican II, it can be surmised from the writings they left behind that they struggled deeply to overcome these vestiges of Christian anti-Judaism.[18] Friedman's story, therefore, provides an important contrast and context for the others who chose more progressive paths in their theologies of Judaism.

REFLECTIONS ON JEWISH-CHRISTIAN IDENTITY

In the midst of the Second World War, a young Jewish woman fleeing Bulgaria arrived on the shore of Palestine during the British Mandate after suffering a terrible tragedy along the route that had claimed the lives of her mother and brother. Within a very short time, she had converted to Catholicism and became a nun by the name of Sr. Regine. She has now been a Sister of Sion for nearly eighty years. Her story is told in more detail in the portrait following this chapter, but a few of her words here serve to illustrate her self-identification as a Jewish Israeli and as a Catholic nun. Her reflections, as well as those of other Jewish converts to Christianity whom I interviewed, express very different theological perspectives and formulations of Jewish identity than those of Friedman and Stein.

Sr. Regine's sense of Jewish identity, which persists strongly despite her spending nearly a century as a Catholic nun, is something that she struggles to find words to describe: "I don't know how to say it. I feel Christian of course, but I feel also very Jewish. And you know, a Jew is a Jew, whatever you do. It's so deep in us; it's in our physical, spiritual everything. You feel it so deeply, and that they cannot take from you."

She had felt this all through the years in every place that she lived. She describes the subtle but clear antisemitism she experienced during her years living in Egypt and says that this experience heightened her sense of Jewish identity. She makes a gesture of being pushed away and rejected, illustrating what she often felt she was subjected to, and says,

> I felt it always. Maybe as Jews we are very sensitive to that. I felt that. I can't say I suffered from that, but I always felt that very often. "If I think like that it's because I'm Jewish; if I act like this it's because I'm Jewish"—they never said it, but you can feel it in the life. . . . I feel myself so strong in what I am, that I have to overcome those little things. They are not little—you can feel them—but I try to not put too much attention to that. Because I know that I am Jewish.

Not far from Sr. Regine, in a cloistered convent on the Mount of Olives, behind a locked metal door over which a sign simply reads "Benedictine," a remarkable woman lived in relative secrecy for many decades. She survived the Holocaust in Poland as a young Jewish girl and converted to Catholicism in the midst of the trauma of the war.[19] Struggling for words to express her identity, she placed English, Hebrew, and French together, announcing simply, "I am Jewish. I am from a Jewish family . . . but *ani* Christian, *ani* Catholic, *ze ne mafriya li.*"[20]

Sr. Paula had longed to be an Israeli citizen since she arrived in Israel forty years ago, which she strongly felt was her homeland. However, she was refused Israeli citizenship, and she explained this rejection by gesturing to and shaking the long black habit that she wears. Because of her faith, signified by the habit, she said, the Israeli government believes she is not a Jew.

Fr. Bruno Hussar also never stopped considering himself to be a Jew after he converted to Catholicism, and even when his Jewish identity might have led to his death, he did not hide it. When Paris came under German occupation, and all Jews were required to register their names, Hussar contemplated the situation and decided that he would abstain from registering his name, but if he were ever asked if he was a Jew, he would not deny it. This moment arrived when he was asked to sign a form at a bank stating that he was not a Jew. He refused to sign the form and told the manager of the bank that he was indeed a Jew. After this incident, his bank account was locked, and realizing that he was in serious danger, he escaped to the unoccupied part of France. There, he looked for work to continue to support his mother, but at the end of every job interview, he was routinely asked, "You are not Jewish, correct?" Every time, he answered that he was, knowing that he would be refused the job but adamant that he would not hide his Jewish identity. From situations ranging from failing to get a job to risking death at the hands of the Nazis, Hussar never denied that he was a Jew.

In 1967, when Hussar was serving as an adviser to the Israeli delegation at a meeting of the United Nations General Assembly, called immediately after the Six-Day War, he addressed a large group at the Israeli consulate in New York. Rising from his seat, he summarized his complex identity to the audience: "I am a Catholic priest, a Jew, an Israeli citizen, I was born in Egypt where I lived for eighteen years. I feel I have four selves: I really am a Christian and a priest, I really am a Jew, I really am an Israeli and if I don't feel I really am an Egyptian, I do at least feel very close to Arabs whom I know and love."[21]

In another generation, and in a very different context, Fr. David Neuhaus converted from Judaism to Catholicism after a long process that began with a visit to Jerusalem in the 1970s when he was fifteen years old. Now a Jesuit priest and the former patriarchal vicar of the St. James Vicariate for Hebrew Speaking Catholics, Fr. David is known as "one of the primary facilitators of the contemporary Catholic-Israeli and Catholic-Jewish relationship" as well as an active voice in Israeli-Palestinian peace initiatives.[22] Fr. David was born to a Jewish family in South Africa, and his parents, concerned about antisemitism in South Africa, sent him to live in Israel as a teenager. Explaining the original purpose of his visit, which was quite the opposite of the eventual outcome, he explains, "That was a decision my parents made, as South African Jews who saw no future for their son growing up in an apartheid society that was coming apart. So it was their decision to send me here. When I came here, I fell in love with Jerusalem—not with Israel, not with the land of Israel, but with the city of Jerusalem—and decided that I would live here forever, with a fifteen-year-old's enthusiasm." While in Israel, he got to know an elderly nun and was struck by her radiant joy. His encounter with this nun began a long journey that led him to Christianity and, eventually, to the priesthood.[23]

Fr. David does not hesitate to say that he is Jewish and Catholic, and in our conversation, he specified the ways in which he bears each identity:

"Being Jewish has always meant, since I was born, belonging to a people, belonging to a history, belonging to a culture. That didn't change when I was baptized. . . . I'm part of a Jewish family, we have a Jewish history, so in that sense, I'm Jewish." He identifies as culturally but not religiously Jewish and is clear that his religious identification is solely Catholic: "There are people who feel both Jewish and Christian from a religious point of view, but I'm not one of them. I'm very Catholic in my religious sentiments. I feel very much at home in the synagogue, not because I pray as a Jew in the synagogue, but because I know the prayers, I know the melodies, I know the culture, I know the language, and there I can pray just as easily to the God that I know through Jesus Christ. But it's very much cultural, historical, familial." He is clear that his faith is not a synchronistic blend of Judaism and Christianity, and yet he feels that as an Israeli Catholic, "I am part of that context. I myself am Jewish and think out my faith as a Jew."

JEWISH-CHRISTIAN IDENTITY IN DIALOGUE

How do these and other Jewish converts to Catholicism contribute to Catholic efforts toward Christian-Jewish reconciliation in Israel, and what role do they play in the Judeocentric Catholic phenomenon explored in this book? For some of those whose views are shared here, these are the wrong questions; they do not understand themselves to be working toward a goal of dialogue or reconciliation but simply have found themselves dwelling along the boundaries between Judaism and Christianity, struggling to reconcile their senses of Jewish identity in the midst of the Jewish people of Israel yet within a Catholic religious vocation. Others, however, do consciously work toward building bridges of understanding between the two religious traditions and find that their Jewish and Catholic identities help them better understand and identify with the views and needs of each community, but this is not without complications.

In contemporary interreligious dialogue, hybrid religious identities are so common as to almost have become the norm. As Catherine Cornille observes, "Multiple belonging has at times been regarded as a virtual condition for interreligious dialogue. Many of the pioneers of interreligious dialogue in the twentieth century have been seen as belonging in various degrees to more than one religion."[24] Cornille argues that those who identify with more than one religious tradition often have the capacity to more deeply understand each community, but this multiple belonging can also be problematic. Those with Jewish-Christian hybrid identities have encountered much resistance in their efforts to be accepted in both communities and also to be deemed as suitable participants in interreligious dialogue. Indeed, most of the pioneers of interreligious dialogue Cornille refers to identified with Eastern religious traditions, such as Hinduism or Buddhism, as well as with Christianity, and these Eastern traditions do not hold the intrinsic and historical relationship to Christianity that Judaism holds.

Dual belonging in Christianity and Judaism is often more problematic than it is between less closely related traditions, and it may be due to precisely this close relationship. Christianity and post–Second Temple rabbinic Judaism developed side by side and contemporaneously, often negotiating boundaries around their traditions in contradistinction to the other, precisely in order to create more distance between the closely related traditions. The deeply rooted suspicions between the two traditions were established in these early years. From Jewish perspectives, Christian intentions to convert Jews remained a source of suspicion, which only intensified through the centuries of forced conversions of Jewish communities and through continuing proselytization efforts. Maintaining distinctiveness and separation is an inherent part of most religious traditions, and this is particularly prominent in Judaism. Any breach in this carefully delineated difference and distance can be challenging for both communities, and claims of dual Jewish-Christian identity very often prove to be not points of mutual understanding but rather sources of dissent. In light of this, the Jewish converts to Catholicism who remain dedicated to Christian-Jewish reconciliation and adamantly opposed to conversion efforts are in a unique position, remaining on the borders of both Jewish and Catholic identity.

When Sr. Regine came trotting down the stairs to meet me, I heard her footsteps before I saw her—a patter of quick, light steps almost like those of a child. A moment later, Sr. Regine appeared at the bottom of the stairs, stepping into the airy, high-ceilinged entryway with a smile on her face. She wears her ninety-five years lightly. She wears her history lightly too—nearly a century of life mapped across a long list of countries, with a vigorously joyful disposition despite the tragedy that marked her life at a young age during the Holocaust. She walks briskly and smiles and laughs easily, and she opened up to me warmly, sharing her life story and spiritual reflections with great directness.

Sr. Regine was born in Bulgaria in 1921 to a Jewish family. Her childhood, as she describes it, was full of joy and ease. Like many other financially secure Jewish families in Bulgaria, her parents sent her to boarding school to receive the best education, and she was happy there, living with the students and teachers who felt, to her, like a family. She always enjoyed returning home to visit her family too, but the surroundings she was most accustomed to were those of her boarding school. Her school was run by the Sisters of Sion at their convent in Rousse, Bulgaria. At that time in Bulgaria, she explained, many Jewish families sent their children to Catholic schools run by the Sisters of Sion because these schools provided the best education, and they respected the Jewish students. When the students had their regular time of prayer, only the Christian students went into the chapel, while the Jewish students went to a different room to pray the psalms. Never, she said, were the Jewish students expected to practice any elements of Christianity.

As a boarding student with the Sisters of Sion, Sr. Regine's Jewish identity was honored and preserved. And yet she had very little sense of what it meant to be Jewish in this context. Living among Catholics, she experienced none of the traditions and customs of Jewish life. Her family was not very religious, although her mother maintained some religious practice, and the young Regine knew little about Judaism. She returned home every year for Passover, but that was the extent of her participation in Jewish ritual life. At school, the uniform included a necklace with a cross for the Christian students and a necklace with a Star of David for the Jewish students, but Regine was never clear about what the Star of David meant to her. Her religious identity was clearly marked and respected, but she lived the same life as the Christian girls in the school.

When Regine was nineteen years old, her peaceful life was torn apart. She had just completed school and was looking forward to the opportunities ahead of her, with her good education and her intelligence. However, the war had begun, and the Jewish families of Bulgaria were being expelled from their homes. Her parents tried to find a way to escape to the only place where they thought they would be safe, in Palestine. However, the British had put a temporary stop on legal immigration. With no other option available, they sought passage on one of the boats making illegal trips to Palestine. Like thousands of others, they boarded an overcrowded boat to sail across the sea clandestinely with the hope of reaching a safe home.

In Sr. Regine's description, even the word "boat" is unfit for the vessel they boarded. Her hands fluttered about a small imaginary object, indicating something fragile, held together by threads, and tossed about violently. This was the same gesture she made a moment later to describe what happened to the boat during a storm. They were in the Black Sea, close to the shore of Turkey. Struggling to find words to describe it, she used the word "collapse" and then "explode." Her hands fluttered to describe the boat shattering to pieces.

The boat, already dangerously overcrowded, shattered under the pressure of the storm, and all the passengers were thrown into the sea. Regine fought to keep her head above water but was weighed down by layers of heavy winter clothing, and the waves crashed viciously in the storm. Far past the point at which she believed she would die, after all her strength had drained, she found herself washed up onto shore. Farther up the shore, her father also washed up, still alive. Her mother died in the sea. Her brother, probably trying to help their mother, also drowned. The world as she knew it was destroyed, and in the wake of the tragedy, she saw faith in God as an impossibility. "I tell you, when it happened," she said, "I wanted to hear nothing: no religion, no God, nothing."

She and the other survivors were captured and imprisoned in Turkey. With time, she was given an opportunity to leave and eventually arrived alone in Palestine. With nowhere to go and nothing left to her name, she was placed in a kibbutz for girls. She could not speak a word of common language with the others and was alone in the world. She said, "When I came here, I had nothing; I didn't even know how to say 'shalom.' I knew nothing. . . . I was so miserable there in that kibbutz, not being able to say a second word in Hebrew." She had just lost her mother and her brother, she had lost her home and everything she knew in life, and she could not even communicate in the language. She was entirely alone in Palestine, having been separated from her father during immigration, and in this kibbutz, nobody seemed to know what she had just gone through, and it seemed to her that nobody cared. It felt like another prison.

It was at this time that she received an unexpected visitor, a Sister of Sion from Jerusalem who traveled to the kibbutz to see how Regine was faring and to offer her comfort. The sister had heard about Regine through a series of messages: the Sisters of Sion in Bulgaria had contacted the Sisters of Sion in Turkey to tell them that their former student had survived the tragedy and was in prison in Turkey. Later, these sisters contacted the Sisters of Sion in Jerusalem to tell them that they had heard Regine was in Palestine.

This visit was a great relief to Regine, and she finally felt as if someone would listen to her and care for her tenderly, as she remembered being treated at the school in Bulgaria. The sister invited her to visit the convent in Jerusalem, and she gladly accepted. She recalled, "Again finding myself in that atmosphere with the Sisters of Sion that I knew in my childhood, I felt happy again." In the wake of the trauma she had just experienced, she felt consoled in this environment: "This visit to the Sisters of Sion convent in Jerusalem opened up a new horizon for me. Memories of my happy childhood in the convent in Rousse returned. All the sisters spoke my language, French; they were very gentle and I felt at ease. I had finally found a place where people were kind and friendly to me, a place where I felt at home."[25]

Not long after this visit, she left the kibbutz for good and moved into the convent to live as a long-term guest. She had no intention to join the sisters as a nun, and indeed at this point in her life, she had no religious faith whatsoever. As she described it, "My move [to the convent] had nothing to do with faith or religion. On the contrary, the tragedy that my family had undergone and the loss of my mother and younger brother had deeply affected my relationship with faith and religion." She explained, "On the night of the tragedy, I had prayed endlessly, asking God for rescue and help, but God had not answered my prayers. At this stage, I wanted to hear nothing about God; I didn't believe in the existence of God and had become an atheist" (72).

She moved to the convent simply because it was a place where she could feel safe and at home. But with time, as she began to heal from the initial shock of the trauma, she became accustomed to life at the convent, and her attitude toward religion began to change. She explained that after the tragedy she lost all faith in God, but eventually her thoughts gradually shifted: "I refused to hear about religion or God, but time passed, and during the first year of my stay in the convent, I had many conversations about these matters, and at night I would think about it. My belief in God and religion changed totally" (77–78).

Sr. Regine described this shift in thinking, and the life-changing choice that emerged from it, quite simply. Laughing, she recalled, "When I was a child, I always said that I would like to be a nun because I found them so nice—they were so nice. So I wanted to be like them, but I never knew that you had to be baptized!" But after the time spent as a guest in the convent, she decided to be baptized in 1941 or 1942, as she recalled.

Sr. Regine was baptized during the height of the war, and although she had suffered greatly from it, she knew virtually nothing of what was going on in the world. In a sense, for her the war was over because her experience of it had ended once she had landed in Palestine. After her tragedy, she had found a place of safety, closed off from the world. In the close community of the convent, she heard very little news of the war that was raging across Europe. She had no idea about the genocide against the Jews and no idea about how her personal tragedy was part of a broader one.

After her baptism, Regine eventually became Sr. Regine, entering into the life of the nuns in the convent. In 1946 she was sent abroad to teach in schools run by the Sisters of Sion, and over the next decades, she lived in Egypt, Tunisia, Turkey, Lebanon, France, England, and Italy. She finally returned to Jerusalem after twenty years abroad. When she had left Jerusalem in 1946, it had been under the control of the British Mandate, but when she was sent back in 1966, Israel had been an independent state for eighteen years, but the convent was located on land that had become a part of Jordan, just beyond the border with Israel. Yet nearly as soon as she returned to Jerusalem, now in Jordan, the Six-Day War began.

Sr. Regine lived through the Six-Day War directly in the center of combat, inside the walls of the embattled Old City. Her convent became a key site for soldiers in need of rest and medical care, and Sr. Regine witnessed it all. She climbed to the roof of the convent, which stands high above all the other buildings within the Muslim quarter of the Old City, and from there she could see the Temple Mount, and on it, a group of Israeli soldiers waving the Israeli flag. Israel had taken the Old City. As she described it, "I was very moved to see the flag of Israel waving on the Temple Mount. My heart was full of happiness, pride, and joy!" (108). After all of her travels, for the first time in her life, she was living with the State of Israel.

A few years later, after a brief time living overseas again, she returned to Israel once more, and this time the congregation sent her to live in the midst of a Jewish population. In line with the changes in the mission of the congregation, she was asked to live in an apartment in Jaffa, on the outskirts of Tel Aviv, where she held a series of secular jobs, doing banking and secretarial work. By then the congregation had abandoned the tradition of wearing a habit, and so Regine was dressed in regular clothing. She was still a nun, but she was also a Jewish woman living in an Israeli city and working regular jobs among her Israeli neighbors, friends, and colleagues. Back in Israel, she renewed contact with her relatives, and although initially her family members were extremely unhappy with her decision to become a nun, with time they welcomed her in the life she chose, and now she regularly spends the Jewish holidays with her Israeli relatives.

As I listened to Sr. Regine tell her story, I wondered how much of her choice to become a nun arose from her response to trauma. It is clear that her tragedy led her to live in the convent as a guest, and that led her to become a nun; what will remain unknown, however, is if she would have ever found herself choosing to become a nun had she not experienced the tragedy. She reflected, "My life would perhaps have been different if the tragedy I experienced had not occurred," but she does not specify how (75).

I asked her about this directly, sensing that she was comfortable enough to have an open conversation about it. I asked her if it was religious faith that made her ask to enter the convent or if it was more about wanting to belong and wanting to feel happy and safe. She answered the question readily, and the quickness with which she responded indicated that it was something she had thought about many times before. "I tell you," she began, "it was more than religious. It's connected to religion, but it was the fact of being a sister, a nun. That, of course, includes the religion, but the first motivation was not to become Christian." In her perception at the time, being a nun was not primarily about the religion but about belonging to the community.

Sr. Regine had lost or been separated from her family and everyone she knew, and with this community, she found a place that offered a sense of family, home, and love. She wanted to belong to that community and to live that life, and being a Christian seemed to be secondary. When looked at this way, her choice to become a nun seems to be a direct response to trauma. However, she clarifies that religious belief arose in her with time, and this religious life has sustained her for the seventy-five years that have passed since that time. Had she never developed faith, she could have left her religious vows at any point in life and began again on her own, but she did not.

When Sr. Regine was baptized as a Christian and became a nun, she did not feel that she was consciously or intentionally rejecting Judaism. To begin, she knew very little about Judaism, having been raised in a nonobservant family and having spent most of her childhood living in the Catholic boarding school. Thinking back to her scant familiarity with Judaism as a child, she said, "When I was in school, we learned the Bible a little bit, but the Bible as the Christians knew it. At home, my father was not a religious man, but my mother, yes, she was from a very religious Jewish [family]. And so we had Pesach—it was a big feast when I was at home—but if not, I had nothing. I didn't know about Judaism, nothing. I knew nothing except what the Bible says." When deciding to convert to Christianity in the midst of the war, she had not known enough about Judaism to be able to conscientiously reject it. In addition, her conversion to Christianity, at least in its early stages, was motivated more by the desire for a community and a way of life than by Christian truth claims. In other words, her conversion seems to have been intended not as the explicit rejection of a tradition or a people but as the acceptance of a new one.

It was this conversion to Christianity, paradoxically, that brought her to a deeper knowledge of Judaism. With a smile of wonder on her face, Sr. Regine marveled, "And through Christianity, I learned Judaism. It's really strange." I asked her to explain how exactly this happened, and she continued, "Well, to be converted, I had to study, I had to learn the gospel, to read. . . . We studied a lot." As she studied, she learned not only about Christianity but also about Judaism, for the history of the two religions are so tightly intertwined. "And so, learning, I entered more into Christianity through Judaism and into Judaism through Christianity. It was such an interaction between the two. And now, always, I understand so much better Christianity when I know Judaism." Today, nearly a century later, she is deeply immersed in both traditions. She remarked, quite simply, "If people ask me 'Are you Jewish or Christian?' I say I am both."

CHAPTER 10

Conversion, Belonging, and Holocaust Trauma

THE INDELIBLE MEMORY

The impact of the Holocaust on the conversion narratives shared in this book cannot be underestimated. For those who survived the Holocaust, the decision to convert to Christianity can only be understood from within the context of this experience. To be clear, this observation does not claim that it was *only* because of the trauma of the Holocaust that each person converted to Christianity; it simply acknowledges that Jewish conversions to Christianity during or immediately after the Holocaust cannot be seen solely as the product of an interior spiritual conviction divorced from the context of the war.[1] Whether they would have ever converted had they not lived through the Holocaust is a question that cannot be answered. However, it remains clear that the experience of the Holocaust and the struggle for survival, both physical and psychological, contributed to the choice of each of the survivors to adopt Christianity.

During the Second World War, uncounted thousands of Jews were baptized in an attempt to survive. Some were baptized as adults, but many other conversions resulted from the baptism of children harbored by Christians despite the fact that conversion to Christianity rarely spared Jews from death. However, in addition to these conversions in the midst of the war, thousands more converted in the aftermath of the war, when they were no longer in immediate danger.[2]

Contemplating the causes of these conversions in the aftermath of the war, after having already survived the greatest danger, Todd Endelman surmises, "The choice of baptism was an emotion-driven response to trauma, an effort to bury the past and at the same time to insure [*sic*] against the unknown, future terrors." He argues, however, that another factor likely drove many of these conversions, seen in "the strength of the desire to begin anew, unencumbered by the past, and the absence of other historically sanctioned ways of doing this."[3]

Although most of the conversion narratives discussed in this book involve the Holocaust in some sense, not all occurred in the midst of existential danger or trauma. For instance, although the story of Edith Stein is now interpreted in the context of the Holocaust, and her death at Auschwitz colors the perception of her entire life story in retrospect, she had converted to Catholicism over twenty years before the war, in 1922. Her decision was unobstructed by the fear and trauma of the war and was reached from a position of free intellectual inquiry. Similarly, although Elias Friedman converted during the war, he was not in any personal danger, working at that time as a medical doctor in South Africa. His personal life was free of the trauma experienced by European Jews, and although in his conversion narrative he refers to his contemplation of the existential threat facing the Jewish people, the threat was far from his personal experience.

The Holocaust continues to be a formative factor affecting the construction of Jewish religious identities. In the personal narratives explored here, the memory of the Holocaust shapes the identity formation of all who walk along the border of Judaism and Christianity—even for those who did not experience it firsthand and for those born after the war. The memory of the Holocaust, whether as a personal or collective memory, is indelible.

CONVERSION NARRATIVES

The narratives collected here are far from a comprehensive survey of Jews who survived the Holocaust, converted to Catholicism, became nuns or monks, and immigrated to Israel, as specific and rare as this narrative may sound. It is only a portrait of a few, including only those I was able to find through long processes of searching, the scouring of directories, many phone calls, and even chance encounters; however, there are many more I did not encounter. A number of my informants told me that there are many people like this, more than can be counted, but at this point in time, few are living, and many of those still living choose to keep their histories private.

In one case, I was already in the midst of an interview with a nun, of whose Jewish identity I was entirely unaware, before I realized that she was a Holocaust survivor. I had requested to meet with Sr. Paula after receiving her name from another nun, who had simply said that Sr. Paula "had a vocation for Israel" and had told me nothing more. After we began speaking, Sr. Paula showed me a family photo, and as she named each person in the photo, I began to sense that some of her family members might be Jewish. When I asked if any of her family members are Jewish, she replied by looking me solemnly in the eye and saying no more than "I am Jewish." From this point on, our conversation took a completely different direction, and we spent the rest of the day talking about her experience during the Holocaust and her aliyah to Israel.

Many of the nuns and monks in Israel who were born to Jewish families congregate at the St. James Vicariate, particularly at its Jerusalem center.[4] Since its early years as the St. James Association, it has served as a central meeting place and as a community for a surprising number of Jews who survived the Holocaust, converted, entered religious life, and then spent the rest of their lives in Israel, living as Hebrew-speaking nuns, monks, and priests while still maintaining links with their Jewish identities and with the Jewish community.[5]

One member of the St. James Vicariate is Fr. Gregor Pawlowski, a retired priest of the vicariate who was born into a Jewish family in Poland in 1931. After both of his parents were killed during the war, he survived on his own as a young boy, hiding and wandering from town to town. Explaining the events leading to his conversion, a brief biography of him narrates, "One day a Jewish boy asked him in the street whether he wanted to live. [Gregor] answered: 'Yes!' Then the boy explained that he need[ed] to acquire a Cath-olic baptism certificate. The boy told him to wait a moment and brought him a baptism certificate."[6] In this telling of the story, this served as the first event that led to his legitimate conversion, although the procurement of a baptismal certificate was simply for survival, and faith was no part of it. A second stage occurred a few years later, when, at the age of thirteen, he was sheltered in an orphanage. When a priest visited the orphanage, Gregor admitted that his baptismal certificate was not authentic, and the priest promptly baptized him. After this unpremeditated conversion, Gregor soon became serious about his new religious identity, and after completing high school, he entered the seminary, keeping his Jewish identity secret for the first years. In 1958, he was ordained to the priesthood and worked as a priest in a number of Polish parishes. In 1966, he published an article in a Polish Catholic newspaper in which he told his conversion story, and the article made it to Israel, where it was read by some relatives and eventually made it into the hands of his brother. Neither brother had known the fate of the other; through this article, they were reunited. In the same years, Fr. Gregor was also in contact with Br. Daniel Rufeisen and began to contemplate making aliyah. In 1970, Fr. Gregor immigrated to Israel and was met at the airport by a large group of people, including Br. Daniel and his own brother, Hayim. He has worked as a priest with the St. James Vicariate since then and has served both Polish- and Hebrew-speaking communities. When Gregor was asked why he wanted to come to Israel, he replied, "My place is here, among the Jewish people. . . . I was circumcised on the eighth day and I belong. I belong both to Poland and to Israel. I cannot speak against Poles because they saved me and I cannot speak against Jews because I am one of them."[7]

Another figure associated with the vicariate is the late Fr. Abraham Shmuelof, born in 1913 in Jerusalem to an Iranian Jewish family. By the time he became involved with the St. James Association, his life had taken many surprising turns along the borders of religious identity. He joined the British Army in 1939 as a Palestinian Jew during the British Mandate and was imprisoned by the Germans in 1941, not because of his Jewish identity, but due to his position as a British soldier. During his four years as a prisoner, he began to read the Bible and experienced a spiritual conversion. Shortly after liberation, he was baptized, and when he returned home to Jerusalem as a Christian, he entered the Benedictine Dormition Abbey in Jerusalem. After a year in the Benedictine monastery, he left Dormition to live in the nearby Trappist monastery in Latrun, but when Latrun became part of Jordan after the war of 1948, he was sent back to Israel for his safety, where he reentered the Benedictine monastery. After his initial radical conversion to Christianity, followed by transitions between two different monastic orders, his life continued to follow an unusual series of changes of position and identity. These transitions include serving as a priest in the Arab-Israeli towns of Nazareth, Jish, and Sakhin, where he was in the unusual position of being a Jewish Catholic priest to an Arab congregation. He later experienced another religious shift and was ordained as a priest in the Byzantine Greek Catholic rite. Eventually he joined the community of Dominican friars in the Isaiah House of West Jerusalem, where he focused on Jewish studies and Christian-Jewish dialogue. Here he recorded the well-known audio collection of the complete readings of the Hebrew text of the Bible, including both the Hebrew Bible and the New Testament.[8] Fr. Abraham Shmuelof's life was characterized by a series of transitions and by shifting expressions of his complex identity, during which he traced multiple paths along the boundary between Christianity and Judaism.

BR. DANIEL'S CONVERSION

Br. Daniel's story was introduced in chapter 6, but in this chapter his conversion narrative is explored in more detail, examining the internal transformation that happened in the brief three weeks that passed between finding a hiding place in a convent after escaping from prison and converting to Christianity.[9] The focus of this reading is on how the context of the Holocaust influenced his conversion and the ways in which he grappled with his Jewish identity throughout this process. In the traumatic context in which he was immersed, he reformulated the way he understood Judaism and the Jewish people through the lens of his newfound Christian faith.

After Br. Daniel, while working as a translator for the Nazis, was accused of assisting in the escape of three hundred Jews from the Mir ghetto, he confessed his Jewish identity under questioning and was imprisoned. He escaped from prison and almost immediately found refuge in a Carmelite convent. The convent was adjacent to the Nazi headquarters where he had formerly been employed and from which he had just escaped as a prisoner, and from the hayloft above the roof where he hid on piles of hay, he was able to peer through an opening and down into the courtyard where he had so recently walked freely in his SS uniform. From this hiding place, he began to read the religious publications that the nuns offered him and, becoming intrigued by the miracles performed at Lourdes, he asked for more reading materials.[10]

Reflecting on this time later, he said that he had felt a need for miracles in the midst of the violence into which he had been plunged. He had experienced great horrors, and although he had managed to remain alive through a series of extraordinarily unlikely events, he had witnessed countless others go to their deaths. In his role as a translator, he had been forced to translate execution orders and then stand by as families were systematically murdered. Even as he fled imprisonment and hid, before seeking shelter within the convent, he had listened to the gunfire and explosions as the remaining members of the nearby Mir ghetto, those whom he had not been able to save, were murdered. And now, nestled in his rooftop hiding place, reading about miracles at Lourdes, he said that he had been "looking for signs of the miraculous, and in the darkness of the surrounding war he found them."[11]

After being moved by the accounts of the miracles at Lourdes, he asked for the New Testament and began to study it. Describing his responses as he read the New Testament for the first time in the midst of the war, he recalled, "I was full of questions. I kept asking why such tragic things were happening to my people. I felt very much like a Jew, I identified with the plight of my people. I also felt like a Zionist. I longed for Palestine, for my own country." It was with this interpretative framework, in a search for answers to explain the horrors to which the Jewish people were being subjected, that he read the New Testament. In the New Testament, he later reflected, he found what he understood to be a book written by Jews in the Jewish homeland two thousand years ago.[12] He read it as a story about his people and about his own search, and he reflected, "In this frame of mind I became exposed to the New Testament, a book that describes events that were taking place in my fatherland, the land I was longing for. This, in itself, must have created a psychological bridge between me and the New Testament" (166).

In a later interview, Br. Daniel recalled the feeling of being entirely alone in the convent, surrounded by strangers, and entirely removed from all things Jewish. And yet in this place, he found a sense of Jewish belonging through the New Testament. He described how he imagined that the two thousand years between the story told in the New Testament and the present time had never happened, and he placed himself within the story, confronted by Jesus. At the end of this reminiscence, he concluded, "If you will not understand this, you will not understand my struggle for the right of my Jewish nationality" (167). For Br. Daniel, this unique encounter with the New Testament was formative to his Jewish identity, his Zionism, and his struggle for Israeli citizenship via the Law of Return.

For Br. Daniel, this transformative experience strengthened his sense of Jewish identity, as he was careful to make clear: "For me the acceptance of Christianity was a Jewish step. It was a move of a Jew toward a certain historical period of the Jewish people" (168). When he spoke of the Jewish friends who visited him in the monastery after he had become a monk and tried to persuade him to return to Judaism, he declared, "But how can I return? I never left!" He continued, "I am all the time on my way back. Back to the source, to the beautiful period, in the faraway past before we split and removed ourselves from each other. I am sure that we will meet again" (247).

He reinforced this connection between his Jewish identity and his new Christian faith by stating, "In the end my conversion was not an escape from Judaism but, on the contrary, a way of finding answers to my problems as a Jew." In the context in which Br. Daniel was then living, the problems to which he referred were intensely existential; it was a problem of survival, and in the narrative of the resurrection, he saw hope for himself and for his people. In his words, "Suddenly, and I don't know how, I identify his suffering and resurrection with the suffering of my people and the hope of their resurrection.... Then I think that if there is justice toward Christ in the form of resurrection there will be some kind of justice toward my people too" (167). Br. Daniel's reflections make the connection between the Holocaust and his conversion clear: in the midst of the trauma of the Holocaust, he converted to Christianity because he found an answer in the story of Jesus to the senseless horror he had experienced, and it gave him a sense of hope, not only for himself, but for the Jewish people as a collective.

COMMUNITY AND BELONGING

A current running through Br. Daniel's conversion narrative and through the narratives of the others discussed here is the desire for a sense of belonging within a Jewish community. This impulse appears to be the main motivating factor in the choice to immigrate to Israel in each person's narrative, and the testimonies show that Israel was seen as a refuge in many ways: as a safe haven from fear and persecution; as an ancestral home, to which immigration was a homecoming; and for many, as a refuge from the sense of aloneness through living with the thriving Jewish community. For those who had lost their families and everything they knew as home, this need for a homeland may have been even more acute.

In these testimonies, the longing for homeland and community, paradoxically, is also met by the newfound Christian community, which provides a much-needed sense of belonging and security. This can be seen in Sr. Regine's narrative, when after surviving a catastrophe that claimed the lives of her mother and brother and finding herself alone and overwhelmed in Palestine, the Sisters of Sion provided her with a community that resembled a family, offering tenderness and security. A similar dynamic can also be seen in Br. Daniel's story, for when he converted in the temporary safety of the convent, he found in the New Testament a renewed sense of identification and belonging with the Jewish people past and present.

The desire for a community expressed in these narratives is also reflected in a personal letter written by another Polish Jew who later went by the name Sr. Paula Palant, who converted to Catholicism and entered a convent after surviving the Holocaust. Unlike the others discussed here, Sr. Palant never immigrated to Israel and spent the remainder of her life in a convent in Poland, but her narrative expresses the impact of this need for a community and home in her decision to convert in the wake of the Holocaust.[13] She was born in Lviv in 1925 and survived both Auschwitz and Ravensbruck. When she returned to Poland after the war, finding that everyone in her family had been killed, she was welcomed into the home of a caring Catholic family. To help her finish the education that she had missed during the war, they enrolled her in a school taught by nuns. Studying under the nuns gave her a sense of security, and she writes that she was so touched by their compassion that after finishing her education, she wanted to stay with them and became a nun. When she writes of entering the convent to become a nun, she uses the words "I was invited to become a part of the family." This emphasis on being accepted into a family, both the Catholic family who took her in and the "family" of nuns, is reinforced in her explanation of her choice to convert and become a nun: "Why did I join the convent and become a nun? No one who did not experience Auschwitz is able to understand what kind of hell it was. Immediately after this hell I found myself in this cloister, able to finish high school in an atmosphere of life, goodness, and love, without concern as to where I came from. I wanted to understand why the sisters were so kind, and [why] they lived in such a way. That was the reason that I came to be a believer."[14] Sr. Palant makes it clear that her transition toward

Catholicism was initially inspired not by faith but by the longing for a safe home and a community and by the desire to understand the source of the kindness she received from the nuns.

Although many of these conversions were fueled by a longing for security and community, conversion to Christianity paradoxically often also entailed rejection by family members and rejection by the greater Jewish community. Br. Daniel speaks of this fear of rejection as he recalls the struggle that he went through when he contemplated converting to Christianity: "I myself had all the prejudices about Jews who convert to Christianity. Aware of these prejudices, I was afraid that my people, the Jews, will reject me. . . . The entire problem was what will be my relationship to the Jewish people, to my brother, possibly my parents if they lived."[15]

Br. Daniel's conversion was in fact received with much anguish by some, including his brother. In a documentary about Br. Daniel, his brother and his brother's wife spoke about their reaction to his conversion. Br. Daniel's sister-in-law responded with less angst than her husband and said that she saw Br. Daniel as a "lonely man who only wanted to do good for everyone" and who sought a life of prayer "in order to find inner calm." His brother, on the other hand, found his conversion to be unforgivable. Shaking his head and clutching his forehead, with a deeply pained expression he said, "There are people who lost an arm or a leg during the war, and there are people who lost their soul. He is one of those."[16]

The pain of being rejected by the Jewish community after conversion is expressed by Sr. Paula Drazek, whose story is told on the following pages. She was reminded of this alienation by her inability to become an Israeli citizen by the Law of Return even after surviving the Holocaust, immigrating to Israel, and living there for forty years. In her testimony, it becomes clear that the pain at being separated from the Jewish community began when she was just fifteen years old, when she converted in the midst of the horrors of the Holocaust in Poland. Remembering that time, she said she continually wished then that she could die, and part of the reason was that she did not want her family to know of the choice she had made.

The narratives gathered here demonstrate the extent to which surviving the Holocaust has influenced both decisions to convert to Christianity and the sense of belonging to the Jewish people. In each narrative, the choices to convert to Christianity, enter monastic life, and then immigrate to Israel are inextricable from the converts' traumatic experiences during the Holocaust and from their identification as members of the Jewish people. Br. Daniel's conversion experience happened while hiding in a hayloft above the Nazi headquarters while they actively searched for him; Sr. Regine converted after surviving the shipwreck that killed her mother and brother; Sr. Paula's conversion experiences happened while she was on the run and in hiding in a cellar after the rest of her family was killed; Gabriel Grossman survived in hiding; Charlotte Klein escaped Germany and converted after making aliyah; Gregor Pawlowski survived as a child alone and on the run—and there are many more like this whose stories are not told here. None had previously intended to become Christian, and only in the terror of the Holocaust and its immediate aftermath did they begin to contemplate conversion. Each of them adopted the Christian faith in the midst of and in response to this trauma and yet maintained a vigorous affirmation of their Jewish identity. It was this assertion of Jewish identity in the wake of the war, coupled with a sense of belonging to the Jewish people and an attachment to the land of Israel as the Jewish homeland, that led many of them to move to Israel.

The search for a sense of belonging after losing everything can be seen in many of the conversion narratives discussed here. However, this observation does not suggest that this is the sole reason the subjects chose to convert and subsequently enter monastic life, nor does it imply that the conversions were not accompanied by profound spiritual experiences or convictions. The complexity of the trauma that each person underwent cannot be fully understood by others, and likewise, the complexity of their emotional and spiritual experiences cannot be summarized by a simple explanation. In these narratives, the desire for Jewish belonging through family, community, history, and homeland runs deep, and conversion quite paradoxically addressed this need while also bringing the converts further away from Jewish belonging.

On the top of the Mount of Olives stands a Benedictine convent. The door looks like any other door set into the long stone walls bordering the street, its dented metal front coated with chipped sky-blue paint. Above it, a sign reads simply, "Benedictines." I rang the bell and waited.

The door was opened by Sr. Gabriele, a reserved German woman with a calm and clear expression. She warmly grasped my hand and smiled and then invited me into a small parlor, where an elderly nun stood to greet me. Sr. Paula is a minute woman, small and frail, with large luminous eyes that gazed deeply into mine as she extended her hands to greet me. The three of us sat down together and began to get acquainted. Sr. Paula is originally from Poland, but she spoke to us primarily in French, the language spoken at their convent, mixed with sentences in English and occasionally Hebrew and Arabic. Sr. Gabriele translated when needed, and the three of us managed to communicate fairly well.

I had requested to meet with them on the recommendation of Sr. Marie Yeshua, who had told me that they were both interested in Judaism. But a few minutes into the conversation, we realized that we had another mutual acquaintance in addition to Sr. Marie Yeshua: Sr. Gemma, who works with Yad Vashem. Sr. Paula excitedly got up and retrieved a photo of herself with Sr. Gemma and some of Sr. Paula's family members. She named the people in the photo and mentioned that one of her cousins is a rabbi. I began to wonder if Sr. Paula might have Jewish heritage, and when I asked, she replied simply, "Ani yehudit" (I am Jewish). Through no more than the photograph of our mutual acquaintance, I realized that I was speaking with a Polish Jew, and likely a Holocaust survivor.

Continuing delicately, and not wanting to make any assumptions about her history, I asked if her family was in Poland during the war. She simply nodded. I asked if her parents survived the war and if she was born before or after the war. A wave of emotion crossed over her face, and she said that she remembered it all over again when I asked. She went on to explain that she was born in 1929, that both of her parents were killed during the war, and that the narrative of her survival is a very long story. And with that, simply from a photograph she showed me of some of her distant relatives, she began to tell her story.

We spoke for hours. Then the monastery bell rang, and it was time to rise and leave for the noon prayer. They asked me if I would like to attend the prayer, and when I accepted the invitation, Sr. Gabriele led me through the guest entrance of their chapel. Inside, the walls of rough-hewn Jerusalem stone soared grandly into a high arched ceiling, and gold-painted icons graced the walls above our heads. I sat on a small wooden chair to the side of the chapel and closed my eyes, listening as the nuns processed quietly in and began to chant. Their voices rose and fell together in the tones of plainchant, measured and hypnotic in the cool of the chapel, resonating off the stones.

After the prayer, Sr. Gabriele led me into the guest refectory, where the table was set for one. On the table were bread, olives, cucumbers in yogurt, a green salad, a pitcher of water, and an open bottle of red Israeli wine. Another nun came in, smiling radiantly, and told me to sit and enjoy. She told me that the fish and pasta would come soon, although there was already more than enough for a meal on the table. I ate voraciously, alone in the silent room, as the warm sunshine poured through the arched window and bathed the high stone walls.

After lunch, Sr. Gabriele and Sr. Paula and I reconvened for another conversation. We had not initially planned this second meeting, but Sr. Paula said that our conversation had made her memories and thoughts open up, and she would like to continue speaking.

She told her story in fragments that were at times difficult to follow, and her eyes shone with emotion as she spoke. Her memories arose as a series of separate stories, often out of sequential order, as the moments that she can never forget rose into her mind one after another.

When she had come to a stopping place, Sr. Paula explained to me in clear and simple Hebrew that the stories she had told me were for me alone. They were not for everybody. She said that a visitor had come from Yad Vashem to ask her about her life, and she had told more to me today than she had to that visitor. If I wanted to write her story, she added, she would like to read the pages before I published them. I assured her that I would honor her wish.

Sr. Paula looked at me meaningfully, and in her eyes was the seriousness of the gift she had offered. I was to protect her story, her eyes told me; I was to honor it and to share it only when she was ready. She repeated that she had told her story only to me and made it clear that she had told the stories not only *to* me but *for* me.

As I was completing this book, I wrote to Sr. Paula to ask for her permission to share her story in this publication. I received an e-mail in response from Sr. Gabriele. Sr. Paula had passed away just a few months earlier, in January 2019. She had remained active up until a few days before her death and passed away in the monastery on the Mt. of Olives in her beloved Jerusalem. It was with great sadness that I received this news, and while Sr. Gabriele communicated the monastery's permission for me to publish this narrative, my heart was heavy with regret that I could not seek this permission from Sr. Paula herself.

I share her story here as she told it to me. It is presented in very simple language without any elaboration and without any commentary, reflecting the way that she told it to me. She had spoken haltingly, with endless emotion in her eyes, and yet with few words on her tongue. This is a story wrenched from the past and shared only in fragments as the images arose in her memory, burdened by the weight of memory.

Sr. Paula's Story
Sr. Paula was between the ages of twelve and thirteen when her family was imprisoned in a ghetto in Poland between 1941 and 1942. Her father, she said with no further explanation, was killed.

A Polish family helped her and a few others escape from the ghetto. She was the last of seven to attempt to leave, and after the first six made it out, the gestapo captured her. They imprisoned her and interrogated her, speaking to her only in German. She did not understand any German, and she could not answer their questions, so they beat her.

She again managed to escape, and this time, she made it out. She remained in hiding for three days and then received the sign that she could run. She ran. Winter was beginning, and it was very cold. Her mother had escaped too, and they survived by hiding in the woods.

She found an opportunity to stay in a home for a period of time, and so she left the woods and was separated from her mother. She later learned that her mother, not knowing where her daughter had gone, had thought she had been captured by the Germans.

Sr. Paula's story becomes unclear at this point, but I gathered that she never saw her mother again after that time and that her mother had died believing her daughter to be captured. "Mea culpa, mea culpa," she said heavily, striking her chest with her fist, and I saw in her eyes, wide and damp, that she has carried this memory as guilt now for over seventy years.

On January 6, 1943, she and a few of the people with whom she was in hiding walked through a village. They had dressed in good clothes to be less conspic-uous, but as the strangers passed through the village on foot on the Christian holiday of Epiphany, the villagers guessed that they were Jewish, and children shouted insults and followed them, jeering and throwing snow at them. They were walking along a road on which Germans often passed, and they were terrified. When they came to the central intersection of the town, they saw a cross standing on the side of the road. In the hope that the village children might be convinced that they were Christian if they prayed before the cross, they all fell to their knees before the cross and made the sign of the cross across their chests. The children believed the farce and turned away.

"It was a miracle," Sr. Paula recalled. The moment when she had fallen to her knees in the snow was, in her experience, not only a miracle of escape and survival but a spiritual miracle as well. "It was the first time in my life that I cried 'Jesus.'"

She said that she cannot explain what happened in her soul then. As she had looked at the cross in that moment of fear, she had found herself contemplating the crucifixion and searching for a reason behind the torture and death of the man on the cross. She felt as though a similar thing was happening to her, and she asked God why. This moment, she said, was the beginning.

Some time passed, and then she found a hiding place in a potato cellar, where she lived for two months. During this time, she asked herself what had happened at that moment when she had knelt in the snow. As a Jew, she was afraid of betraying God with these thoughts about Jesus. She spoke to God, asking, "My God, you're the God of my fathers. I don't want to betray you. Tell me, who is Jesus?"

In those months of darkness, hiding in the damp potato cellar alone at the age of thirteen, after both her mother and father had been killed, she wanted to die. Dying was her only wish, but she did not want the Germans to take her life; she wanted nothing more than to fall asleep and never wake up.

In that darkness, she wondered if God might want her to survive— and might even want her to become a Christian. She promised that if God showed her that he wanted her to survive, she would become a Christian.

However, she did not wish to become a Christian, and she did not want to survive. She wanted neither; she wanted only to die and to die as a Jew.

But she did not die. God took care of her, she said, and she survived. And so, with time, she became a Christian.

On March 27, 1945, she was baptized at the age of fifteen. She says that Christianity did not feel like a new faith for her. She now believes it was the same faith she had always had as a Jew and the same God of her fathers. When she began reading the New Testament, she said she felt like it was her own book, the book of her people.

"Nobody has seen God," she said, "and this is faith, this is hope." She always feels like somebody is holding her in his hands. Everybody suffers, she said, but despite her great suffering, she feels that she was always carried; she was always held.

"So one might ask, what is faith? It is night. Nobody knows what it is."

When she heard that the war was over, she set out walking toward a monastery seventy kilometers away from where she had been hiding at the time. She was offered a ride by Soviet soldiers, and she accepted despite her fear. They treated her kindly and drove her thirty kilometers, and she walked the remaining forty. She eventually arrived at the monastery, which had been destroyed during the war, just as the nuns were beginning to return. She asked to enter their community and to become a nun.

Two months later, some surviving members of her family tracked her down and found her at the monastery. They asked her to leave with them, but she did not want to. She stayed and took monastic vows. For the next thirty years of her life, she remained in that monastery.

After thirty years had passed in the Benedictine monastery in Poland, Sr. Paula was offered an opportunity to travel to Israel for three months follow-ing communication with two other Polish Jews who, like her, had survived the Holocaust, converted to Catholicism, and entered monastic life. They each had immigrated to Israel to be in the Jewish homeland and had entered monasteries there. They were the well-known Br. Daniel Rufeisen and a woman by the name of Stella Tsur, and together they encouraged Sr. Paula to visit them in Israel.

Sr. Paula recalled that she went to Israel to be with these people who had experienced what she lived through and who had made a choice like hers, but that is not the only reason; she also went to Israel to be with her own people in what she believes is the Jewish homeland and her own homeland. After the three months had passed, she asked to stay for one year and, even-tually, to stay for life. She was accepted into the Benedictine monastery on the Mount of Olives in Jerusalem to live there permanently. Another forty years passed in the monastery on the Mount of Olives.

Sr. Paula said that she has always had a longing for a Jewish homeland even when she was a young child in the shtetl before the war began. When she first set foot in Israel in the 1970s, she felt immediately as though she had come home. "This is my land. This is my land," she repeated.

She intensely wanted to become an Israeli citizen, and she applied for citizenship through the Law of Return. Her application was denied, as it is for most Jews who have converted to Christianity, as Br Daniel's court case brought to light. She wanted to be accepted as a member of Israeli society, and she wanted to belong, but Sr. Paula has not felt as if she belonged any-where that she has lived. She says that when she was in the monastery in Poland, she always felt like an outsider as a Jew. And in Israel, she is treated as an outsider as a Christian. However, she doesn't *feel* different, she said; she feels Israeli.

Recalling the months when she lived in hiding in the cellar, praying to die, Sr. Paula said that she had asked God to let her fall asleep and not wake up. This was her prayer and desire every day of her life during that time. This desire, she made clear, ended only on the day that the State of Israel was declared. When Israel was born, for the very first time, she stopped praying to die. She wanted then to live and to help Israel survive.

At this point in her story, when she spoke of her love for Israel, she stopped and made a firm declaration: "God exists. God exists." Of this she is absolutely certain, and she said that when Israel was founded, she finally knew it for sure.

Sr. Paula believes that God kept her alive during the war, and she believes that God keeps her alive still. And now she believes she knows why God has kept her alive: "I give my life for Israel. I love Israel so much that God keeps me alive for Israel."

CHAPTER 11

Theology After the Holocaust

INTRODUCTION

Following the exploration of the impact of the Holocaust on the formation of Jewish identity in chapter 10, the current chapter discusses the way that it has shaped Christian thought. In the wake of the Holocaust, as the world began to gradually comprehend the extent of the atrocities that had been committed, the calcified anti-Judaism lodged deep within Christian theology began to be brought to light, examined, and questioned. As awareness of the Holocaust grew, Christians were forced to critically reevaluate their own tradition and to take stock of the ways that Christian theology had contributed at least in part to the systematic genocide of Jews. Gradually, the ingrained and intransigent teachings of contempt began to be shaken. This chapter considers the ways that the Holocaust has impacted and continues to impact Christian perceptions of Jews in two distinct parts: first, it examines the profound changes in perspective and recognition of collective culpability in Christians who lived through the war as well as in the generations that have followed; second, it engages in a critical analysis of problematic issues regarding Christological interpretations of the Holocaust.

CULPABILITY AND ATONEMENT

For many Catholics who witnessed the Second World War, the realization
of the atrocities committed against Jews instigated an awakening to the reality of Jewish life. Br. Yohanan Elihai's experience, introduced in chapter 6,
expresses this well, as he recalls a sudden moment of shock and awakening
when, while attending a victory celebration in Paris at the age of eighteen,
he came upon a photograph of a concentration camp. This moment and
this image awoke in him an awareness and sense of urgency that defined
the course of his life, eventually bringing him to live in Israel. In his recollection, at that very moment he recognized the link between the anti-Jewish
sentiments he had encountered in the Catholic community in which he
had grown up and the horror that he saw in the photograph. In his telling,
this recognition was instantly followed by a drive to work toward changing
that legacy in Christian thought. It was this response that led him to live in
Israel, and to this day he insists, "The Holocaust made me want to live with
this people and share its experiences in Israel."[1]

Similarly, Fr. Marcel Dubois's experiences helping hide Jewish children
in France also awakened him to the reality of Jewish life in a way that forever
changed his understanding of Jews. The experience changed him and drew
him to move to Israel, where he lived until his death, teaching at Hebrew
University and developing a Catholic spirituality attuned to Judaism and
to Christian-Jewish relations.

The experiences of many Sisters of Sion also contributed to the eventual changes on the institutional level within the congregation. During the
war, many of the sisters worked within the resistance movement, harboring
Jews in convents and schools. Paradoxically, it was the closeness of these
relationships that enabled the sisters to realize how very little they understood of Jewish life and how distant they were from Jewish experience.
Since its inception, the congregation had operated on the assumption that
they understood Jews and Judaism enough to pray for them—that is, they
understood Jews through the lens of the Christian perspective, which held
that Jews had failed to recognize Jesus as the messiah and that a good Christian response to Jews was to pray for them so that they might see the truth.
Members of the congregation had occasionally taught Jewish students in
their schools, but there was very little interaction or familiarity with Jews

beyond that. It was in the midst of the war and in its immediate aftermath that they realized how insufficient their vision was. Through these experiences during the war, and in the shock of the Finaly Affair, when they recognized that their actions had led to a shameful disrespect of Jewish identity, they began to recognize their own blind spots; they finally began to know enough to understand what they did not know about the Jewish people.

A radical self-transformation in response to witnessing the Holocaust is also evidenced in the testimony of Jan Karski, the Polish courier who was the first person to issue an eyewitness report of what he saw at the Warsaw ghetto, delivering the message in person to Franklin D. Roosevelt. Witnessing these horrors changed him radically; it altered his understanding of the Jewish people, his understanding of his Catholic faith, and even his understanding of his own identity. He later declared at a conference in 1980, "The war made me a Jew. I am Jewish, I want to be Jewish. I am a Christian, but I am a Jew." He continued, "And all the murdered Jews became my family. But I am a Christian Jew. I am a practicing Catholic. And although not a heretic, still my faith tells me: There, the second original sin had been committed by humanity." He concluded, "This sin will haunt humanity to the end of time. It does haunt me. And I want it to be so."[2]

Many of the individuals discussed in this book were young adults during the Second World War, and the experience of it marked them deeply. However, a number of others were either born after the war or spent the wartime years outside of Europe, shielded by distance, and yet they also feel that the impact of the war has shaped their consciousness. Many speak of a sense of collective culpability for the antisemitism that made the Holocaust possible, which they feel they carry through the history of their faith and for which they feel accountable. Sr. Talia expresses this when she reflects, "It is our pain: in the name of Brother Jesus, what we have done in history, from the first persecutions in the first church down to Auschwitz. It was not me, not my family, but at least I'm part of it now. I have the Catholic heritage on my shoulders, and I think the pain is here, whether I want it or not." A similar feeling motivates Sr. Gemma, the founder of the Catholic Institute for Holocaust Studies, in her work in Holocaust education at Yad Vashem. She recognizes the collective culpability of Christian theology in contributing to anti-Judaism and has dedicated herself to teaching Christians about the Holocaust.

This sense of collective culpability takes on a specifically theological character in the concept of atonement.[3] Sr. Michaela very directly expresses this desire to atone for the history of Christian anti-Judaism. She did not witness the Holocaust in her own life, but she exhibits a Christian spirituality that is deeply shaped by a response to the Holocaust. Expressing a profound sense of sorrow for the history of Christian anti-Judaism, she said that this feeling of atonement is at the center of her spiritual life. She believes she has received a call—that is, a mission spiritually granted to her—to offer her life in atonement for the history of Christian persecutions of Jews. She feels that her choice to live as a cloistered nun, praying specifically for these sins, is her way of offering her life as an atoning sacrifice.

Sr. Marie Yeshua has long been motivated by a similar desire for atonement. She first traveled to Israel as a young woman as part of a pilgrimage organized by an ecumenical group with the intention of asking for forgiveness for the Christian history of anti-Judaism. That pilgrimage was so transformative that she decided to become a nun and remain in Israel for life, and she soon entered monastic life with the Poor Clare Sisters in Jerusalem. Referring to her involvement with another Christian group seeking forgiveness, she recalls, "When Israeli people came here, we spoke a lot, and they asked, 'You asked forgiveness? You asked forgiveness for all the history?' And one was crying and took me in an embrace." She concludes, "When [Israeli Jews] know that really you are asking forgiveness, with conscientiousness of all the suffering that the Church brought to the Jewish people for a long time—with the pogroms, with the Inquisition, with replacement theology, and many, many things—they receive you like a sister, like somebody who prays for them and with them, and you are part of the body."

AN ANALYSIS OF CHRISTOLOGICAL INTERPRETATIONS OF THE HOLOCAUST

The culpability of Christian theology in the anti-Judaism that fueled racial antisemitism, culminating in the Holocaust, was finally officially acknowledged by the Catholic Church with the 1998 document "We Remember: A Reflection on the Shoah." A follow-up statement entitled "Catholic Teaching on the Shoah" directly acknowledges this Christian culpability. It admits that "Christian anti-Judaism did lay the groundwork for racial, genocidal antisemitism by stigmatizing not only Judaism but Jews themselves for opprobrium and contempt. So Nazi theories tragically found fertile soil in which to plant the horror of an unprecedented attempt at genocide." The document continues by affirming that Christian anti-Judaism is a "necessary cause" for explaining the development of Nazi antisemitism.[4]

Today, many discussions seeking theological meaning in the Holocaust attempt to be sensitive to Jewish self-understanding and to maintain awareness of the distinction between Christian and Jewish interpretations. Many Christian scholars direct their efforts in theological responses to the Holocaust in a self-reflexive direction, asking how Christians may theologically understand the Holocaust rather than suggesting universal theological truths about it. This approach addresses only Christian theologies and refrains from drawing conclusions about Jewish experience. However, not all Christian interpretations of the Holocaust are this careful and sensitive.

Many other theologians readily, and without apology, apply theologies of the crucifixion to Jewish suffering and death during the Holocaust. This can be an offense to Jewish self-understanding in multiple ways. These theologies apply Christological concepts that are entirely external to Jewish tradition to the genocide against Jews, and in addition, they attempt to make sense of a tragedy that was spurred, in part, by precisely the same Christian tradition. John T. Pawlikowski argues that these parallels between the crucifixion and the Holocaust are not only offensive to Jews but also inconsistent with Christian thought: "Christian theology has always described the Cross as a voluntary act on the part of God and Jesus. And the Cross can be properly interpreted in a redemptive fashion only when viewed as a culmination and consequence of Jesus' active ministry. The Shoah was neither voluntary nor part of a redemptive mission in any sense."[5]

Theological interpretations of Holocaust victims serving as atoning sacrifices can also be found in a few Jewish sources after the war, but they are rare and highly controversial, such as that offered by Rabbi Reuven Katz, the chief rabbi of Petah Tikvah, who held that Jewish victims of the Holocaust "constituted a complete burnt offering" and that "the innocent blood of the sacrificial victims (*Korbanot*) atoned for the collective sins of Israel."[6] Interpretations such as these are not widely accepted within Jewish communities, but they still are less controversial, from many Jewish perspectives, than Christian interpretations that link the victims of the Holocaust to the crucifixion of Jesus.

Contemporary Catholic theologian Eugene Fisher, who has long been active in Christian-Jewish dialogue and reconciliation, is careful in his enunciation of any possible connection between the crucifixion of Jesus and the death of Holocaust victims. Discussing the hope inherent in Christian interpretations of the crucifixion, he writes, "If this sense of hope amidst despair is true because of the death of one Jew long ago, Christians will inevitably ask themselves, might it not also be true, and much more so, of the deaths of six million Jewish women, men, and children consigned to the most diabolical hell humanity has ever created for itself?" Here Fisher does not claim that Jesus is engaged in any salvific activity in the death of Holocaust victims; he merely suggests that hope might somehow be found in the midst of utter despair. Aware of the sensitivities surrounding these issues, he clarifies that he is not equating the deaths of six million with this one death. He also insists that he does not "seek to absorb the deaths of the six million into the theological categories developed by the Church to articulate its faith that the death of Jesus, and therefore death itself, has some purpose, that there is reason to hope even in the face of the most awesome evil, evil understood as a mysterium tremendum."[7] Fisher is careful to clarify that he does not intend to absorb these deaths into a Christian theological worldview. However, regardless of the best of intentions and the most careful use of language, when Christians make theological interpretations of the deaths of six million Jews in the Holocaust, using Christian theological categories to make sense of a Jewish tragedy, they inevitably sublimate Jewish experience and Jewish religious tradition under the symbols and systems of Christian thought.

When the Catholic Church chose to use Edith Stein as a symbol of Jewish-Christian reconciliation, under the religious name St. Teresa Benedicta of the Cross, it was far less restrained in its application of theologies of the crucifixion to Stein's death at Auschwitz. Pope John Paul II wrote of what he saw as the eschatological implications of her death, which the Church interprets as a martyrdom: "Her voice merged with the cry of all the victims of that appalling tragedy, but at the same time was joined to the cry of Christ on the Cross which gives to human suffering a mysterious and enduring fruitfulness."[8] According to this interpretation, through her suffering, she linked the suffering of many to that of Jesus, which Christians believe to be a redemptive suffering. In this way, her death is framed as an atoning sacrifice, uniting human suffering with the mystical body of Jesus. Such connections are deeply problematic from Jewish perspectives, both through the notion that the murders of Jews during the Holocaust were somehow redemptive, and through placing these deaths in a Christological framework.

This type of post-Holocaust theology can be seen in the work of many theologians, even including some of those who understand themselves to be working toward Christian-Jewish reconciliation. For example, in "Christian Reflections on the Holocaust," Fr. Marcel Dubois begins with a sensitive and humble argument for abstention from theological interpretations of the Holocaust: "More often than not we are incapable of understanding in the light of the Cross our own trials, small and great; what right have we then to speak to our Jewish brothers of the abyss of suffering into which their people has been plunged? What is more, what right have we to justify an event of which so many Christians are unaware either because they knew nothing about it, when they should have known, or because like distant and help-less spectators they looked at it from outside only."[9] However, immediately afterward, he departs from his own advice, concluding, "And yet, has our faith nothing to say to us about the martyrdom of millions of Jews? Has it nothing to discover in this martyrdom? There is a Christian way of looking at the history of Israel and at the entire destiny of the Jewish people; there should also be a Christian way of looking at the Holocaust."[10] Developing his Christological reading of the Holocaust further, Dubois writes, "The transcendent intelligibility of the Holocaust can be granted only by light from above, and for us Christians, that light passes through the mystery of Golgotha." Dubois is careful to qualify his interpretation; Christians seek that heavenly illumination through Christian means, and implied in this is that Jews follow Jewish means. In the next lines, however, he carries this to a point that risks collapsing that distinction: "What the Christian can truly say is that to the eye of faith, Jesus fulfills Israel in her destiny of Suffering Servant; and that Israel, in her experience of solitude and anguish, announces and represents even without knowing it the mystery of the Passion and of the Cross."[11]

Dubois was deeply dedicated to Christian-Jewish reconciliation and dialogue, and yet in the theologies of this exemplary and conscientious opponent of antisemitism, a lurking supersessionism can be seen. Claiming that Jesus fulfills Israel, he alludes to the supersessionist tradition so embedded in Christian theology. Furthermore, the suggestion that Holocaust victims unwittingly "announce" and "represent" the crucifixion of Jesus is, by many standards, an injustice to the Jewish victims of the Holocaust. It dishonors their suffering and deaths as Jews, and the suggestion that they unwittingly participated in proclaiming Christian truth claims is an injustice to their memory. It challenges their own self-awareness and self-determination as Jews and posthumously applies a Christian function to their suffering and death. "The Calvary of the Jewish people," Dubois concludes, "whose summit is the Holocaust, can help us understand a little better the mystery of the cross."[12] He may be right in concluding that this theology is helpful to Christians who wish to better understand a Christian mystery, but despite his influential service in Christian-Jewish relations, in this case he fails to understand the need for abstaining from universal theological conclusions.

None of these theologies are as egregiously offensive, however, as that put forth by Fr. Elias Friedman. Friedman, the Jewish convert to Catholicism discussed in earlier chapters who spent the wartime years in the safety of South Africa, writes with a sense of ownership of Jewish history, which he seems to believe gives him license to give an unapologetically supersessionist interpretation of Jewish history as a whole, particularly the Holocaust.

In a chapter entitled "The Historical Consequences of the Sin of Disbelief" in his book *Jewish Identity*, Friedman goes so far as to suggest that the Holocaust is the consequence of the Jewish "sin" of refusing to recognize Jesus as the messiah. He writes, "The blindness of post-Christic Jewry to the infinite treasures of grace earned for mankind by the mediation of Jesus was and remains a terrible consequence of unbelief, one which has jeopardized the salvation of many. What is more, forty years after Calvary a chain of disasters overtook Jewry."[13] In the list of disasters that follows, Friedman begins with the failed revolt against the Romans and ends with the Holocaust, making clear his conviction that the Holocaust was the consequence of the Jewish "blindness" and "sin of disbelief."[14]

Later in the same chapter, Friedman offers a more detailed explanation of his theological interpretation of the Holocaust and claims that Jews fail to understand the Holocaust because they don't understand its connection to the crucifixion of Jesus. After quoting a number of notable Jewish figures, such as Abraham Heschel and Golda Meir, who each stated that there is no explanation or answer for the Holocaust, Friedman counters, "Yes, there is an answer to Auschwitz, God's answer, the ingrafting of the Jews and the glory of the 'resurrection of the dead' to follow."[15] In other words, he believes that the answer to the Holocaust is the eventual conversion of

Jews to Christianity. Finally, Friedman expresses the stunningly offensive notion that the Holocaust was a theological necessity to urge Jews toward the recognition of Jesus as the messiah. To explain this, he asserts that Jews needed to experience a form of crucifixion. Through the Holocaust, he says, "the people of the Messiah had to be molded into the image of their Messiah, in order to learn who the true Messiah was."[16]

Friedman's theologies evidence interpretations of Christian theology of the kind that have inspired some of the worst acts of antisemitic violence throughout history. If Friedman were the only one to sanction these views, then perhaps he could be shrugged off as an aberration. However, even more disturbing than the work of this one individual theologian is the fact that the Vatican gave the seal of its official approval to Friedman's book. This approval is made explicit on the copyright page of the book, which is imprinted with the *nihil obstat* and *imprimatur*, which the Vatican defines as "official declarations that a book or pamphlet is free of doctrinal or moral error." One might hope that this official Vatican statement was issued prior to the theological reforms of Vatican II; alas, it was issued in 1987.

In his discussion of the cross standing outside of Auschwitz, James Carroll succinctly summarizes the problematic nature of Christian theologies of Jewish suffering during the Holocaust: "The cross signifies the problem: When suffering is seen to serve a universal plan for salvation, its particular character as tragic and evil is always diminished. The meaningless can be made to shimmer with an eschatological hope, and at Auschwitz this can seem like blasphemy." He continues, "Here is the question a Christian must ask: Does our assumption about the redemptive meaning of suffering, tied to the triumph of Jesus Christ and applied to the Shoah, inevitably turn every effort to atone for the crimes of the Holocaust into a claim to be the masters of Jews in the other world?"[17] As Carroll points out, there is a triumphalism implied when theologies of the crucifixion are applied to the Holocaust, one that claims the ultimate superiority of Christian belief over not just Jewish belief but also the afterlife.

Christian theological interpretations of the Holocaust, although in some cases developed with the intention of honoring Jewish religious traditions and Jewish suffering from Christian perspectives, falter on many accounts. These theologies provide even more examples of Christian colonialization of Jews and Judaism. They use a weapon as a balm, in effect, through applying the supersessionist theologies that undergird centuries of Christian violence against Jews to explain or even justify the Holocaust. In Christian attempts to interpret Jewish suffering, Jewish experience can be forced into and disfigured within a Christian narrative, erasing the particularity that is so central to the survival of Judaism and the Jewish people.

PORTRAIT: SR. MICHAELA

She came out to greet me with paint still on her hands from icon painting. Sr. Michaela, who has been living at the Benedictine monastery in Abu Gosh for thirty-four years, laughs often and is never at a loss for words. She confided in me with a relaxed comfort, as if she had known me for years, and she rarely paused in her stories, which piled one on top of the other. She is vibrant, verbose, and full of a bubbling energy that can be almost brash, although always warm.

Since early on, Sr. Michaela has felt a call to dedicate her life to Christian-Jewish reconciliation and has longed for the Catholic Church to more fully recognize its historical involvement in antisemitism. "My dream," she said, "was that a pope would go to Yad Vashem. . . . When that finally happened, when John Paul II went to Yad Vashem, I was in floods of tears. I felt that I could then sing the *nunc dimmitis*—you know, 'You can let me depart in peace according to your word, because my eyes have seen your salvation.' It was like the fulfillment of my dreams so I could die." She laughed richly and said, "That was fifteen years ago, and I'm still here!"

When I asked her how she first became interested in Judaism, she traced it back to her youth: "I think I was about the age of seventeen when I started this whole journey toward a love of Judaism, of the Jewish people, and of Israel. At the same time, my Christian faith was growing in me, and it was a bit confusing, quite frankly, at times." She related that this developed further in college, when she began to learn more about Judaism: "[I learned about] the whole history of Christian persecution of the Jews, and I took that very, very personally. I took this so much to heart at that age, and I really felt a personal call. . . . I felt a personal call for the Jewish people and for Israel. But I never planned on it, or even thought of it, as ending up living here."

For many years, this call remained unrealized, even when as a young woman she entered a congregation of religious sisters in the United States. Describing her original intention when entering that congregation, she said, "I was going to become a nun in a nursing order and go off to Africa or whatever and just keep this personal call and love [for the Jewish people] in my heart. That's why I joined a missionary community." However, after she left that congregation, a decade later she decided to return to that early call she had felt. She visited Israel in 1982 to spend Easter at the Abu Gosh monastery at the invitation of a friend of hers who was then at the monastery, and she described a powerful sensation that hit her as soon as she walked onto the monastery grounds, which she likened to being hit over the head with a lead weight. At that moment, she felt that this was where she belonged and where she was to spend the rest of her life. This sense of belonging was a surprise to her, and she reflected, "This original call for the Jewish people surprisingly led me here. It wasn't like I wanted to live in the land [of Israel]." Contemplating this strong sense of connection, she said, "It's not just my community and my monastic life, but I *had* to be here."

She paused, looking into the air as if to gather her words there, and began to speak seriously about the spiritual call that she believes she has received: "I don't want this to sound morbid, and I've never really known how to describe it properly, but it was a call to give my life for the sins of Christians of the past—and that we would change that, that the Church would change that, that Christians would change that, and that we would learn to love the Jews, and love Israel, and recognize our sin, and repent, and reconcile."

Looking at me frankly, Sr. Michaela continued, "That's not something you go around advertising. . . . It's a very silent offering, it's very personal. It's me and God; it's not something that I talk about at all." She acknowledged that this call is not often well received and is sometimes misunderstood. She rarely communicates this sense of a call to others, but simply her presence as a nun wearing a habit in Israel at times makes her the recipient of resentment. "It's not easy in this country," she conceded, "and in this city in particular. I can't go to Mea Shearim. There are parts of the Old City where if I walk through dressed like this, I guaranteed will be spat at—or at least, spoken to not very politely. I've had things thrown at me; I've had the car rocked from side to side when I was stopped by a yeshiva. I've had things like that, and so you have that kind of very negative experience."

This treatment is certainly frightening and disturbing, but when she experiences it, she is always reminded of her deep sense of a call to offer up her life in atonement. "It's like something deep down inside me goes back to that offering and says, 'You don't know what you're doing, but honey, my life is yours anyway.'" Although it can be challenging, for her, it's part of the call: "It's what gives my life meaning, and it's a gift that God asked me to give, and so it's given. It's not something you take back—even when the giving is difficult and even when it's not understood. And I guess it's in that sense of offering, because that's what atonement is."

Sr. Michaela finds that "atonement" is a good word to describe what she feels called to, although she admitted that it often has dark associations: "I think it's something true and deep and important. But as a word, what it evokes can be negative, can be dark. For those who were Catholics pre–Vatican II, it can have kind of Jansenistic overtones of punishment." However, she clarified, "It's none of that for me." She reflected, "I think your life is only completely fulfilled if it's offered. People are not always consciously aware of that, but a wife offers her life for husband and children, and vice versa, and there are so many vocations in this world that are called in his world to offering." She concluded, "I have felt since I was very young that my life was meant to be offered for the Jewish people."

It was September when we met for the second time, and the high holidays of Rosh Hashanah and Yom Kippur were approaching. Connecting her personal call to atonement to Yom Kippur, the Day of Atonement, she described a Jewish ritual act of atonement occasionally practiced in the days preceding Yom Kippur, which is controversial and practiced by only very few Jews today: "If you're ever in Jerusalem in the market area just before Kippur, you will see certain religious Jews with the chicken, alive still, whipped around their head." Laughing, she lamented, "Oh, the poor chicken!" But she became more serious again and said she sees this rite of atonement as an analogy of her own offering of her life in atonement for the sins of Christians against the Jewish people: "But that's what it is too. I don't know if I know how to describe it any other way."

PART 4

Praying for the Jews

When she gave me directions, Sr. Rebecca had told me to turn left around the monastery walls, walk up the hill, and keep going up and up until I reach a large gate. Be sure to wear a hat, she had added, because it's a long walk. There was nobody else on the village road that baked under the midday sun. Eventually I reached a steel gate, and behind it, a long, narrow road disappeared between tall scrubby pines, continuing up the endless ascent. Just as I approached the gate, I saw Sr. Rebecca making her way down the winding lane. She greeted me with a warm smile and led me up the dusty road. She strode up the steep hill easily, explaining that she walks twice a day down the hillside to attend mass and vespers at the nearby monastery, and then back up again, even in the heat of summer.

Sr. Rebecca lives as a hermit in a low one-room structure at the top of the hill. After many decades in apostolic life as a Sister of Sion, she had requested to live as a hermit and asked that she be allowed to do so in Israel. She explained her religious vocation in very simple terms as a call to be present in Israel: "I know part of my vocation is to be here, in Israel. . . . For me, it's simply a call to be here with the people who are also my people, and to love." Solidarity and love for the Jewish people are central to her religious vocation, and she knows that this is a rare thing. She remarked, "People like us, who are here for love of the Jewish people, are a tiny minority."

Sr. Rebecca lives in solitude, removed from the regular patterns of interaction with the world around her, and yet she feels that in her own case, the hermetic life only makes sense if she practices it in Israel. Describing the foundations of hermetic life and why she feels that it is necessary to live in

Israel if she is to be a hermit, she said, "The basic is the relationship with God, and that I live it in silence and solitude, and that doesn't have to be in Israel. But it's also a relationship with God's people, who are my people. . . . And believe me, living here is not easy, but I'm really convinced this is where I belong. This is where God wants me."

When Sr. Rebecca speaks of "my people," she is referring to her Jewish heritage and her deep sense of connection with the Jewish people. She was raised by a Jewish father and a Catholic mother, and although she is not halachically Jewish by birth or religious practice, she strongly identifies as Jewish. Her sense of Jewish identity, she explained, stems from identification with the shared history of the Jewish people: "I often say to other people that being Jewish, aside from the religious roots . . . is being part of this people even if I'm not accepted halachically, which means that I share in a history. It has to do with the history of this people, of which I am a part." She added, "I do think that history, attitudes, ways of thinking, are passed on in our bodies, in our minds."

Sr. Rebecca feels that because of her identity, the Sisters of Sion's work in Christian-Jewish reconciliation comes very naturally to her: "I've always said it's in my flesh and blood because I'm of Israel and of the nations, I'm Jewish and Christian, and that has been important for me, and that's why I entered Sion. The work I used to do was very much an expression of that." But now that she lives as a hermit and is no longer actively engaged in that kind of work, she feels that she is still working toward that goal, but in a different way: "Now, it's just being here." She clarified, "What is my mission? Just to be here with, for—whatever you call it—God." She reflected, "I know part of my vocation is to be here in Israel. And that has to do with my own biography, aside from the fact that for [the Sisters of] Sion, Israel and Jerusalem are the heart of our vocation. For me, it's simply a call to be here with the people who are also my people and to love."

While many Christians identify Israel first and foremost as the land of Jesus, Sr. Rebecca sees it differently. She is no stranger to multiple theological perspectives on the land of Israel and indeed holds a PhD in this topic, having completed a doctoral dissertation on the land of Israel in rabbinic literature and the New Testament. Now living a life of solitary prayer in Israel, she reflected, "For me, Israel is not first of all the land of Jesus. Of course it's the land of Jesus, and it's the land of the Incarnation, and that's extremely important, and the Incarnation is essential to me—to us as Christians but also to me personally. But it's the land of the people of Israel. . . . So for me, the primary reason why I felt called to live here in Israel is not because it's the land of Jesus but because it's the land of Israel, of the people of Israel."

She is careful to qualify, however, that seeing Israel as the land of the Jewish people is not without complications in the contemporary political situation, and she feels torn by what she recognizes as injustice in the political conflict. As she expressed it, "I've sometimes asked myself, 'Can I continue to live in Israel, with the government as it is, and doing what it does, and things developing as they are?' But I always come back to . . . solidarity." Despite all of her conflicted feelings about the political conflict, her sense of solidarity with the Jewish people is not shaken.

Elaborating on the meaning of "solidarity," she referred to her long process of trying to obtain Israeli citizenship and having her application repeatedly refused: "I used to say, and in a certain sense I still say it, that I wanted Israeli citizenship as an expression of my solidarity with the Jewish people, and I very often have added that's not saying with the government. . . . In the meantime, because of this injustice, and the government, the word 'solidarity' has become a little difficult for me, and what has come into the foreground is much more that it's simply out of love for this people." She added, "And solidarity with the *peoples* of this land. My emotional solidarity is Jewish, so my first solidarity is with the Jewish people, but the sense of being torn, and of horror at things that happen, [is] on both sides. . . . So that sense of tremendous suffering is there, and it's very real, and if anything, it's bigger than it was."

She reflected, "Many Christians whom I deeply admire say that we as Christians cannot take sides. Part of me agrees with that, but part of me knows my emotional reactions are Jewish. I can't change that, and I don't really want to change that. But that's the way it is." However, she clarified, "It doesn't exclude for me that I see the suffering of the Palestinians and want that to be changed. It also doesn't change for me that I think present-day politics on the Israeli side are awful, and it becomes harder and harder for me to live in Israel. I'm not intending to leave, but it's no longer something that's just a pure pleasure. But that doesn't prevent my emotional reactions from being Jewish."

As our conversation continued, Sr. Rebecca spoke of her struggle to find a place where she belongs as someone who identifies as both Catholic and Jewish. The search to find this place—whether that is manifested in a community, or a formulation of religious identity, or even a physical place—is something that she often struggles with. As an American nun of Jewish heritage living in Israel, she feels always on the outside, never fully accepted as a member of Israeli society or as a Jew, and she also feels different than the other non-Jewish sisters in the Sisters of Sion. In the shadowed room of her hermitage, she said that she recently realized that perhaps the condition of not belonging is precisely where she belongs. Whether she wants it or not, she added, maybe it is within the condition of not belonging that she will find peace.

When we had finished speaking, and after she had brought out a tin of cookies to share with me, Sr. Rebecca walked me back to the gate in the afternoon sun, through flowering gardens and down the dusty, winding road, and said good-bye. I walked back down the village road to the nearby Benedictine monastery in Abu Gosh, where Sr. Rebecca attends the daily liturgies as a guest. I had scheduled a few more hours of interviews there, and when they were over, I followed the monastic community to their church for the service of vespers. I sat in the back of the church under the vaulted stone ceiling and listened to the psalms in an antiphonal Gregorian chant as the voices gently arced across the church and back again. As they chanted in French, I read along in the English translation, "Happy are those whose strength is in you, in whose heart are the highways to Zion" (Ps. 84:5), and gazed out the open door toward the road that I would soon take back to Jerusalem, the modern-day highway to Zion.

CHAPTER 12

Interreligious Dialogue and Monasticism

CONTEMPLATIVE LIFE

Life behind the walls of a cloistered contemplative monastery may seem like a rather odd context for work in Christian-Jewish relations. The latter suggests an active engagement in social activities and the world outside the monastery, while a contemplative monastic vocation traditionally requires remaining within the enclosure of the monastery, living a solitary life dedicated to prayer.[1] However, while a notable number of those whose stories are shared in this book live within such monasteries, they do not consider themselves to be dedicated to Christian-Jewish relations *despite* the parameters of their contemplative vocations; rather, they understand the practice of contemplative prayer to be the ground from which their dedication to the Jewish people is expressed. In their understandings, their vocations provide a foundation through which they may dedicate themselves to the contemplation of the "mystery of Israel" and prayer for the Jewish people.

This chapter explores the link between the dedication to Christian-Jewish relations and vowed religious life, finding aspects of monastic life that are conducive to close interreligious relations. Although religious life is a life of solitude, prayer, and contemplation, even for those in an active apostolic vocation, this interiority in the monastic tradition is not insular. Vowed religious life is not only solitary, in the sense that one lives without family and marital life, but also intensely communal and relational. In monastic theology, the solitary life is also relational, oriented toward a relationship with God, relationships with others, and a relationship with God through relationships with others. As the reflections of the nuns and monks in this study reveal, a life of prayer is a life of linking private and interior experience to the lives of those in the surrounding world.

After living in Israel for twenty-five years as an apostolic sister of the Sisters of Sion, Sr. Pilar relocated to Europe and then returned to live in Israel again, this time as a contemplative nun in La Solitude, the contemplative monastic branch of the Sisters of Sion. She believes that she is called—in the sense of a spiritual "call" from God—to love the Jewish people, and she finds that she is able to express this love differently now as a contemplative nun than she did in the past as an apostolic sister. During her many years as an apostolic nun in Israel, she expressed this love through interaction with others in the world around her, but in the years since she has become a contemplative nun, she has expressed it mostly through prayer. She gestures to the plunging hills outside of the open window and says that the convent is perfectly located for prayer for the Jewish people. Sr. Pilar points to one side of the hills, where the Hadassah Medical Center stands, and then to the other side, where the Yad Vashem Holocaust Museum and Memorial are located. She explains that as she sees it, her convent is located between two centers of the suffering and healing of the Jewish people. From her hilltop perch, enclosed within the walls of the convent, she says that she first prays for the Jewish people in her immediate surroundings, and from there, she moves on to praying for the entire world.

On another high peak not far from Hadassah Medical Center yet very far from the commotion of city life, a soft-spoken monk lives as a hermit in a little hut on a cliff above the monastery of St. John of the Desert. After many years of living in a Benedictine monastery in Jerusalem, Fr. Bernard now lives on this cliff overlooking a sweeping vista. He lives in solitude and silence, and yet he is not cut off from the world. Many Israelis visit the monastery to see the historic site, and he finds that they are often eager to engage in deep conversation, and they ask him probing questions. Although his mother tongue is Polish, he speaks Russian fluently, and many Russian Israeli Jews come to the monastery to meet with him and discuss issues of faith. In addition, every year he teaches a new group of students who visit

Jerusalem from Rome, instructing them about Judaism and Jewish life in Israel. He says he sees it as his task to bring Jewish life closer to these students through organizing lectures by visiting rabbis and Jewish educators. He takes them to services in a synagogue and teaches them about the Jewish holidays. And yet, after all of this activity, he returns to his life as a hermit, alone and in contemplation in his little desert garden high above the valley.

Behind the high stone walls surrounding the Benedictine monastery in Abu Gosh, where Sr. Michaela has been living for forty years, she feels that she has "found a way to live this [love for the Jewish people] in a life of prayer." She recognizes that the utility of contemplative life is not easy to understand and that perhaps the notion of utility is simply not applicable to contemplative life in the same way that it is to many other vocational paths. She notes that monasteries have been likened to "a powerhouse, almost like electricity" due to the power of prayer. She continues, "I think if you accept the crazy idea that prayer is . . . like an electrical station, what better place to have a source of prayer that mounts to God than here at the center of the world? In places of violence and discord, there's no better place to have a source of prayer. There must be something that influences the world around us—even though it has nothing to do with us, it has everything to do with God. It's not understood; even we don't understand it."[2]

As Sr. Michaela remembers the struggle that her father had over her choice to become a contemplative nun, she explains that he had wanted her to go out into the world and engage in activity to make a change, and he felt that contemplative life was a life wasted. She recalls, "I tried to explain [contemplative life] to him when I was coming here, and he said, 'But it's useless!' and I said, 'Yeah, exactly!'" She concedes that "humanly speaking, it's not serving any purpose other than God asking it of us." Pondering the utility, or lack thereof, of contemplative life, she continues, "Hopefully, I think if God asks this prayer of us, then there is something that God alone can take and use for the world, and first of all, the world around us, a world of discord and even of hate. But we hardly ever see any results, and we're not asking to see results, and we're not asked to see results. It's that kind of trust: okay, here is my prayer, take it and do what you want."

Sr. Anne Catherine also reflects on the utility and meaning of monastic life even though her own life as an apostolic Sister of Sion is far more immersed in the public sphere. Sr. Anne Catherine teaches in many different institutions and maintains a busy schedule, yet still she is adamant that the true purpose of her life as a religious sister is found not in these activities but in contemplative prayer. She explains, "We did not enter for *doing* things. And contemplatives, they witness that—the efficiency of prayer, of not doing anything; the efficiency of presence, the quality of presence." In Sr. Anne Catherine's view, the "utility" of religious life is not in action but in intangible elements such as the "efficacy of prayer" and the "quality of presence."

When Sr. Marie Yeshua, who lives as a cloistered contemplative nun in Jerusalem, describes the "utility" of contemplative life, she uses an architectural metaphor. Describing the architecture of the Church of the Nativity in Bethlehem, located just a few miles from her monastery, she picks up a piece of paper and draws the wooden post that serves as the cornerstone. On the paper, she indicates one vertical piece of wood attached to the peak of the roof, which descends a few feet and then ends, not attached to anything beneath it and not visibly supporting anything. This, she says, is like the role of contemplative monasticism in the world: "It's not useful, but if you take this off, the whole edifice will fall down."

MONASTIC INTERRELIGIOUS DIALOGUE

In *Monastic Quest and Interreligious Dialogue*, Gilbert G. Hardy writes that monastic life "is uniquely all-embracing: it is an act of radical conversion, a total reorientation of one's life toward some newly perceived goal of unlimited greatness," which requires a "disposition of heart and mind" characterized by "a primordial openness toward the Absolute, a deep-seated inclination to reach out toward Being and to yearn for its perfection."[3] Internal to monastic life, Hardy argues, is an orientation toward openness in encountering the other, which can engender a receptivity to meaningful, open, and potentially transformative meetings with the religious other. Matteo Nicolini-Zani proposes that this dimension of monastic life has been coming to the forefront in recent years and that a collective move toward greater openness to religious otherness can be seen in monastic life across cultures. He observes that "monks—at least some of them—belonging to all religious traditions are experiencing a transformation, a sort of alchemical *transmutatio* in their respective monastic identity as a response to the multi-religious context in which they live and as a result of their personal contacts, at different levels, with spiritual seekers walking in different religious ways."[4]

One manifestation of this has been the practice of monastic interreligious dialogue, which has become prominent in the years since the Second Vatican Council. Monastic interreligious dialogue, as it is known now, is based on the goal of deepening mutual understanding and respect through dialogue between monastics of different religious traditions. However, it did not begin that way. Many of the early pioneers were initially inspired by a missionary impulse for conversion, and they traveled to Asia to "convert pagans" and to work toward deeper inculturation of Christianity in Asia.[5] Dialogue, in these cases, was intended not to allow mutual learning and respect but to convince the other to accept Christianity.

In 1960, this impulse inspired the establishment of the Secretariat to Aid the Implantation of Monasticism, also known as AIM. Although its original intent was to spread the Christian faith through the establishment of monastic communities in Africa and Asia, the organization gradually shifted away from this goal, and in 1965, inspired by *Nostra Aetate*, AIM suggested that learning about monastic practices in non-Christian religions could contribute to a renewal in the Christian faith.[6] This shift was reflected in a series of changes to the organization's name, from the Secretariat to Aid the Implantation of Monasticism, to Aid Among Monasteries, and finally to Alliance Among Monasteries, emphasizing dialogue rather than conversion.[7] Today, monastic interreligious dialogue is fairly common between Christian monastics and monastics from a variety of Eastern religious traditions, and it is based on the understanding that the dialogue is intended for mutual learning and not for any conversionary intentions.[8]

MONASTIC HOSPITALITY AND INTERRELIGIOUS DIALOGUE

The Rule of St. Benedict, which has served as a template for many other monastic rules and governing principles of religious congregations, places hospitality as one of the highest virtues and obligatory of monastic life. When the rule instructs, "Let all guests who arrive be received like Christ, for He is going to say: 'I came as a guest, and you received Me,'" it does not simply encourage warmth to outsiders; it declares that a monk must treat an outsider as if he or she were Jesus Christ. The passage continues,

"In the greeting let all humility be shown to the guests, whether coming or going; with the head bowed down or the whole body prostrate on the ground, let Christ be adored in them as He is also received."[9] The emphasis on hospitality does not end with this passage but runs throughout the rule, concerning the treatment of fellow monks, the relationship between the abbot and monks, and all forms of interpersonal relationship.[10] Hospitality, in the monastic context, is an attitude with which one may approach all encounters, and this opening of the self to otherness, so foundational to monasticism, can allow meaningful interreligious dialogue to occur.

In her study of the virtues required for effective interreligious dialogue, Catherine Cornille identifies hospitality, defining it as "an attitude of openness and receptivity to those very differences as a possible source of truth."[11] Through hospitality, the religious other can be welcomed without being distorted—that is, neither being kept at too far a distance and seen only in its otherness nor brought in so close that its difference collapses. In other words, a disposition of hospitality is capable of respecting alterity, neither refusing the other nor sublimating the other within an illusion of sameness.

Exploring the role of hospitality in interreligious dialogue, Marianne Moyaert argues that one of the keys to hospitality lies in recognizing the otherness or strangeness of one's self. Moyaert observes, "As long as identity and otherness are thought of as opposites, openness for the strange other will be difficult. It is only to the extent that the strangeness of one's own identity is acknowledged that one can open oneself to the strangeness of the other."[12] Christians of Western origin in Israel are doubly outsiders or strangers, but the position of being an outsider, on the margins of social life in a culture that is not one's own, may in fact foster this hermeneutical openness, for "a living retention of the memory of being a stranger oneself promotes hospitality. Because we ourselves are strangers, we must be hospitable to other strangers."[13]

Fr. David Neuhaus of the St. James Vicariate for Hebrew Speaking Catholics discusses how living as the constant outsider or religious other, as members of his parish live as Catholics in Israel, can lead to a greater spiritual openness. He reflects, "So what it means all the time is the awareness of going out and not staying in . . . the realm of safety, where we all share the same language and so the questioning is muted, but going out into the world, where the questions sometimes become very challenging. [This is] very challenging in terms of trying to make sense of what we are saying, which obliges us to try to make sense of what we are thinking." He continues, "That is woven into our lives, and I think that's the experience of someone who lives on the margins and doesn't have the luxury of being part of the dominant culture, where things are taken for granted."[14]

A condition of radical openness to the unknown in oneself and, by extension, to the other allows difference and otherness to be welcomed on very deep levels, even within oneself. It may be precisely this disposition and awareness that the Benedictine monk Fr. Jacques expressed as we sat in the shade of the monastery garden, where his monastic community lives as the Christian outsiders in the middle of an Arab Muslim village in Israel. He spoke about the existential mystery of encountering the other:

> You may think that when you talk about something, you understand the same things. But in fact, each of us is dealing with many things in his life. Always, even when we have no consciousness of it, we are dealing with the mystery of our existence at every second. At every second, we are dealing with this. It's sort of printed in our deep memory. We don't lose anything; it's here. And then, when you start to know those people a bit more, and a bit closer, then you experience that in fact, when they speak of anything, even concrete realities of daily life, they speak from a point at the heart of themselves, which is the focus point of an internal and inward universe that is not yours. So you think you understand. But the immediate connection that some reality produces in his own world is definitely not the same connection that the same reality produces in your own interiority.

After this profound reflection, Fr. Jacques concludes with a simple call to hospitality: "So, once more, what's the possible connection? Probably charity, and that's all. To give a glass of water."

Sr. Michaela met with me in front of the church to lead me into the cloister of the Benedictine monastery, where I was invited to join the nuns for lunch. She led me into the antechamber to the refectory, where the nuns were waiting, standing silently around the sides of the room. The prioress said a few words and welcomed me as their guest, and when the other nuns processed into the refectory, the prioress softly said that she would remain behind with me. When the prioress and I entered the refectory together, we paused before a nun who held a jug of water and a glass basin. The prioress guided my hands over the basin, and she lifted the pitcher, generously pouring cool water over my hands. Then she was handed a perfectly ironed white linen cloth, which she ceremoniously opened, and holding both my hands in hers, she dried my hands with tender care and attention. She pressed my hands lovingly with the immaculately soft linen cloth, as if my hands belonged to a person who had been lost forever and had returned miraculously, when in fact I was nothing to them but a stranger at their gate. In a final gesture, she lifted my palms and placed on each one a long and tender kiss.

The refectory was full of light from the long, narrow windows that rose from the floor to the ceiling. All the nuns stood along the walls until the prayer was completed, at which point each pulled out a wooden stool at the same moment and sat down. The nuns sat at long tables along three sides of the wall, facing the center. The meal was taken in complete silence but for the voice of the reader, sitting at a desk in the corner of the room. The reading, in French, was a reflection on the relationship between Christianity and Judaism.

When the meal was over, all the nuns processed out together across the garden to a small oratory for the midday prayer. At each of the four corners of the oratory were glass doors, all of them open, so that the room appeared to have no corners but was open to the gardens—more like a tent than a chapel. They chanted the psalms of the midday prayer in Hebrew, in the language in which these poems were written, and in the land in which they were written thousands of years ago.

The village of Abu Gosh sits in a plunging crevasse between two steep hill-sides. The main road is a narrow strip running along the length of one of the hills, unprotected from the sun. The village spreads out below and scales up the next hillside, and somewhere in the middle of it, I had heard, is the Benedictine monastery. I was told that I couldn't miss it, and no more directions were necessary. There are only a few small roads in the center of the village, yet after I had walked their lengths, I still could not find the monastery. I stepped into a café where a few young men sat smoking and asked where the monastery was located. Two young men jumped up to show me, and both of them eagerly walked me to the gate. I thanked them, but they did not leave. I rang the bell and spoke into the intercom, and when the gate opened remotely, the two of them quickly slipped in before me. When a monk came immediately forward to greet me, he quietly asked them to leave, and they ducked out without protest.

Behind the gate was an oasis. The broad leaves of stately palms bent to the ground, and along paths through carefully tended grapevines, the sound of motors and stereos that filled the streets outside the monastery walls was replaced by the sound of birds. Across this garden, Fr. Jacques strode toward me in his long white habit. We walked to a gathering place in the garden composed of rows of long benches under a canopy. The birds sang on all sides. He looked intently at me as he spoke with a deep and steady gaze, and he answered my questions thoughtfully and with gravity.

Fr. Jacques began his vocation as a Benedictine monk at his community's monastery in France and later requested to relocate to the monastery in Abu

Gosh. Benedictine monasticism, unlike many other forms of contemplative monasticism, includes a vow of stability through which the monk vows to remain in one place, living at his monastery for the rest of his life. A move to another location is not undertaken lightly, but at his request, he was invited to come to Israel. He has now been living here for twenty years and has no intention of ever leaving.

The monastery grounds hold a large church built by the crusaders, who believed it to be the site of the biblical Emmaus. The current Benedictine abbey was established on this site only recently, in the late 1970s, when a community of Benedictines from France became caretakers of the ancient church.

The purpose of the Benedictine community's presence in Israel, as Fr. Jacques described it, is "to be a friendly presence of the Catholic Church in the midst of the Jewish people on His land, on this promised land, and as monks." He slowed down to give extra emphasis to the phrases "Jewish people," "this promised land," and "as monks."

Commenting on the importance of the Jewish people and the land of Israel to his spirituality, Fr. Jacques brought up the wordplay among three Hebrew words that are connected through alliteration: *shem, sham,* and *am.*[15] *Shem* literally means "name" and is also used as a title of God; *sham* means "there," and *am* means "people," often used to refer specifically to the Jewish people. He spoke of a spiritual connection that he sees among God (*shem*), the land (symbolized by *sham*), and the Jewish people (*am*), and he said, "As you see, that's the way we connect the land and the people here."

Referring again to the *shem-sham-am* wordplay, he spoke of the vocation of the monks, who live together as one people (*am*) in one place (*sham*) praising God (*shem*). He understands the religious purpose of the monastery's presence to be connected to the Jewish presence in Israel: "We are brothers, just like the Jews are a people, in a place, and praising the name, in the hope of the kingdom that is to come." He continued, "So it's very similar. I like this comparison. Certainly it makes sense, and certainly it makes us sensitive to the difficulties for the Jews to dwell in this land. I'm not talking about political difficulties, which are just one aspect of the challenge of dwelling in this land, and not the major aspect. Because living in Benedictine life is difficult, and you go through—or you may be led to go through—any kind of human fragility but also of human dignity and beauty." In Fr. Jacques's very philosophical interpretation, the essential challenges of being a human being and living in relation to others are brought into sharper focus in monastic life. And as a religious community whose members take vows to remain living at the monastery in Israel, he feels an affiliation with Israeli Jews as members of a religious community who are committed to life in Israel.

The Benedictine vow of stability is an important part of the link between the monastery and the Jewish people of Israel, in Fr. Jacques's interpretation: "The Benedictine vocation itself is very similar to the Jewish vocation. . . . For us, being here in stability makes us still closer to the challenge that they are going through because we also will not escape our responsibility. . . . We came to be with [the Jewish people] to be in the same boat, so once the boat has left the shore, you don't leave the boat." He finds that this commitment to remaining in Israel for life, as determined by the monastic vow of stability, helps Israeli visitors to the monastery feel a sense of connection. He explains that many Israeli visitors ask how long the monks intend to stay in Israel. When the monks answer that they plan to stay permanently, Fr. Jacques said the visitors often react with "a smile on their faces, and they sort of breathe fresh, so they understand. . . . Of course, they appreciate it, and they immediately get the message of our presence, which is only to be in the same boat."

Fr. Jacques is careful to note that the vocation of the monks is purely religious and eschews any side-taking regarding the Israeli-Palestinian conflict, which is a political issue. He explained, "As for us, here in Abu Gosh, we only have a religious purpose, and we have to very humble, maybe a bit ethnographic regarding those realities [of political conflict]—ethnographic in a more comprehensive and affective way, probably—to try to understand and to love the people as humbly as we can." In a context of political conflict and religious diversity, he believes that his duty is simply to remain humble about the limits of his understanding, recognizing that he cannot know the whole story or ever fully understand the experiences of others and to respond to the other with love.

Fr. Jacques spoke freely and openly, rarely breaking eye contact. He spoke as if he were widely opening the door to his self, just as the gate had swung open widely when I had entered the monastery a few hours earlier. The two young men had seized that opening as an invitation, and as Fr. Jacques spoke, he seemed to be opening himself up in invitation as well. And yet he also seemed to hold within himself a carefully disciplined reserve, a contemplative silence like an interior monastery wall.

As we spoke, the sound of the birds was broken by music from a car stereo. It sounded as if the car were parked right behind the monastery wall, and the Arabic pop music grew louder, asserting itself and claiming territory proudly. The outside world reaches into the monastery, and the lives and prayers of Fr. Jacques and his brothers extend out.

CHAPTER 13

Between the Synagogue and the Church

CHRISTIAN LIFE BY THE JEWISH CALENDAR

The start of Shabbat is marked in Jerusalem with a siren, which extends for many long moments, signaling the break between the profane rush of the weekdays and the sacred time of the Jewish Sabbath. As the steady tone of the siren carries on the wind across the city, reminiscent of the long wail of the shofar, time seems to momentarily stop. The silence that settles onto Jerusalem, beginning at that moment and remaining throughout the night and the daylight hours of Saturday, is profound. This great stillness is broken on Saturday night after the sun sets, and the next morning, the city is entirely back to normal as a new work week begins on Sunday. In Hebrew, Sunday is called *yom rishon*, "the first day," and it signals the return to mundane time after the sacred time of Shabbat. But for Christians living in Israel, Sunday is the Sabbath, and so the Christian weekly experience in Israel is of a Sabbath after the Sabbath.

For some, this is interpreted as an experience of the "eighth day," a theological concept dating back to the early church in which the Christian Sabbath, falling a day after the Jewish Sabbath, was counted as the eighth day in a seven-day week, symbolizing both the beginning of time and the end of time.[1] Sr. Rebecca feels that she experiences these temporal overlaps within her own life, living in Israel and feeling so connected to the Jewish liturgical calendar. She feels that the theology of the eighth day has taken on a deeper meaning for her in the years that she has lived in Israel.

Another notable overlap in the Jewish and Christian calendars occurs at the time of Passover and Easter, which very often fall during the same weeks. Sr. Rebecca attends the Passover Seder with her Jewish relatives in Israel every year, as do most of the Christians of Jewish heritage whose narratives are shared in this book. In some years, as it was during the year in which we spoke, the Seder falls on Good Friday, and so a day of fasting for Catholics coincides with a day of feasting for Jews. Sr. Rebecca found a way to celebrate both at once, reflecting her own understanding of herself as both Catholic and Jewish.

The overlap between the holidays is not coincidental; the Christian celebration of Easter developed out of the Passover tradition, based on the New Testament narrative of Jesus's crucifixion occurring at the time of Passover. Early Christians drew a symbolic connection between the Passover sacrificial lamb and Jesus, portraying him as the new sacrificial lamb. For Christians in Israel who celebrate Easter with their religious communities and Passover with Jewish family members or friends, these two commemorations are tightly interwoven both through this theological link and through the calendar. Indeed, this sense of interconnection between the Jewish and Christian liturgical calendars extends into almost all aspects of ritual markings of time for Christians who live in Israel. Within a nation where Jewish holidays become national holidays and where the world seems to come to a stop on every seventh day, Christians observe their own religious traditions from within the framework of Jewish markings of time.

ST. JAMES VICARIATE FOR HEBREW SPEAKING CATHOLICS IN ISRAEL

The St. James Vicariate for Hebrew Speaking Catholics in Israel is very much what it sounds like—that is, a community of Catholics in Israel who speak Hebrew in their day-to-day lives and who celebrate mass in Hebrew. The phrase "Hebrew Speaking Catholics" in name of the vicariate distinguishes it from "Hebrew Catholics," a phrase used by Fr. Elias Friedman and others to denote Catholics of Jewish heritage. The St. James Vicariate does not distinguish between Catholics of Jewish or non-Jewish descent and is quite simply a place of community and prayer for Catholics who use Hebrew in their daily lives. Despite the fact that Hebrew is the official language of Israel, Hebrew-speaking Catholics comprise a rather small community, for unlike most other countries, in Israel the language that one speaks is very often associated with the religion one practices; most Hebrew speakers are Jewish, while most Christians in Israel are Arab Israelis who use Arabic as their primary language of community life and liturgy. However, the St. James Vicariate provides a spiritual home for those Catholics who are not Arabic-speaking and who live in Israel for family, employment, or refuge.[2]

Since the Second Vatican Council, Catholic masses have been celebrated in the vernacular, reflecting the languages spoken by the parishioners, and in that sense, the St. James Vicariate is not unusual. However, the vernacular in Israel holds a special place in both Christian and Jewish traditions as the modern adaptation of the ancient biblical language. Prior to 1956, no Catholic mass had ever been celebrated in Hebrew.[3]

The vicariate comprises a Catholic community unlike any other in the world in that it is located in the midst of an Israeli Jewish milieu and intentionally assimilated into that culture. It not only is located within a Jewish majority—for the same could be said about a Catholic parish located in certain neighborhoods in Brooklyn, New York, for instance—but is fully immersed in a culture and society that is thoroughly Jewish in both the private and public realms. While other Christian communities in Israel, recognizing their minority status, have aimed to maintain a distinct separation from the Jewish milieu, the vicariate was established to embrace and adapt to the Jewish context in which it exists. This aim can be seen in the "Statutes of the Work of Saint James" (the original title of the group in its early years, when it was generally called the St. James Association), which outlined the five following goals:

- to develop Catholic communities;
- to ensure among the faithful a solid Christian spirit sensitive to "the mystery of Israel" (Romans 11:25), steeped in both a Biblical formation and a spirituality sensitive to Jewish-Christian culture;
- to work for the full integration of Jews who have become Catholics in the Church and in Israeli society;
- to continue to sensitize the Church to her Jewish roots;
- to combat all forms of anti-Semitism.[4]

These goals were issued in 1955, ten years before the promulgation of *Nostra Aetate*, and when these statues were drawn up, there was little discussion of Judaism in official Catholic texts. Mention of "the Jews" in Catholic theological material of this time generally referred to the Jewish people of biblical times, with little regard for the two thousand years of rabbinic Judaism that had evolved since then or for the experience of Jewish people in the contemporary world. The statutes, in this context, show that the St. James Association held views of Jewish-Christian relations that were before their time in a pre–Vatican II Catholic Church.

The St. James Vicariate is unique in its dedication to healing relations between Christians and Jews today, and its recent pastoral letter claims, "In particular, we are inspired in our identity and mission by the teaching of the conciliar document *Nostra Aetate* and all the documents that have followed, which contribute to one of the greatest revolutions in the 20th century, the revolution in relations between Jews and Christians."[5] It also aims to present the Christian history and narrative more clearly within its originally Jewish context so that it may be better understood. As the recent pastoral letter of the vicariate "Sixty Years: A Pastoral Letter" expresses, "We seek to make Jesus of Nazareth known as a son of this Land and of the Jewish people. It is important to restore the New Testament to its place within the Jewish literature of the Second Temple period." The vicariate understands itself to play an important role in furthering Christian-Jewish relations, and according to its own self-understanding, "an Israeli Catholic community of believers in Jesus, living integrated in Jewish Israeli society, serves as a bridgehead for profound healing and reconciliation between Jews and Christians in the land of Jesus."[6]

Today the vicariate serves the needs of two basic demographic groups, as Fr. David Neuhaus, the former patriarchal vicar of the vicariate, explains.[7] The first is "people who are Israeli citizens, Hebrew-speaking, part of the Jewish milieu, and are Catholic. That's a group of about 800 people; we have seven parish communities spread over the country." Of the people in this group, he continues, "A small minority are Jewish, like myself. The majority are of a variety of backgrounds, and many of them are members of Jewish families. In other words, the spouses of Jews, the baptized children of a Jewish parent, distant relatives of Jews, or simply people who live in the Jewish milieu."[8] However, the vicariate is clear in its rejection of all forms of proselytization and never seeks to bring Jews into the Christian faith. Rather, it provides a welcoming place for Jews or members of religiously mixed families who, on their own accord, had already become Catholic. Recognizing the struggles that Jewish converts to Christianity often face in Israeli society, the vicariate aims to offer them a Christian community attuned to Jewish Israeli society, and it holds that Jewish Christians are "encouraged to take pride in their roots and remain united with their people."[9] The Jerusalem community of the vicariate, known as the *kehilla*, also serves as a meeting place for Catholics in Jerusalem who are engaged in the study of Judaism or with Christian-Jewish dialogue in some form. Many religious sisters and brothers from congregations across Jerusalem come to the kehilla to attend mass, and at a Sunday vigil mass, many of the people whose narratives are shared in this book can be found greeting each other in the pews. Even those who live within cloistered monasteries occasionally visit the kehilla when they have the opportunity to leave the monastery.

The second demographic group in the Vicariate, Fr. David says, is much larger, and it is composed of "the migrant workers and the asylum seekers who work in Israel and live in Israel and are here long-term. Some of them have children that are growing up here and are Hebrew-speaking as their first language." When St. James was founded in 1955, the first group was proportionately much greater, but in recent years a second group has grown substantially, and today this second group composes the vast majority of members of the Hebrew-speaking Catholic communities across Israel.

The Jerusalem kehilla is unique within the vicariate. It sits in a peaceful corner within the city center of West Jerusalem, tucked away on a quiet side street just a half block away from Yafo Street, the shopping district, where a tangle of stores announce their sales to a bustling crowd. The elegant old building where the kehilla meets is surrounded by a spacious courtyard separated from the street by an iron gate and is a sanctuary resting quietly behind the busy street. Inside, the chapel is very spare, and unlike most Catholic churches, there are few representational images. The walls are mostly bare, with a stripped-down ornamentation reminiscent of many synagogues, and handwritten Hebrew signs indicate the daily readings and songs.

The Jerusalem kehilla sees itself to be in lineage with the early Christian community of Jerusalem during the time of Jesus. The St. James Vicariate was named after James in the New Testament, who was the head of the Jerusalem community of early Christians, according to the Acts of the Apostles. In the Jerusalem kehilla, this name is particularly meaningful, for it points to the connection between the community today and the early Christian community headed by St. James. As explained in "Sixty Years," "We pay particular attention to the Jewish milieu in which our *kehillot* live, breathe and have their being. A 'church' in the midst of the Jewish environment, particularly sensitive to the inner life of the Jewish people, recalls the most primitive '*kehilla*,' the church of the first disciples of Jesus."[10]

NUNS IN SYNAGOGUES

Many of those whose voices are heard in this book incorporate aspects of Jewish practice into their own liturgical practices. For some, it's through no more than recognizing the holiness of Shabbat for their neighbors and marking the day by being more restful and reflective when the busyness of regular weekday life comes to an end. Others, however, attend synagogue services every week or incorporate aspects of Jewish ritual into their community's life.

Sr. Gemma, the founder of the Catholic Institute for Holocaust Studies, regularly observes elements of Jewish practice and attends the Shabbat morning service at a synagogue nearly every week. She explains that out of respect for the congregants, many of whom would be upset by a Christian joining the services at an Orthodox synagogue, she attends one of the few Reform synagogues in the predominantly Orthodox city of Jerusalem. She would prefer a more rigorous and traditional liturgy and regrets that the Reform synagogue does not read the weekly Torah passage in its entirety, but she still finds great meaning in the services.

Sr. Gemma began the practice of studying the weekly Torah passage in its entirety decades ago with Fr. Isaac Jacob at the religious community he founded at Tel Gamliel with a focus on studying Jewish tradition in the context of Benedictine monastic life and spirituality. The community at Tel Gamliel did not last, and when Sr. Gemma moved to Jerusalem after the community project came to an end, she tried to maintain some of its practices. She adds that although she also attends mass daily, the weekly Torah study adds a great deal to her spiritual life. Going to the synagogue every Shabbat allows her to maintain this practice with a Jewish community. In addition, she says it also gives her a greater insight into the New Testament and the words of Jesus through understanding Jewish scriptural interpretations and traditions. This was one of the primary reasons that the Tel Gamliel community studied the Torah, and now, living in Jerusalem, this practice continues to connect Sr. Gemma not only to her own Christian scriptural text but also to Jewish thought and experience.

Maureena Fritz, a Sister of Sion, also attends synagogue services every week at the Reform congregation Kol HaNeshama, and she says that she feels very much at home there, as if she belongs there. She finds that the recitation of the Shema is of particular importance to her due to its centrality in Jewish spirituality and also because of the way it became one of the teachings that Jesus passed along into Christian tradition. As Maureena points out, in the biblical text of Mark 12:28, when a person asks Jesus for the most important commandment, he answers by reciting the Shema.

Sr. Rebecca often participates in Jewish liturgical celebrations, and she feels that her identification as someone who is both Catholic and Jewish influences her experience in a way that might not be shared by Christians without Jewish heritage. Referring to the phrase "our fathers" as it is used in Jewish liturgy, she wonders, "What does the phrase 'our fathers,' for example, mean to [other Christians]? To me, it's *our* fathers and our mothers; I mean it's *my* history . . . for me, that is very much what this Jewish people is."

Others in this study do not regularly attend synagogue services but instead draw aspects of Jewish liturgy into their Christian liturgical practices. For some, this is as simple as the use of the Hebrew language in prayer. The Hebrew language holds a unique place in prayer; indeed, it holds three unique places: First, as the language of the Hebrew Bible, it is regarded by both Jews and many Christians as the ancient language of scripture and as the language through which God's revelation was made known. Second, for Jews, it is the sacred language of prayer and has held that privileged position throughout the centuries, regardless of the vernacular spoken by Jewish communities across the diaspora. Third, in Israel, Modern Hebrew is the vernacular, spoken today by Israelis of all religions. When Christians in Israel choose to pray in Hebrew, each of these aspects of the language adds weight to its significance.

At La Solitude, the community of contemplative nuns at the Sisters of Sion's convent in Ein Kerem, the Liturgy of the Hours is chanted in Hebrew twice a day, as it is at the Benedictine monastery in Abu Gosh. At La Solitude, the nuns pray a total of four offices a day, and while lauds and vigils are in French, they chant the midday office and vespers in Hebrew. They gather in a small, minimal chapel, where a wall of windows looks out into the garden. A simple altar stands in the middle of the unornamented room, with the greenery of the garden visible behind it. A small pile of collections of Tehillim (the psalms of the Hebrew Bible in Hebrew) rests on the shelf just inside the chapel door. These booklets are not Christian publications and contain nothing but the psalms—no additional prayers, and no Christian additions—used by the nuns as they chant vespers and the midday office. Sr. Pilar explained that the purpose of praying the psalms in Hebrew is to symbolically pray alongside the Jewish people, to "unite our prayer to their prayer." Through the simple act of chanting the psalms in the Hebrew language in which they were written, her community feels that it engages in an expression of spiritual solidarity with Jews, praying with the very same words.

INTERRITUAL SHARING OR APPROPRIATION?

These individuals and communities have brought aspects of Judaism into their Christian thought and practices, making it a more Jewishly attuned faith. The Western Catholics in Israel whose stories are told here are adamant that they reject all forms of appropriation of Judaism, but what are the implications of these practices of interreligious and interritual borrowing? Is there a point at which Christian practices of Jewish liturgy might become inappropriate? When does it challenge the boundaries of each religious tradition, stretching the limits of Christian faith and practice, or diluting or disrespecting the distinctiveness of Jewish thought and ritual practices by placing them in Christian contexts? And on the other hand, when can it serve as a vehicle for greater interreligious understanding?

At Sr. Talia's monastery, the community of monks and nuns celebrate Kabbalat Shabbat together every Friday evening and invite guests to join them weekly.[11] On the Friday evening when I joined them, the monastic community and the guests gathered around a long table. Booklets for the service were passed around the table, written in Hebrew with French translations provided. With minimal ceremony, the celebration began with singing. The community sang all the psalms of Kabbalat Shabbat as printed in the booklet. As the superior of the monastery began each new melody, the others gradually joined in until everybody sang together.

When asked if her monastic community practices any other elements of Jewish liturgy, Sr. Talia responded definitively, "No, we do not, and I don't think we should. I definitely do not think we should because we are not Jews. . . . I don't think we should do more because we are different, we are Catholic. It is very important to keep our Catholic identity, to be clear." She concludes that the importance of a clear separation between religious identities is something that she learned from living in Israel: "It is another lesson of this country, that the identities are very clear, and it is very important."

The little booklet of psalms that the monastery follows for its Kabbalat Shabbat service is composed of the psalms recited during the Jewish Kabbalat service, and it contains no reference to Jesus or to any other specifically Christian beliefs with the exception of one notable addition: the Lord's Prayer in Hebrew. This addition, however, could easily go unnoticed by one not familiar with Jewish liturgy, for when recited in Hebrew, the Lord's Prayer appears to be a Jewish prayer. It begins with the word *avinu* (our father), reminiscent of the Jewish prayer *Avinu Malkenu*, and contains no reference to Jesus Christ, the Holy Spirit, or any other specifically Christian concepts. It fits into the service nearly seamlessly, but despite the lack of specifically Christian concepts in the prayer, it is nevertheless a Christian prayer inserted without commentary into the text of the Jewish liturgy. This Christian addition, presented in the language of Jewish prayer, functions to subtly but powerfully blur the distinction between the specifically Jewish tradition of the Kabbalat service and Christian theology.

When the psalms had all been sung, the superior stood and said the Shabbat blessing over wine and a loaf of challah, precisely following the Jewish ritual while speaking the blessing in Hebrew, and following this, as it would be done in a Jewish home, the meal began. The recitation of the blessing over the bread and wine had no Christian additions—it was performed exactly the way it would be in a Jewish setting—but in this context, the blessing inevitably took on Christian associations. Here stood a Catholic priest, standing and raising bread and saying a blessing over it, then raising wine and saying another blessing. In his hands, the bread and wine recalled the elements of the Eucharistic rite, which itself has roots in ancient Jewish practice. Although there was nothing overtly Christian in this ritual, in the hands of one who daily raises bread and wine in the rite of the Eucharist, the associations were clear to all present.

Sr. Gemma, who attends the synagogue every Saturday, admits that Jewish prayers and Christian prayers at times blend and overlap in her thoughts and sometimes in her ritual practice as well. She often goes to pray at the two main pilgrimage sites of Jewish and Christian spirituality in the Old City of Jerusalem, the Western Wall and the Church of the Holy Sepulchre, respectively. When she prays at these places, she explains, she does not focus on the difference between Christian spirituality and Jewish spirituality. Instead, she thinks simply about the human longing for the divine. "When I go to the [Western] Wall," she says, "I'm hardly thinking about the Temple. I don't think I think much about the Temple at all. But I think about all the people there and all the prayer. Because you have all those *petics*, all those little pieces of paper, and all that prayer. And people are very, very in earnest, especially the women there—they're very taken up by their prayer; it completely envelops them. It's very moving."

When Sr. Gemma visits the Western Wall and the Church of the Holy Sepulchre, she finds that Jewish or Christian prayers often spontaneously arise in her at the wrong place: Jewish prayers come to mind at the Christian site and Christian prayers at the Jewish site. She laughingly comments, "I probably pray the Our Father at the Wall, and I probably pray the Shema in the Holy Sepulchre. But it doesn't matter. Really, it doesn't matter." Sr. Gemma believes that it is inconsequential if Christian and Jewish religious practices meet and mix in her own spiritual experience. But does it matter to others, and if so, then to whom and why?

For her weekly synagogue attendance, Sr. Gemma has chosen a synagogue that accepts her, and the congregation knows that she is a nun. Sr. Gemma remains discreet and respectful at all times. Her participation in Jewish liturgy and her visits to the Western Wall are undertaken with profound respect for Judaism, and as evidenced by her decades of work with Yad Vashem, she is passionately committed to addressing the history of Christian anti-Judaism through educating Christians about the Holocaust. She and the others discussed here are extremely careful to cause no offense. They bring elements of Judaism into Christianity, but they do not bring elements of Christianity into Judaism.

The adoption of elements of Judaism into Christianity is an inherent part of the development of Christianity from its very beginnings; indeed, the earliest Christian movement cannot be understood apart from its origin as a movement within Judaism, which carried its Jewish theological and ritual background with it as it developed into a distinct religion. However, in the Christian interpretation of this historical borrowing, it is seen as an appropriation justified by supersessionist theologies. For these reasons, Christian practices of Jewish traditions are often received with ambivalence and with a suspicion founded on a history of supersessionism. It is weighted with a dark history, and there is no assurance that this history will not be repeated in such borrowing. Consequently, Christian practices of Jewish traditions, even when well intentioned, can easily slide into religious appropriation, carrying with it the suggestion of Jewish sublimation into Christianity if not sensitively monitored and considered.

A rite will always change when performed outside of its home tradition, just as the Shabbat blessing of bread and wine changed in the hands of the Catholic priest at the monastery. This, however, can be threatening to a religious tradition that has historically preserved its boundaries with great struggle and trial. The preservation of Jewish tradition and the Jewish people is one of the central concerns of Judaism, and when Christians practice Jewish rituals and traditions, it can be seen as eroding this important distinction. This may be ameliorated by the fact that any risk of religious synchronism is on the part of Christians, not Jews—that is, it is not Jews performing Christian rites but Christians performing Jewish rites. The latter may be less challenging to Jewish continuity and survival than the former, but both challenge the borders.

Sr. Gemma has forged a path of her own. She entered the Sisters of Charity in the United States in 1950, over a decade before the reforms of Vatican II. She rose to academic success rapidly, receiving a PhD in history, and eventually became the chair of the history department at Seton Hill University. In 1975, she moved to Israel and began to be deeply involved in Holocaust education. Recognizing the need for Catholics to study the Holocaust, she founded the Catholic Institute for Holocaust Studies in 1989, based at Seton Hill University in Pennsylvania. The institute brings Catholic educators to Yad Vashem to study the Holocaust and to receive pedagogical instruction for teaching about the Holocaust. In 2007, Sr. Gemma became the first non-Jewish and non-Israeli recipient of the Yad Vashem Award for Excellence in Holocaust Education.

By the time I met with her in Jerusalem, Sr. Gemma had been living in Israel for forty years. She lives in Jerusalem not with members of her own congregation but with members of the Sisters of St. Joseph of the Apparition in a room in their estate hidden behind a high gate on HaNevi'im Street. A petite woman with white hair and large dark eyes, she arranged to meet me in Mahane Yehuda, the crowded street market in central Jerusalem. With a wide smile on her face, she gave me a hug and then pressed through the crowds, buying her fruits and vegetables for the week. As she pushed her shopping trolley through the chaotic narrow aisles of the *shuk*, speaking with all the vendors in Hebrew, she seemed to be entirely assimilated into Israeli culture.

Sr. Gemma's engagement with Jewish and Israeli life and culture goes deep; she has made Israel her home and has brought aspects of Jewish tradition and thought into her Christian faith. She said, "I try to observe some of the things that are observed in Judaism," and explained that attending synagogue services nearly every Shabbat is one of the ways that she keeps a close sense of connection with Jewish life in Israel. In addition to sharing in Jewish prayer, she finds that speaking Hebrew also keeps her in touch with Israeli life and allows her to be immersed in an Israeli mind-set.

She also feels that this connection with Jewish Israeli life is deepened through experiencing Shabbat in the city of Jerusalem: "Even here, in this house, which is definitely not Jewish, when Erev Shabbat comes, everything quiets down—the house quiets down—and we have a holy hour. When you hear the whistle in the neighborhood saying that it's Shabbat . . . it touches you in some way." She finds that this gives her an experiential connection to what she sees as the sacredness of the land: "It's really in some ways the holiness of Shabbat that's one of the most convincing things, to say that there's something about the holiness of the land." In this marking of sacred time, she finds a way to experience sacred place: "[Shabbat] has been a way for me to really experience that there is something holy about this land and about the people."

Sr. Gemma finds that Jewish holy days that set aside sacred time, such as Shabbat and the high holidays, also give her a sense of the sacredness of the land and people of Israel. She related that she feels this during Yom Kippur, when the city of Jerusalem becomes completely silent, with all traffic stopped: "There is a heaviness in the air, so you do experience—I think you can tangibly experience—God's presence here in some way. Maybe other people don't feel that way, but I feel that's very powerful, and it reflects on something about the land—or the people in the land, that's a better way to say it."

Sr. Gemma's feeling of connection to Israel and to Jerusalem in particular is powerful, and her participation in Jewish rituals reinforces and marks that connection. She expresses this by describing what she feels when she travels back to visit her congregation in the United States: "When I go back to the States, our motherhouse is in a small town, and so there's only one synagogue. And I go to the Friday night [service] there because it's very small, and they don't have [a Saturday service]. But then there's no Hebrew, and then there's nobody saying 'Quiet down, this is Shabbat.' There's none of that. So when I'm there, I'm thinking, 'I've got to get back, I've got to get back.' Even spiritually, I have to get back."

CHAPTER 14

The Problematics of Prayer for the Jewish People

NEW FORMS OF PRAYING FOR THE JEWS

The intention to proselytize, whether overt or hidden, hovers like a shadow over the practice of praying for the Jewish people. The practice is burdened by a history of Christian prayer for the conversion of Jews to Christianity, which is not only offensive to Jewish self-understanding but also historically associated with a wide range of acts of oppression and violence. In short, the concept of Christian prayers for the Jewish people is problematic enough that any treatment of it, whether the scholarly analysis of it or the spiritual practice of it, requires careful enunciation and specification.

The voices that have spoken throughout this book express views of what it means to pray for the Jewish people that are dramatically different than the earlier precedents. Their own practices of prayer for the Jewish people, as they explain it, are undertaken in recognition of the injustices perpetuated throughout the history of the Christian desire for Jewish conversion. They do not merely abstain from the desire for the conversion of the Jewish people to Christianity; rather, their spirituality and theological outlook are characterized by an explicit rejection of precisely this problematic history. This approach, however, is far from the norm in Christian attitudes toward Judaism. Outside of this group, there are many other Catholics today who are unashamed to speak of their desire for Jewish conversion. Despite the statements made in recent Vatican documents declaring that Christian missionary efforts to Jews are inappropriate, many still see the desire for Jewish conversion to Christianity to be intrinsic to the Christian faith and hold that Christians are bound by faith and duty to evangelize to all people. The following pages explore this traditional theological starting point and the attendant problems it raises. It also analyzes new, theologically inclusive and pluralist Christian practices of praying for Jews, remaining alert to the tangle of beliefs and intentions that lie beneath these practices, in which the theological visions of Christianity often clash against those of Judaism.

Sr. Pilar sits in front of a window that opens onto a sweeping view of the hills to the west of Jerusalem. She is uncompromisingly direct in explaining what he sees as her purpose in living as a contemplative here: "For me, the purpose of being here—we say we contemplatives live a life of praise and intercession—[is to] to pray to the God of Israel and to intercede for the Israel of God." Prayer for the Jewish people is central to her personal sense of mission within her religious vocation. What, however, does she pray *for* when she prays for the "Israel of God"? Without pause, she answers, "We pray that they are faithful to their vocation. It's beautiful, the vocation of the Jewish people. . . . And praying that the Church understands this richness of the Jewish roots and the richness of the Jewish people that is always there. It has a lot to teach us." When asked to clarify what she means when she refers to the "vocation of the Jewish people," Sr. Pilar counts the points off on her fingers as she answers, "To be faithful to God, one; to be a witness to the unicity of God; and to be a witness for the nations. The vocation of the Jewish people is for the nations; they are the people who say to the nations that God is one." She adds that not only does she pray *for* the Jewish people, but as she understands it, she symbolically prays *with* them: "I pray for and with the Jewish people. . . . In the midday and the afternoon, we pray the psalms in Hebrew to pray with them, it's the psalms that they pray. . . . So we pray with them. So we unite our prayer to their prayer." As discussed in the previous chapter, her community's practice at La Solitude of chanting the psalms twice a day in Hebrew does not introduce any Christian additions into Jewish prayer but simply engages in the ancient practice of ritually reciting the psalms of the Hebrew Bible in their original language.

A similar practice of praying for and with the Jewish people is also expressed by Sr. Carmen, who regularly prays the Amidah, a lengthy central prayer in the three daily Jewish prayer services. From her home located across the street from the house of the president of Israel, where she prays for the leaders of Israel, Sr. Carmen expressed that praying for the Jewish people is absolutely central to her religious vocation. When asked what precisely she prays for, she responded, "I pray that they may be faithful to their call. And their call is not isolated from the call of *Benei Noah*. There's a big call, and there's a specific call. So there is no division, but it's a continuity."[1] In Sr. Carmen's interpretation, the specific "call" of the Jewish people is closely related to the universal "call" of all people, or *Benei Noah* (sons of Noah). She sees these two calls as existing in unity—as part of the same interaction between God and humanity.

The desire to pray for the Jewish people is behind the name that Sr. Michaela took when she became a nun. When she entered the monastery and was clothed in the Benedictine habit, she was given the opportunity to choose the name she would take on as a nun. She had been beginning to learn Hebrew and had learned that the name Michael was from the question "Who is like God?" (*Mi-cha-El?*). The meaning of the name struck her deeply, and it also seemed to express an experience she had in her own practice of prayer. She explains that she had learned that "Michael in the Talmud is the angel who gathers up the prayers of Israel and brings them before the face of God. That symbolizes fairly well what my prayer is. It's part of this gathering up the prayers of Israel." Even at that early stage in her religious vocation, Sr. Michaela felt that her practice of praying for the Jewish people was essentially fueled by the desire to help lift up the prayers of the Jewish people. She was not praying for certain outcomes in her prayer; she was merely gathering and holding up the prayers of the Jewish people as if ushering those prayers along their way toward God.

Praying for the Jewish people, particularly for those living in Israel, is also a regular part of the spiritual life of Fr. Bernard, a Benedictine monk who lives as a hermit on a cliff above the monastery of St. John of the Desert. However, he clarifies that these prayers are without a specific goal: "I never ask God to do one thing or another for Jews. I just pray for them. God knows what to do. God knows that they need peace. I just pray for them." He believes "that the first thing on God's heart [is] his own people. God said, 'I'm sent to these people.'" Therefore, he believes, it is neither his right nor in his power to engage in petitionary prayer for specific outcomes for the Jewish people or for Israel. "Israel has deep problems," he adds, "and God doesn't need hints for how to solve them. The problems have no solutions; they only have histories." Fr. Bernard has a deep respect for Jewish religious traditions, and when he prays for Jews, he often uses prayers taken from the Hebrew Bible rather than using Christian prayers. This, he explains, is a reflection of his theological perspective on the nature of religious truth and the path to salvation. He firmly believes that there are many paths to salvation and that Christians can never assume that Judaism is incomplete without belief in Jesus. That does not diminish his Christian faith in any way, he says, but it allows him to be humble about God's ways: "For us as Christians, Jesus is the savior for all of us. But the road to salvation, there are as many of them as there are people in the world. Only God knows how to save all people."

EVANGELIZATION

The notion of Christian prayer for Jews is complex and problematic despite the good intentions of those discussed here. At the root of the problem is the tension between the conviction that Christian claims about salvation are universally true, on the one hand, and the belief in God's enduring covenant with the Jewish people, on the other. The former conviction is expressed through evangelization, which holds a central position within Christianity. As the Catholic Church makes clear, "Confessing the universal and there-fore also exclusive mediation of salvation through Jesus Christ belongs to the core of Christian faith," and this injunction to witness the exclusiv-ity of Christian truth claims extends to Christian-Jewish relations as well; indeed, this line occurs in a document written by the Vatican Commission for Religious Relations with the Jews.[2] Those who wish to rethink Christian theologies of Judaism and to develop progressive understandings of the ongoing validity of Judaism must grapple with the theological prerogative to evangelize. Evangelization is distinct from proselytization and does not necessarily involve an explicit intent to convert; however, the lines between evangelization and proselytization can easily become blurred. Given the dark history of Christian anti-Judaism and the forced conversions of Jews, this creates a theological obstacle to the task of reconciliation in Christian-Jewish relations.

Although the individuals whose stories have been told here hold new
pluralist understandings of evangelization, the traditional attitude about its
necessity remains prevalent in Catholic thought. Indeed, the conversionary
intentions that this study identifies as problematic are not seen as such by
many Christians today; instead, this is generally seen as part of the foundation of Christian faith, and most Christians believe that their faith carries
with it the duty to guide others to share in the same faith. In the course of
my fieldwork, as I interviewed people representing a range of Catholic views,
I found many whose views were surprisingly inclusive concerning issues of
salvation and truth. However, I also encountered others who, although they
expressed a particular interest in Judaism and Jewish-Christian dialogue,
maintain very traditional views on the necessity of evangelization. One
young priest in Jerusalem who claims to be invested in Jewish-Christian
relations and is active in Jewish-Christian dialogue admitted, "If you have
good friends, even if they are Christians who don't believe, you wonder why
they don't take part in this joy. I pray for the same for my Jewish friends.
I don't pray that they will become Christian, but more and more, [I pray]
that they will be open to the reality that Christ is the messiah." He recognizes that an explicit intent to encourage Jews to convert to Christianity
is unacceptable (and also forbidden by the Israeli government), and so
expresses his wish in carefully chosen language. However, the message in
his statement is clear: recognizing Jesus as the messiah is the central faith
claim of Christianity, and so he prays, in effect, for the conversion of Jews.
This desire, expressed in indirect terms such as these, is certainly far from
unusual among Catholics but becomes particularly problematic among
those who are actively involved in Jewish-Christian dialogue.

A similar view was expressed by a nun of Jewish heritage who asked
that neither her name nor the name of her monastery be mentioned. Before
entering a cloistered monastery outside of Jerusalem, she had first come to
Israel when she was an evangelical Christian attracted to Messianic Judaism. She immigrated to Israel motivated by a Christian Zionist vision and
tried to integrate into Israeli society while secretly remaining active with a
Messianic group. A number of years later, she converted to Catholicism and
eventually entered a contemplative monastery outside Jerusalem. When
she explained her monastic community's sense of connection to Judaism,
she began very unobtrusively, "Our prayer embraces the Jewish people as
our older brother and truly as our brothers and sisters. And our prayer is

always that God's will for the Jewish people will be accomplished." When she specified what she and her monastic community believe God's will for the Jewish people consists of, however, it became clear that she prayed for Jewish conversion to Christian faith. "Ultimately," she confessed, "we have the prayer that the day will come when they will recognize the messiah in Yeshua [Jesus]. That is our prayer, but we don't force anything on anyone. We have many Jewish friends who do not believe in Yeshua, and we don't press anything on them. . . . The prayers in the liturgy are for God's blessing to be fulfilled for his people and ultimately seeing their messiah in Yeshua." Like the young priest and many others with whom I spoke, she does not use the word "conversion" for this; nevertheless, the hope that Jews will recognize Jesus as the messiah is still essentially a desire for conversion.

These sentiments are not surprising, for they are standard within Catholic discourse. When these views are expressed by Catholics who are active voices in Jewish-Christian dialogue in Israel, however, it is less expected. Such is the case with Fr. Marcel Dubois, who was so influential in Jewish-Christian dialogue in Jerusalem. In an interview in 1997, toward the end of his life, he admitted a theological view that seems to contradict his decades of work in Jewish-Christian dialogue and reconciliation: "Recently I said to someone in the University—who does not agree at all—that as Christians we are convinced (though this is difficult to express) that a Jew who becomes a Christian accomplishes the vocation of Jewry, and so is more Jewish than his brothers. And on the Christian side we have to accept that he is naturally more Christian than his Christian brothers. Why? Because in the presence of the grace of God he has done something that was prepared for the Jews."[3]

Dubois's admission of this view is surprising, particularly given that on two separate occasions in the same interview, the interviewer had pushed him to address the small number of Jews who had frequented the Isaiah House and had then converted to Christianity. Both times, Dubois responded that they never encouraged conversion at the Isaiah House, and he clarified that those who wished to convert from Judaism to Christianity were always told to go elsewhere for the conversion process. He added that it would be potentially damaging to the effectiveness of his community in Jewish-Christian relations if these conversions became a publically discussed issue. However, he felt comfortable expressing his theological view regarding the status of Jews who become Christian: he believed they become more

Jewish than other Jews and more Christian than other Christians because they have accomplished God's plan for the conversion of Jews to Christianity. Despite his substantial work in Jewish-Christian reconciliation, Dubois failed to realize that "holding Jewish existence up to a unique form of Christian scrutiny could never be acceptable to Jews," and his legacy ultimately "reminds us again why Jews are perhaps not altogether wrong to experience anxiety 'when a Christian loves Israel.'"[4]

The Catholic Church has released many documents on Christian-Jewish relations, beginning with the promulgation of *Nostra Aetate* during the Second Vatican Council, and although the general prerogative to evangelize is unambiguous throughout the documents, they remain unclear on the issue of evangelization specifically to Jews. *Nostra Aetate* emphasizes the spiritual bond between Judaism and Christianity while also suggesting the ongoing necessity of evangelizing, referring to "the burden of the Church's preaching to proclaim the cross of Christ as the sign of God's all-embracing love and as the fountain from which every grace flows."[5] The document avoids direct discussion of proselytization and therefore does not explicitly reject the proselytization of Jews. The follow-up document, "Guidelines and Suggestions for Implementing the Conciliar Declaration Nostra Aetate, 4," clarifies that evangelization is part of the "very nature" of the Catholic Church: "In virtue of her divine mission, and her very nature, the Church must preach Jesus Christ to the world (*Ad Gentes*, 2). Lest the witness of Catholics to Jesus Christ should give offense to Jews, they must take care to live and spread their Christian faith while maintaining the strictest respect for religious liberty in line with the teaching of the Second Vatican Council (Declaration *Dignitatis Humanae*)."[6] In this statement, the document urges sensitivity when evangelizing to Jews, clarifying that it must not disrespect religious liberty, but nevertheless, it upholds the necessity of spreading the faith to all, including Jews.

The recent Vatican document "The Gifts and Calling of God Are Irrevocable: A Reflection on Theological Questions Pertaining to Catholic-Jewish Relations on the Occasion of the 50th Anniversary of 'Nostra Aetate' (No. 4)," specifies this issue far more than the earlier *Nostra Aetate*, but it still leaves the tension unresolved. It clarifies that "the Catholic Church neither conducts nor supports any specific institutional mission work directed towards Jews." However, it continues, "While there is a principled rejection of an institutional Jewish mission, Christians are nonetheless called to bear witness to their faith in Jesus Christ also to Jews, although they should do so in a humble and sensitive manner, acknowledging that Jews are bearers of God's Word, and particularly in view of the great tragedy of the Shoah."[7] Despite the slight amelioration caused by the "humble and sensitive manner," this renewed injunction for Christian evangelization to Jews reinforces the image of the Jewish people as "bearers of God's Word" and yet ultimately wrong and in need of evangelization.

A recent debate between theologians Gavin D'Costa and John T. Pawlikowski, OSM, published in *Theological Studies*, addresses this issue of mission to Jews. D'Costa argues that Catholic teaching holds that the Church's mission is not directed to any one particular group of people, nor is it forbidden to any one group; mission must necessarily be directed toward all people. Therefore, he argues, mission is as necessary to Jews as it is to all people. Enumerating his points, D'Costa argues, "(1) The magisterium teaches that mission to the Jewish people and individuals is required if Catholics are to be faithful to the truth of the gospel. (2) There is also recognition that Jews may adhere to their ancient religion in good faith ... which contains true revelation, but that this revelation is completed in historical and eschatological time, in Jesus Christ."[8] D'Costa believes that his view "avoids traditional supersessionism and abrogation, and affirms the continuing validity of the Jewish covenants and promises." He concludes, "But there should be no misunderstanding of the basic principle: mission to the Jews is theologically legitimate. Learning how best to implement that principle is the complex task that still awaits the careful attention of the contemporary Catholic Church in honest dialogue with Jewish groups and individuals in their great diversity."[9]

Pawlikowski, a longtime advocate of Jewish-Christian reconciliation and a practitioner of Jewish-Christian dialogue, disagrees with D'Costa's methods and conclusions. He criticizes D'Costa's "neglect of the emerging theological consensus on continued Jewish covenantal inclusion as a central argument against missionizing Jews."[10] Arguing for the inclusion of social and interpersonal concerns in any effective and theologically sound approach to the issue of mission, Pawlikowski counters that "authentic dialogue has to bring together the theological tradition of the church past and present with the personal experience of encounter with members of other faith communities—Jews in particular." He concludes, "The question of mission to Jews, or mission to any other faith community in the context of interreligious dialogue, cannot be determined solely through theological reflection, as vital as that reflection remains."[11]

This debate reflects the concerns that the voices heard in this book grapple with. Motivated by the recognition of the validity and rich distinctiveness of Judaism and yet also compelled to address in some way the fundamental Christian imperative to evangelize, each voice heard here negotiates his or her own way of understanding what evangelization and mission should mean in today's world and in relation to the Jewish people.

This process of negotiation can be seen in Sr. Rebecca's reflections. She is adamantly opposed to any form of evangelization to Jews and indeed feels that it is against God's will for Jews to convert to Christianity in today's world. She elaborates, "I am profoundly convinced that God wants the Jews to remain Jews. I think the Jewish presence is necessary for the Church and for the world." Sr. Rebecca's reasoning for the ongoing necessity of Judaism is profoundly different than the reasoning upheld by Christian tradition for millennia, which held that the presence of Jews in exile is necessary to serve as a reminder to the world of their sin in failing to recognize Jesus as the messiah. Using a radically different rationale, Sr. Rebecca explains the reasons she believes that Jews should not convert to Christianity and that the presence of Jews is "necessary for the Church and for the world": "One reason is when you think of Church history, the Church had forgotten so much that the Jewish people proclaims—not necessarily in words but as a light for the world, and that's necessary. And so I think their presence is necessary for the world, and for the Church, to remind the Church of things that are essential and that the Church had forgotten or had never really received." And so, she concludes, "I *never* pray for the conversion of the Jews to Christianity."

Yet this strong assertion is nuanced by Sr. Rebecca's reflections on secular Judaism. She notes that the Jews who are closest to her, including her own Jewish family members, are secular. She expresses, "I wish for them that they could in some way come to faith," but clarifies, "Now, that doesn't have to be Christian faith." However, she concedes with great carefulness and hesitancy: "I know there are many secular Jews who are fascinated by Christianity, so I think sometimes, well, maybe if they come to faith in Jesus, it might be a source of great happiness for them. But that's not the same as wanting, working, praying, for their conversion to Christianity." The central desire motivating Sr. Rebecca's prayer for Jews is not for Jews to develop faith in Jesus; indeed, she had already clarified that she believes that it is God's will that Jews remain faithfully Jewish. Her desire, rather, is for secular Jews without any religious faith to experience faith in some form—if not within the boundaries of traditional Jewish faith, then perhaps in another form. Sr. Rebecca is fully cognizant of the sensitivity of this subject and its many nuances, as one who holds a doctorate in Jewish studies, is from a Jewish family, and has been living in Israel for decades. And with all this in mind, when she is deeply honest, she acknowledges that in wishing that secular Jews might experience the joy of faith, she does not rule out that they might find this joy through faith in Jesus if they are led to it on their own accord and not through persuasion.

Sr. Rebecca's reflections resonate in many ways with those of Sr. Talia, who expresses feeling torn between the natural desire to share what brings her joy with her Jewish friends and the cultural awareness and sensitivity that holds her back from doing so—to avoid allowing her religious self-expression to verge onto evangelization. Sr. Talia explains that Jesus "is the one that separates me from my Jewish friends. The one that is supposed to unite us and to be a source of joy and celebration, he's the one that is a source of incredible pain." The source of this pain, she clarifies, lies in "knowing something that is so precious and not being able to share it."

In Sr. Talia's own experience, God's love is experienced through Jesus, and she explains that she naturally wants to share the source of her joy with those whom she loves. However, she recognizes that she cannot share this without falling into evangelization and thereby disrespecting those whom she loves. So when speaking with her Jewish friends, she adamantly refuses to express her faith, and she feels that this choice causes her pain. She describes it as "a burning fire in my heart and a suffering at the same time. A huge suffering. This is the cross. This is exactly the cross for me." The conflict between the desire to express and share her faith and the decision to abstain from doing so for the sake of respect for Judaism, as made clear in her words here, is a central theme in her spiritual struggle.

"I'm speaking as a nun," Sr. Talia continues, "as somebody who is praying nearly all the day long, so it is a mystical approach, but it is my approach." The narrative of her experience in prayer is reminiscent of the experiences documented by the women mystics of the Middle Ages, who claimed to gain an intimate knowledge of Jesus's pain through prayer. As she expresses it, "My approach is that sometimes in prayer, I feel this deep, deep, incredibly deep pain in the heart of Jesus for his people." Despite this mystical and intimate sense of Jesus's own pain, as she describes it, Sr. Talia also readily admits the limits of her understanding. Retaining an attitude of humility, she adds, "And at the same time, I feel that there is something that I do not understand. I do not understand what he is doing with his people. I don't. I do not have all the keys. I have some keys, but not all the keys, because I have not finished my journey." And so, she concludes, she simply remains within this state of tension, feeling the "burning fire" and continuously abstaining from any expression of faith that could be construed as evangelization to Jews. She feels that only Jesus can decide if Jews should have faith in him: "If he wants to convert them, it's his problem, not mine."

A THEOLOGICAL PARADOX

Evangelization is essentially a soteriological issue, as it is fueled by the conviction that one must have faith in Jesus to be saved. Within Catholic thought, however, the conviction that faith in Jesus is necessary for salvation becomes a point of theological irresolution, and even paradox, when coupled with the recognition of God's enduring covenant with the Jewish people and the ongoing validity of Judaism. This is a perplexing issue for Catholics dedicated to Christian-Jewish dialogue and to prayer for the Jewish people without evangelization.

Charlotte Klein, the Sister of Sion who made aliyah to escape antisemitism in prewar Germany, expresses precisely this tension: "For Christians, there exists here a genuine dilemma for which no perfect solution has yet been found. If Jesus is the Christ, is he not God's revelation for all people, Jews as well as Gentiles? Is his significance not universal?" She answers these questions with the suggestion that no theological resolution has been found that, in her reckoning, satisfactorily accounts for the covenantal validity of Judaism. She continues, "Several answers, none of them completely satisfactory, have been proposed. It may be that Christian claims for Jesus are too absolute, even in the New Testament, and Christians might need to rethink their Christology and perhaps to qualify the titles they have given to Jesus."[12] Klein proposes a reenvisioning of Christology reminiscent of some of the theological concepts expressed by the voices heard in this book, radically opening up current Catholic notions of the identity and role of Jesus.

These views, however, do not align well with the current Christology and soteriology of the Catholic Church. Indeed, these questions are addressed directly in "The Gifts and Calling of God Are Irrevocable," which observes, "Another focus for Catholics must continue to be the highly complex theological question of how Christian belief in the universal salvific significance of Jesus Christ can be combined in a coherent way with the equally clear statement of faith in the never-revoked covenant of God with Israel." While this suggests that the paradox might remain unresolved, the following line suggests otherwise in an unambiguous conclusion: "It is the belief of the Church that Christ is the Saviour for all. There cannot be two ways of salvation, therefore, since Christ is also the Redeemer of the Jews in addition to the Gentiles." With this, the document seems to suggest that the paradox has been resolved; Jews can find no way to salvation except through Christ. The paragraph concludes, "Here we confront the mystery of God's work, which is not a matter of missionary efforts to convert Jews, but rather the expectation that the Lord will bring about the hour when we will all be united, 'when all peoples will call on God with one voice and "serve him shoulder to shoulder."'"[13] In short, the document instructs that Christians should not work toward Jewish conversion; however, in the same breath, it asserts that God will take care of it himself. It concludes that the Christian understanding of salvation is the one and only universal way and that Jews too must find salvation in Jesus if they are to be saved at all. Although "The Gifts and Calling of God Are Irrevocable" has been hailed by many as a breakthrough in Catholic theologies of Judaism and as a major step forward in Christian-Jewish dialogue, the document makes it clear that the official teaching of the Church is still adamant that Judaism will be complete only with faith in Jesus, which effectively calls a halt to efforts to seek an understanding of the validity of Judaism in and of itself.

Many of the individuals whose narratives have been discussed in this book have moved beyond the assumption that the Christian understanding of Jesus is the absolute truth and have broken away from the traditional theologies that have resulted in centuries of anti-Judaic teaching. While their views often tend toward philosemitism, thus swinging beyond the range of normalization in their understandings of Jews and verging onto the territory of essentializations, their lives, practices, and theologies exhibit a remarkable departure from the centuries-old patterns of Catholic understandings of Jews and Judaism. They push the boundaries of Catholic thought on

Judaism, and although they do not represent the mainstream, the views they express may suggest future directions in Catholic thought if recent developments are indicative of future shifts.

PORTRAIT: SR. MAUREENA

When Maureena Fritz opened the door, I was immediately struck by her strong, controlled presence. She stands straight and tall, with an energy that's both tensely alert and graceful. Her ninety years of age seem impossible, as if she has moved through the century with only increasing vigor. Maureena, as she prefers to be called, without the title "Sister," is a Sister of Sion, originally from Canada. When I met with her, she had just returned from an overseas trip, one of the many that she frequently makes, to lecture and conduct workshops in Christian-Jewish relations, theology, and Jewish studies. She welcomed me into her home in a beautiful neighborhood in Baqa and led me to a table, where she sat and fixed her gaze on me intently and unwaveringly.

At first, Maureena was very reluctant to allow herself to be recorded and was wary of being misquoted or misinterpreted. She told me that too many interviewers in the past had not listened carefully enough and had misrepresented her. However, she eventually consented, and when she began to speak about her life, a remarkable narrative of intellectual and spiritual inquiry emerged. She spoke of seventy years of professional life as an academic, which began when she became the principal of a high school when she was only in her twenties. She later pursued graduate work and earned a doctorate in religious studies from the University of Ottawa, followed by a period of postdoctoral research. She served for a time as the superior of her community and taught at St. Michael's College in Toronto, where she was known around the college not only for her scholarship as a professor but also, as a former colleague described, for how she arrived at her classes:

"She came by motorcycle. Not the polite European scooter style, but a great big Harley hog of a bike."[14]

Since its inception in 1983, Maureena has been the director of the Bat Kol Institute, an educational organization based in Jerusalem that she founded to provide courses in Jewish studies for Christian students. Explaining one of the many reasons that Christians should study Judaism, she argued, "In order to understand the New Testament, one needs to study Judaism. The Gospels are Jewish books. Not to have a minimal knowledge of Judaism leaves one insensitive to misinterpretations of Jews in the New Testament. A good exercise for a Christian is to sit beside a Jewish person when someone is explaining to a Christian a New Testament text, especially the problematic texts in the New Testament that refer to Jews."

The study of Judaism, Maureena believes, is also necessary for Christians wishing to engage in interreligious dialogue with Jews. She explained, "Many people are involved in Jewish-Christian dialogue, some on a very superficial level. Entering into dialogue means trying to get to know the other and to understand the person. Dialogue of Christians with Jews who are interested in their own roots means getting involved in Jewish studies." She added that being involved in Jewish studies includes not simply reading about Judaism but also engaging in the study of rabbinic literature, a practice that is central to Judaism.

Recounting how her engagement in Jewish studies began, Maureena recalled, "My own involvement in Jewish studies, and by that I mean the religious traditions of the Jewish people, began with my desire to know Jesus, the Jew. If I knew something about the Jewish traditions of his time, I would know something about him. For example, he would have kept the Sabbath and not abolish it, as some seem to say."

She speaks of "redeeming Jesus's name," but what she means by this is far from what many others might mean. Her goal is not to influence or change those who do not believe in Jesus; she feels that is neither her responsibility nor her right. Rather, she wants to redeem his name from the way it has been misused by many of his believers. As she explained, "As for Jesus, I believe his name has been maligned by many of his followers—by those who claim he is the answer to all the questions of life. In his name, people have been persecuted and killed." She continued, "I am writing a book entitled *Who Is Jesus* for me, a ninety-year-old nun. In it, I hope to redeem the name of Jesus from followers who have demeaned so many others in his name. I believe

Jesus was a prophet. He had a great impact on people. I want to know who he is. In doing that, I have no intention of trying to convert others, but if I am asked about him, I want to be able to tell them who I think he is and to correct the false teachings about him."

Maureena studies Judaism to learn and expand her horizons from the richness of the tradition as well as to inform her own Christian faith. She clarifies that this study is intended not to reinforce what she already knows about Christianity but to open up and deepen her understanding of the Jewish identity of Jesus and to break open received assumptions. She is careful to not interpret Judaism only through Christian lenses; she studies it with the intention of allowing Judaism to transform her faith. She feels that this study has indeed shed new light on her faith and continues to do so. "As I studied," she reflected, "I found myself in harmony with much of the Jewish tradition. I often feel I have a Jewish soul. My spirituality is centered on God, not on Jesus, as was Jesus's own spirituality as portrayed in the synoptic Gospels."

"Questioning one's faith is a good exercise," she said. "Here Jews give us a good example. Their educational system is built on text study and questioning. To question can be frightening, and [it can] shake one's faith." Her many years of study have provided this challenge time and again, and as she explained, it has been very difficult: "My own experience of questioning really shook up what I believed. I dropped old understandings for new understandings. Even the word 'God' was emptied of content and refilled with new content for me, and this is an ever-continuing process. Sometimes I feel I am walking in a barren wasteland with no faith." However, she believes that this process of losing and finding faith, and of always being open, is crucial to belief. As she expressed it, "But that is the only way, I believe, to claim one's faith as one's own. It's not enough to simply believe what one was told to believe. . . . If one feels one is on the edge, it can be a good sign that one is taking one's faith seriously and asking questions."

These chapters have explored and analyzed the emergence of a Judeocentric Catholic phenomenon in Israel and have analyzed it in relation to the greater context of Christian responses to Jews, Judaism, and the State of Israel. This book has traced the origin of the phenomenon to responses to the Holocaust and to the lives of a number of Christians who developed Catholic communities in Israel engaged in the study of Judaism and attuned to Jewish Israeli experience; it has observed how the phenomenon departs from earlier philosemitic views as well as from contemporary responses to Israel; it has explored the impact of the Holocaust on Jewish conversions to Christianity and on the formulation of religious identity; and finally, it has investigated the theologies and internal religious motivations undergirding this Judeocentric phenomenon, addressing monastic traditions, boundary-crossing ritual practices, and notions of salvation in relation to Jews and Judaism. And yet this book intentionally comes to a close without a concluding evaluation of the phenomenon explored in its pages.

The phenomenon is cast here neither as an unequivocally positive development in Catholic theologies of Judaism nor as a pluralist movement of great benefit to Jewish-Christian relations. Nor, on the other hand, is it portrayed as a subtle attempt to recast Judaism within a Christian theological framework, appropriating and ultimately sublimating Jewish traditions and identity into a Catholic context while veiling the old intransigent desire for Jewish conversion under the cloak of a philosemitic adoration. Certain aspects of each of these polarized evaluations may indeed be found in some expressions of this Judeocentric Catholicism, but it is far too varied and multivalent to be conclusively evaluated in such terms. In conclusion, this book can argue only that the phenomenon it has identified and described is equivocal, particularly in its more overtly philosemitic expressions, which have the potential to be either beneficial or harmful for Jewish-Christian relations and Christian understandings of Jews in a post-Holocaust world.

In presenting this phenomenon as it takes shape in the lives of individuals and is expressed through personal narratives, this book has approached it as a case study in Christian perceptions of Jews and Judaism in a time of rapidly changing theological and cultural contexts. These contexts continue to evolve, and as religious demographics and cultural trends continue to swiftly change on a global scale, this phenomenon will undoubtedly take on new and very different forms. In many ways, this phenomenon is a reflection of larger shifts in Christian thought, and if these shifts continue in the same general direction, toward a relaxing of soteriological and ecclesiastical exclusivity, this phenomenon may serve as a harbinger of future developments.

However, the narratives shared here also reflect cultural and historical experiences that are quickly receding into the past. Many of the factors that influenced these developments are specific to the generations that lived during the Second World War and in the decades immediately following it, and many of those memories are disappearing with the lives of those who held them. Indeed, at the time of this publication, these shifts are already occurring, as so poignantly evidenced in the very recent loss of Sr. Paula. In the few years that have passed since these interviews were recorded, a number of the others whose voices are heard here have dealt with age-related health struggles that have taken them away from their beloved land of Israel. As the times continue to change, and as memories of the Holocaust grow more distant, I am grateful for the immense privilege of having had the opportunity to listen to the narratives shared here and to be offered a glimpse into the inner worlds of these lives on the border.

Maureena sits bolt upright in her chair, her tall frame rigid with the conviction of her words, her posture as straight and proud at ninety as it must have been at twenty. She declares, "As to the question [of] whether Jesus is the only way to salvation, my answer is no. And I claim that no one can say yes to that question. Who has absolute truth except God? So I am against all those who are out there trying to convert others to believe in Jesus as their savior. Let each one seek the truth and be faithful to their own search. ... If there is a God and if there is an afterlife, they will be there with God."

In a café not far from Damascus Gate, Sr. Talia leans eagerly across the table. Her eyes flashing with intensity, she explains that when she prays for the Jewish people, she does not pray for any particular outcome whatsoever except that God's will might be accomplished. She sits back suddenly and raises her hands in the air as she says that we can never know, or even pretend to know, what God's will consists of. "I'm not going to interfere in these kinds of things—who am I?" she asks. And then she makes it clear that while her own faith is entirely rooted in Jesus, she does not dare to claim that she knows what God desires for Jews and what role Jesus has in this context. She says that she prays "that these people will be ready to receive the incredible gift of the love of God" and then adds, "But which form is it? I do not have a clue. Once again, I don't know."

Across Jerusalem, in the apartment where she prays for the political leaders of Israel, Sr. Carmen reflects, "For me, I think the Jewish people will be saved on their own premises, on their own teaching. How, I don't know. It's God's wisdom. . . . I can accept that God does it, in his or her own way, beyond me. Maybe in a few more generations, somebody will have a little something about that, maybe."

In a shadowed room in the Ecce Homo convent in the Old City, as the Muslim call to prayer sounds outside, Sr. Maureen asks, "Is Jesus the savior of the world? And if he is not, what is he? How does that fit into our whole concept of Judaism and Christianity walking together—walking together differently?" She herself has no answer and does not expect to find one soon. "There are all sorts of analogies, as you know, about the relationship, and it remains a mystery," she says. "It feels like a cop-out when you say that, but I guess we're still in transit."

To the west of Jerusalem, in the cloister of the Benedictine monastery, Sr. Michaela leans back and laughs. Speaking of the paradox of her own faith in Jesus along with her belief that Judaism is indeed complete without Jesus, she says, "I think it's a little bit narrow minded to not be able to relax into paradox, because what do we understand? And I think the temptation is always to choose one way because it's too uncomfortable to be open to two or more. But I feel that's my call, and so I just accept the discomfort that comes with it sometimes."

Over the hills and into the valley beyond Mt. Herzl, in the flower-filled gardens of the Ein Kerem convent, Sr. Anne Catherine speaks softly as she states simply, "Nobody can say 'The truth is in my hands.' Nobody can say that. We are all walking toward an unknown. But the unknown that we know belongs to God. We cannot say 'I know who Jesus is exactly.' No. I do not know."

Chapter 1

1. "Anti-Judaism" refers here to specifically religious discrimination levied against Jews as members of Jewish religious traditions. "Antisemitism," on the other hand, refers here to a racist ideology founded on notions of the racial distinction of Jews.

2. This change is expressed in the 1965 conciliar document *Nostra Aetate*, the fourth section of which discusses the relationship of Christianity to Judaism and God's covenant with the Jewish people. This document has since been followed by a number of subsequent works further specifying and expanding on the changes in Church teaching on Judaism.

3. The term "Judeocentric Catholicism" for this phenomenon is my own. It is distinct from a far more general and public direction in Christian thought that John T. Pawlikowski has called the "re-Judaization of Christianity," which he sees as manifested by "a marked increase in Christian acknowledgment of the ongoing validity of the Jewish covenant, as well as an enhanced awareness of the church's intimate connection with this covenant" (Pawlikowski, "Re-Judaization of Christianity," 60).

4. For the sake of simplification, the term "monastic" is used here to refer to a wide variety of vowed Catholic religious communities, including communities of apostolic religious sisters and brothers, hermitages, cloistered monasteries and convents, and so on. Similarly, the terms "nun" and "monk" will often be used to refer to a wide range of vowed Catholic "religious," as they are generally called, in which "religious" functions as a noun rather than an adjective. In this very broad usage, it includes religious sisters, religious brothers, nuns, friars, and monks.

5. The designation "Israel" here refers to the land inside the Green Line, or pre-1967 borders, within which Jews are the ethnic and religious majority.

6. All Bible citations used in this book are from the New Revised Standard Version (NRSV).

7. "Making aliyah" generally refers to Jewish immigration to Israel, motivated by the Zionist desire to live in the Jewish homeland. It literally means "going up" and is drawn from the biblical language of going up to Jerusalem. Its usage in this context, referring to Christian immigrations, is playfully unorthodox.

8. Orsi, "Study of Lived Religion," 173.

9. McGuire, *Lived Religion*, 4.

10. This critique "presupposed that researchers were riddled with many barely perceptible self-interests and/or assumptions which distorted and biased their observations, leading them to construct more than to reveal their object in ways that rendered their object oppressed" (Davies and Spencer, *Emotions in the Field*, 2).

11. Responding to this issue as it is presented in this book, Gavin D'Costa argues that a "liberal assumption of a neutral way of looking at the world" is not feasible. Furthermore, he argues that a true Catholic theological pluralism is not possible given the foundational tenets of Catholic faith (from personal correspondence, January 24, 2019).

12. This is evident, for example, in efforts to understand the magnitude of the impact of the Holocaust. Numbers and other forms of hard data alone cannot communicate the reality of the Holocaust; it can only begin to be understood through narratives. It is only in the empathetic identification with human experience that something resembling an accurate understanding can be reached.

Chapter 2

1. In the course of this research, I interviewed approximately eighty bishops, nuns, monks, religious sisters, and religious brothers, the majority of whom were Catholic. Of them, twenty-five exhibited what I would identify as a Judeocentric Catholicism and are discussed in this book. However, this group cannot be considered statistically representative. Those with whom I met for interviews were already a select group not representative of vowed religious in Israel and the Palestinian territories as a whole for a number of reasons: they were the few who felt comfortable being interviewed by a stranger, they had a particular interest in interreligious relations and were willing to speak about their experiences in interreligious encounters, they had responded to my emails or calls while countless others had not, and they were receptive to participating in this research.

2. See chapter 4 for a deeper discussion of this.

3. Karp and Sutcliffe, *Philosemitism in History*, 1.

4. Levenson, *Between Philosemitism and Antisemitism*, xii.

5. Ibid.

6. Ibid., ix.

7. Judaken, "Between Philosemitism and Antisemitism," 23.

8. Ibid., 30.

9. Karp and Sutcliffe, *Philosemitism in History*, 7.

10. Some argue that it originated in the late nineteenth century in France, in part as a response to the Dreyfus Affair, while others place its development after the First World War and still others place it much earlier, as evidenced by the founding of the Association of Prayer for Israel in 1905 (Deutsch, "Journey to Dialogue," 9). Finding a much earlier point of origin, Robert Whalen argues that "its origins are English, and it drew continuously on two centuries of British research into biblical prophecy from the seventeenth century onward. Philo-Semitism was, however, soon 'domesticated' and adapted to the political and theological climate of America after independence" (Whalen, "'Christians Love the Jews!,'" 225). According to Karp and Sutcliffe,

the term was developed in Germany in 1880, intended specifically as the exact antonym of antisemitism, and was originally used in a derogatory manner—"invented by avowed antisemites as a sneering term of denunciation for their opponents" (Karp and Sutcliffe, *Philosemitism in History*, 1).

11. Karp and Sutcliffe, *Philosemitism in History*, 1.

12. Ibid.

13. Bauman, "Allosemitism," 143.

14. Ibid.

15. As Yaakov Ariel argues in his work on philosemitism among evangelical Christians, "A major feature of the Christian philosemite relation to the Jews has been the mission. Since the rise of the pietist movement in central Europe at the beginning of the eighteenth century and the evangelical movement in Britain at the beginning of the nineteenth century, missions to the Jews have occupied an important place on the Christian philosemitic agenda" (Ariel, "It's All in the Bible," 276).

16. The desire for Jewish conversion to Christianity can also be seen in some more progressive movements in modern history. One example is the literary circle of three Jewish converts to Catholicism in early twentieth-century France: Charles Péguy, Léon Bloy, and Raïssa Maritain. These three literary figures developed a kind of philosemitism intended as an alternative to what they saw as two unacceptable norms: the French secular insistence on the suppression of Jewish particularity and the long tradition of Christian teachings of contempt for Judaism. In place of these two modes of relating to Judaism, these writers "created a highly aesthetic and imaginative philosemitic alternative that advocated the unity between Jews and Christians, and occasionally supported resistance to antisemitism" (Moore, "Philosemitism Under a Darkening Sky," 262). They developed creative models of philosemitic thought, and yet they were not immune to the tendency to express the standard stereotypes of Jews. And like so many other instances of philosemitism, their love of Jews was paired with the hope for conversion.

17. Pointing to this ironic outcome, Celia Deutsch observes, "Philosemitic responses, in contrast to the better-known anti-Semitic

ones, reflected an assumption that Jews could be assimilated if they converted. Jews thus should cease to be Jews, preserving no Jewish particularity or distinction" (Deutsch, "Journey to Dialogue," 9).

18. Sartre, *Anti-Semite and Jew*, 13.

19. Stern, *Whitewashing of the Yellow Badge*; Levenson, *Between Philosemitism and Antisemitism*; Rubinstein, *Philosemitism*; Edelstein, *Unacknowledged Harmony*; Karp and Sutcliffe, *Philosemitism in History*.

20. See, for example, Ariel, *Unusual Relationship*; Goldman, *Zeal for Zion*; Shapiro, *Christian Zionism*.

21. Stern, *Whitewashing of the Yellow Badge*, 392.

Chapter 3

1. A well-known example of this tension arises in the Law of Return, the Israeli law that holds that anyone with at least one Jewish grandparent may be granted citizenship due to Jewish identity. In contrast, other legal determinations of Jewish identity in Israel, such as marital law, follow the halachic definition of what constitutes Jewish identity, which is far more exclusive.

2. A longer discussion of this issue can be found in chapter 9.

3. Steinsaltz, "Is There Such a Thing," 46.

4. Soloveichik, "How Not to Become a Jew," 42.

5. Despite Soloveichik's use of the concept of a "blood community," it is not necessarily biological, for a convert to Judaism also becomes a part of this family. Ibid., 44.

6. Neusner, "Toward a Zionism," 14.

7. Said, *Orientalism*.

Chapter 4

1. Sabella, "Comparing Palestinian Christians," 1. This statistic is drawn from the Palestinian Bureau of Statistics, "Demography of the Palestinian Population in the West Bank and Gaza Strip," *Current Status Report*, no. 1 (December 1994); and Israeli Central Bureau of Statistics, *Statistical Abstract of Israel* (Jerusalem: Israeli Central Bureau of Statistics, 1998).

2. For a more detailed treatment of Palestinian identity, see Khalidi, *Palestinian Identity*.

3. Palestinian Christians represent a complex array of denominations, which the Middle East Council on Churches divides into the four following groups: (1) Oriental Orthodox, non-Chalcedonian (including Armenian, Syriac, Coptic, and Ethiopian); (2) Eastern Orthodox, Chalcedonian (Greek Orthodox); (3) the Catholic family; and (4) the evangelical and Episcopal family, which includes all Protestant denominations (Bouwen, "Churches of the Middle East," 27–28).

4. Sabbah, "Reflections on the Presence," 9.

5. Neuhaus, "Jewish-Christian Dialogue in Israel," 77.

6. Ibid., 77–81.

7. Khader and Neuhaus, "Holy Land Context," 69.

8. Neuhaus, "Jewish-Christian Dialogue in Israel," 77.

9. See, for example, Ateek, *Justice and Only Justice*; Raheb, *I Am a Palestinian Christian*; and Katanacho, *Land of Christ*.

10. Ateek, *Palestinian Christian Cry*, 11; Raheb, *I Am a Palestinian Christian*, 103.

11. Khader, "Christian-Jewish Dialogue," 86.

12. Prior, "State of Israel," 145.

13. Reuther, "Christian Zionism," 185.

14. Kairos Palestine, Kairos Document. Khader and Raheb, who are both quoted in this chapter, are two of the numerous coauthors of this document.

15. Ibid., 2.3.3.

16. Ibid., 4.2.1.

17. Raheb, *I Am a Palestinian Christian*, 103.

18. Kairos Palestine, "Year of Painful Memories."

19. Khader and Neuhaus, "Holy Land Context," 70; Assembly of Catholic Ordinaries in the Holy Land, "Relations with Believers," chap. 13.

20. Sabbah, "Reflections on the Presence," 8; Assembly of the Catholic Ordinaries in the Holy Land, "Relations with Believers," chap. 13.

21. Khader, "Christian-Jewish Dialogue," 88.

22. Goldman, "Christians and Zionism," 249.

23. Evangelicalism can be found across Protestant denominations, primarily in the congregations outside of mainline Protestant denominations but also in the mainline churches. It can be generally categorized by "a belief in a few theological essentials that include the authority of the Bible, the divinity of Jesus, the Trinity, salvation by faith, eternal life for the saved/damnation for the unsaved, the importance of evangelism, and a need for a personal conversion experience for each individual" (Shapiro, *Christian Zionism*, 5). Whereas some of these points are rarely emphasized in nonevangelical forms of Christianity (e.g., damnation of the unsaved, the importance of evangelism, and the need for personal conversion), other points are foundational to Christian faith in general (e.g., the divinity of Jesus, the Trinity, and the authority of the Bible). However, the distinction is in the literalist way that these elements are interpreted in evangelicalism.

24. Engberg, *Walking on the Pages*, 26. In this passage, Engberg paraphrases common misconceptions about Christian Zionism.

25. Shapiro, *Christian Zionism*, 12.

26. Ibid.

27. Ariel, *Unusual Relationship*, 3.

28. Shapiro, *Christian Zionism*, 74.

29. Ibid., 82.

30. Ibid., 75.

31. It must be clarified that belief in Jesus is not identical to being a Christian, as seen in the self-identification of Messianic Jews. While some would identify Messianic Judaism as a movement within Christianity, others consider it a Jesus-believing movement within Judaism.

32. Although this eschatological view is found most clearly in dispensationalism, it is not restricted to it. Rather, it permeates Christian teaching even in the most moderate forms, for essential to most modes of Christian faith is the belief in the eventual return of Jesus at the end of time and the recognition by "all Israel" of Jesus as the messiah. This teaching is also found in the Catechism of the Catholic Church despite the headway the Church has made in changing its teachings about Judaism:

The glorious Messiah's coming is suspended at every moment of history until his recognition by "all Israel," for "a hardening has come upon part of Israel" in their "unbelief" toward Jesus. St. Peter says to the Jews of Jerusalem after Pentecost: "Repent therefore, and turn again, that your sins may be blotted out, that times of refreshing may come from the presence of the Lord, and that he may send the Christ appointed for you, Jesus, whom heaven must receive until the time for establishing all that God spoke by the mouth of his holy prophets from of old." St. Paul echoes him: "For if their rejection means the reconciliation of the world, what will their acceptance mean but life from the dead?" The "full inclusion" of the Jews in the Messiah's salvation, in the wake of "the full number of the Gentiles," will enable the People of God to achieve "the measure of the stature of the fullness of Christ," in which "God may be all in all." (Catechism of the Catholic Church, #674)

33. Ariel, "It's All in the Bible," 276.

34. Ibid., 278.

35. Engberg, *Walking on the Pages*, 73.

36. Ariel, *Unusual Relationship*, 246.

37. Its roots can be traced back to early nineteenth-century Britain, and the emergence of Messianic Judaism as it is known today began in the United States in the 1960s with the movement known as Jews for Jesus. Messianic Judaism grew rapidly in the 1970s, composed of Jews who confessed belief in Jesus but also wanted to continue to identify as Jews and to maintain aspects of Jewish tradition and practice.

38. Ariel, "Different Kind of Dialogue?," 318.

39. Ibid., 323.

40. Shapiro, "Jews for Jesus," 1.

Portrait: Sr. Talia

1. This phrase refers to a passage in the Letter to the Romans (11:15) that addresses the paradox, from a Christian viewpoint, of the role of Jews as God's chosen people and Jewish unbelief in Jesus.

2. Zech. 2:8.

Chapter 5

1. "Statutes of the Work of Saint James," promulgated in 1955. Cited in Neuhaus, "Sixty Years."

2. Although the Congregation Notre Dame de Sion was founded in the nineteenth century with the intention of praying for the conversion of Jews, in the twentieth century they became one of the first groups in the Catholic Church to recognize the error of anti-Judaic theologies, and they preceded the Second Vatican Council in revising their teachings and practices regarding Judaism. See chapter 7 for a more detailed discussion of the congregation.

3. There are also a number of Christian lay communities in Israel that express interest in Jewish-Christian relations, and many people I encountered in the course of my research spoke positively about a few such communities in this regard. However, I was unable to find sufficient external evidence or first-person testimonies supporting this and have chosen to address only traditional vowed religious congregations in this study.

4. Three monks from the Benedictine Abbey of Bec-Hellouin in France arrived in Israel in 1976 with the intention of starting a Benedictine community in the Holy Land, although they had no plan as to where they might settle and remain. They were offered the opportunity to reside on the grounds of the ancient Crusader church, and in 1977, three nuns joined them. In the forty years that have followed, the monastery has continued to grow, with separate men's and women's communities living side by side within the monastery walls.

5. Gourion was elected as the abbot in 1999 after serving as the superior of the community since its founding. Beginning in 1990, he simultaneously served as the patriarchal vicar of the Hebrew-speaking Catholics. Racionzer, "Hebrew Catholicism," 412.

6. The Catholic Institute for Holocaust Studies, based at Seton Hill University in the United States, provides scholarships for educators to study at Yad Vashem.

7. Sr. Francine is a pseudonym, at her request.

Chapter 6

1. With the exception of Br. Yohanan Elichai, whom I had the honor of meeting and interviewing in 2016, all of the others discussed in this chapter passed away before research for this book was begun.

2. Hussar, *When the Cloud Lifted*, 12.

3. Ibid., 23.

4. Ibid., 23–24.

5. Yudelman, "Christian Theologian of Zion," 23.

6. Hussar, *When the Cloud Lifted*, 79–80.

7. Rist, "Interview with Pere Marcel Dubois," 187–88.

8. Hussar writes delicately of the resistance he encountered by many at the council and the anti-Judaism it reflected. In other passages in his memoir, however, he writes far more directly about the anti-Judaism and antisemitism that he encountered from a number of Catholic clergy who were unaware of his Jewish heritage. In one example, he writes of a disturbing response from the superior of a convent in Jaffa when Hussar had asked him if he might use the convent's guesthouse to hold mass for a number of Jewish converts to Catholicism who were afraid to attend mass in public. The superior responded, "If you darken the doors of my convent with your Jews, I shall jump out of the window: it's them or me!" This serves as a testament to the anti-Judaic teachings embedded in Christian thought and the antisemitism that was still evident in clergy even after the Holocaust (Hussar, *When the Cloud Lifted*, 64–65).

9. Hussar, *When the Cloud Lifted*, 86–90.

10. Rioli, "Christian Look," 37.

11. Yudelman, "Christian Theologian of Zion," 23.

12. Goldman, *Zeal for Zion*, 197.

13. Yudelman, "Christian Theologian of Zion," 24.

14. Goldman, *Zeal for Zion*, 197.

15. The others included Fr. Joseph Stiassny, NDS; Fr. Jean-Roger Héné (Assumptionist); Martin Weinhoben; and Yosha Bergman. Neuhaus, "Sixty Years," 1.

16. The St. James Association is now the St. James Vicariate for Hebrew Speaking Catholics and is discussed in more depth in chapter 13.

17. Neuhaus, "Sixty Years," 1.

18. Ibid., 9.

19. Miller, "Zionist Monk."

20. His first dictionary of colloquial Palestinian Arabic was for French-speaking readers, published in 1973. He followed this with a dictionary of colloquial Palestinian Arabic for Hebrew speakers and also a similar textbook published by the Israeli Ministry of Defense.

21. His dictionaries and textbooks include *Dictionnaire de l'arabe parlé palestinien: Français-arabe* (Paris: Klincksieck, 1973); *Hebrew-Arabic Dictionary for Palestinian Spoken Arabic*, parts 1–2 (Jerusalem: Yanetz Press, 1977–79); *Arabic-Hebrew Dictionary for Spoken Arabic* (n.p.: Ministry of Defense Publishing House, 1999); *Speaking Arabic: A Course in Conversational Eastern (Palestinian) Arabic* (Jerusalem: Minerva, 2009); *The Olive Tree: A Transliterated Dictionary of Conversational Eastern Arabic (Palestinian)* (Jerusalem: Minerva, 2012).

22. Elihai, *Juifs et chrétiens.*

23. Shuali, "New Testament Translated," 518.

24. St. James Vicariate for Hebrew Speaking Catholics in Israel, "Gabriel Grossman."

25. From my interview with Sr. Gemma Del Duca, SC, on September 16, 2015. Sr. Gemma had worked closely with Fr. Jacob throughout his twenty years at Tel Gamliel.

26. Jacob, "Rule of Benedict," 399–400.

27. Ibid., 400–401.

28. The monastery at Tel Gamliel is now occupied by the Order of St. Bruno.

29. Kelly, "Pioneers in the United Kingdom," 9–13.

30. Tec, *In the Lion's Den,* 45–47. Shalom Goldman tells the story of his escape differently, writing that Rufeisen managed to escape while he and other "necessary Jews" were being transferred to another prison (Goldman, *Jewish-Christian Difference,* 132).

31. Tec, *In the Lion's Den,* 66–67.

32. Goldman, *Jewish-Christian Difference,* 133.

33. Tec, *In the Lion's Den,* 134–38.

34. Ibid., 156–59.

35. Ibid., 163.

36. The details of his conversion are discussed in chapter 10 of this book.

37. Tec, *In the Lion's Den,* 185.

38. Ibid., 167.

39. Ibid., 241.

40. Goldman, *Jewish-Christian Difference,* 140. Friedman worried that many Jews would resist conversion because they would be expected to abandon their Jewish identity. He proposed a community in which converts would retain elements of Jewish identity, hoping to attract more converts.

41. Ibid., 142.

42. Ibid., 143–46.

Chapter 7

1. These three commitments are specified in the Constitution of the Congregation of Our Lady of Sion, article 13.

2. Klein, "From Conversion to Dialogue," 389.

3. Deutsch, "Journey to Dialogue," 2.

4. Boys, "Sisters of Sion," 34–35.

5. Deutsch, "Journey to Dialogue," 2.

6. Ibid., 10–11.

7. Boys, "Sisters of Sion," 38.

8. Klein, "From Conversion to Dialogue," 398.

9. Klein observes, "According to the Jewish religious experience there is no sign that the Messiah has already come," and "in the light of their particular experience, they cannot accept the idea of a Messiah who has come but whose coming not only has not changed anything but has made their fate even worse" (ibid., 398–99).

10. Deutsch, "Journey to Dialogue," 9–14.

11. Ibid., 17–18.

12. Ibid., 26.

13. Ibid., 27.

14. Boys, "Sisters of Sion," 37.

15. Deutsch, "Journey to Dialogue," 19–20.

16. Boys, *Has God Only One Blessing?,* 20.

17. Deutsch, "Journey to Dialogue," 18.

18. Gros, "Congrégation Notre-Dame de Sion," 489. Translated in Deutsch, "Journey to Dialogue," 19.

19. Deutsch, "Journey to Dialogue," 23–24.

20. Boys, "Sisters of Sion," 38.

21. Deutsch argues that although the 1964 General Document discussed changes in theological approaches to Judaism, advocating that Jews be seen as "engaged with us in

the Mystery of Salvation that unfolds through time," it also revealed itself to be still mired in supersessionism, writing of "the real though incomplete religious values" of Judaism. Deutsch, "Journey to Dialogue," 33–34.

22. Klein, "From Conversion to Dialogue," 396.

23. Deutsch, "Journey to Dialogue," 4, 14.

24. Ibid., 4–5.

25. Ibid., 8.

26. The Bat Kol Institute has now become a part of the Christian Center for Jewish Studies, directed by the Brothers of Sion, under the name Bat Kol–Christian Center for Jewish Studies. The institute is housed at Ratisbonne, founded as the Institute Saint Pierre de Sion by the Congregation of Notre Dame in the nineteenth century. After Vatican II, it became the Christian Center for Jewish Studies, directed by the Brothers of Sion, with the goal of providing a place for "Christians to study Judaism and to have contact with the Jewish people in their own country" ("About Us," ISPS-Ratisbonne, October 11, 2019, http://www.ratisbonne.org.il/about-us/).

27. Fritz, "Ecclesial Copernican Revolution," 68.

28. All of Maureen Cusick's quotes are drawn from my interview with her.

29. Congregation Notre Dame de Sion, *Constitution*, 13.

30. In the street name "HaLamed He," the two Hebrew letters *lamed* and *he* equal the number thirty-five in commemoration of thirty-five soldiers killed in an ambush during the war of 1948.

Chapter 8

1. Promises of the land and traditions associated with it are referenced in Gen. 12:7; Gen. 13:15; Gen. 26:2–5; Exod. 6:8; and many other passages. For a brief summary of rabbinic perspectives on the land, see Visotzky, "Aspects of Rabbinic Literature," 1–13.

2. Despite the sizable role that the concept of the Holy Land has played in Christian pilgrimage and popular culture throughout the centuries, the notion that the Holy Land is indeed a holy land is not an established and widely accepted Christian teaching. Indeed,

many scholars argue that the New Testament exhibits a rejection of the theological value of the land. See, for example, Burge, *Jesus and the Land*; Wilken, *Land Called Holy*.

3. In Revelation, the extended apocalyptic vision that serves as the closing of the New Testament, the heavenly Jerusalem is a part of a new earth and a new heaven that emerge after the destruction of the current heaven and earth. This new Jerusalem descends from heaven: "Then I saw a new heaven and a new earth; for the first heaven and the first earth had passed away, and the sea was no more. And I saw the holy city, the new Jerusalem, coming down out of heaven from God, prepared as a bride adorned for her husband" (Rev. 21:1–2).

4. Jacob, "Preface to the Hebrew Translation," 1.

5. Ibid., 9–10.

6. Jacob, "Rule of Benedict," 406.

7. Whereas most Catholic responses to Israel generally avoid addressing any potential theological implications of Israel, Gavin D'Costa puts forth the unique and rather controversial argument that the Catholic Church is moving toward a Catholic form of Zionism. He claims that this can be seen in "evidence residing not only in post–Vatican II speeches and papal pronouncements . . . but also in several different official documents whose cumulative significance has yet to be recognized." D'Costa writes that if his assessment proves to be true, then "in a Europe threatened—haunted—by the return of anti-Semitism, it [will be] nothing short of countercultural in the most auspicious sense of that word" (D'Costa, "New Catholic Zionism").

8. In 2016, Pizzaballa was named the apostolic administrator of the Latin Patriarchate of Jerusalem, serving as the head of the patriarchate.

9. Sr. Rebecca is a pseudonym, at her request.

10. Goldman, *Zeal for Zion*, 266; Yudelman, "Christian Theologian of Zion," 24.

11. McGarry, "Land of Israel," 214.

12. McGarry, "Preface," xi.

13. The name Fr. Jacques is a pseudonym, at his request.

Chapter 9

1. Soloveichik, "How Not to Become a Jew," 44.
2. When the Israeli High Court determined that Br. Daniel was not a Jew, as discussed in chapter 6, they were not taking the halachic position, which would have held that he was indeed still a Jew, albeit an apostate.
3. Oz, *Amos Oz Reader*, 235–36.
4. Cohn-Sherbok, *Messianic Judaism*, 191.
5. Kavunguvalappil, *Theology of Suffering*, 16.
6. Berkman, "Esther and Mary," 55.
7. Borden, *Edith Stein*, 15.
8. Pope John Paul II, "Proclaiming St. Bridget," 9.
9. National Conference of Catholic Bishops, "Bishops' Conference."
10. Novak, "Edith Stein," 16.
11. Banki, "Some Reflections on Edith Stein," 47.
12. Solle, *Silent Cry*, 148.
13. The 2015 Vatican statement on Christian-Jewish relations, "The Gifts and Calling of God Are Irrevocable," notes that supersessionism, also known as replacement theology, had been the primary model for Christian theologies of Judaism from the Middle Ages up until the Second Vatican Council. It defines supersessionism as the belief that "the promises and commitments of God would no longer apply to Israel because it had not recognised Jesus as the Messiah and the Son of God, but had been transferred to the Church of Jesus Christ which was now the true 'new Israel,' the new chosen people of God" (Catholic Church, "Gifts and Calling," 17).
14. "Branch, Re-ingrafted," 17. Subsequent references to "Branch, Re-ingrafted" appear parenthetically in the text.
15. In 1982, his concept of a "Community of Israelites in the Church" was supported by the South African Catholic Bishops' Conference.
16. See "About the ACH," Association of Hebrew Catholics, April 16, 2017, http://www.hebrewcatholic.net/about-the-ach/.
17. Friedman, "Branch, Re-ingrafted," 21.
18. See, for example, Dubois, "Israel and Christian Self-Understanding," 63–90; Jacob, "Rule of Benedict"; Tec, *In the Lion's Den*.

19. Sr. Paula's story is told in detail, in her own words, after chapter 10.
20. She intersperses English and Hebrew and inserts the French negation *ne* in the Hebrew phrase: "I am from a Jewish family . . . but I am Christian, I am Catholic, it doesn't matter to me."
21. Hussar's speech followed those of luminaries such as Abba Eban and Abraham Heschel. Hussar, *When the Cloud Lifted*, 9–10.
22. Goldman, *Jewish-Christian Difference*, 110.
23. When he told his parents about the outcome of his time in Jerusalem, which led him to want to convert to Christianity, they were shocked and dismayed, and so he promised them that he would wait ten years before converting, with their promise that if he still wanted to convert after ten years, they would accept it. "They agreed," he said, "hoping that by the time ten years had passed I would have come to my senses" (Swanson, "Israeli Priest"). All other information and quotes are drawn from interviews that I conducted with Neuhaus.
24. Cornille also notes, "On the other hand, multiple religious belonging may also become an impediment to serious interreligious dialogue insofar as it tends to move away from commitment or belonging to a particular religious tradition and engagement in dialogue" (Cornille, "Multiple Religious Belonging," 324).
25. Danon, *Sister of Sion*, 68. All information and quotes in this chapter are drawn from my interview with Sr. Regine, with the exception of a few passages drawn from Ruth Danon's biography of Sr. Regine, which are cited parenthetically, with page numbers, hereafter.

Chapter 10

1. No conversion can properly be understood as a merely personal experience without attention to the social context. Jewish conversions during the Holocaust are not unique in this regard, but the impact of the social context in these cases is particularly pressing.
2. The number of Jewish conversions to Christianity both during and after the war was so large that, as Todd M. Endelman observes,

"the French rabbinate launched a public campaign to prevent further defections and to urge those who had converted in desperation to return to Judaism" (Endelman, *Leaving the Jewish Fold*, 192–93).

3. Ibid., 192.

4. For a more detailed discussion of the St. James Vicariate, see chapter 13.

5. The St. James Vicariate does not intentionally aim to be a gathering place for Catholics of Jewish heritage, and the vast majority of its congregants have no Jewish heritage but are Catholics from many parts of the world who now live in Israel and speak Hebrew. Nevertheless, it serves as a natural home for Hebrew-speaking Jewish converts to Catholicism.

6. "Father Gregor Pawlowski's Story," St. James Vicariate, October 20, 2016, http://www.catholic.co.il/index.php?option=com_content&view=article&id=285:father-gregors-story&catid=38&lang=en&Itemid=145.

7. Ibid.

8. "Abraham Shmuelof," St. James Vicariate, April 17, 2017, http://www.catholic.co.il/index.php?option=com_content&view=article&id=281:abraham-shmuelof&catid=38&lang=en&Itemid=145.

9. Goldman, *Jewish-Christian Difference*, 134.

10. Tec, *In the Lion's Den*, 166.

11. Goldman, *Jewish-Christian Difference*, 134.

12. Tec, *In the Lion's Den*, 208. Subsequent references to this work are cited parenthetically with page numbers.

13. Her correspondence was eventually published in *Commonweal*. Palant, "I Do Not Look Jewish," 31.

14. Palant, "I Do Not Look Jewish," 31.

15. Tec, *In the Lion's Den*, 167.

16. From the English subtitles of the 2001 film *Brother Daniel: The Last Jew*, directed by Amir Gera.

Chapter 11

1. Miller, "Zionist Monk."

2. Greenberg, "Holocaust as a Source," 2.

3. While atonement can refer in a secular context to reparation for harm, in Christian theological contexts it takes on another dimension, referring to reparation for sin, or to reconciliation between God and humanity through Jesus. The atonement discussed here is the former, as reparation for Christian sins against Jews.

4. National Conference of Catholic Bishops, "Catholic Teaching on the Shoah," 10.

5. Pawlikowski, "Shoah," 155.

6. Greenberg, "Holocaust as a Source," 4–5.

7. Fisher, "Mysterium Tremendum," 67.

8. Pope John Paul II, "Proclaiming St. Bridget," 9.

9. Dubois, "Christian Reflections," 4.

10. Ibid., 5.

11. Ibid., 15.

12. Ibid.

13. Friedman, *Jewish Identity*, 111.

14. Friedman's writing style cannily evades a direct assertion of this in any single sentence, but his argument here and throughout this chapter of his book leaves no doubt that this is his conclusion.

15. Friedman, *Jewish Identity*, 127.

16. Ibid., 125.

17. Carroll, *Constantine's Sword*, 6–7.

Chapter 12

1. Catholic religious vocations are often categorized by the terms "active" and "contemplative," the former involving work outside of a monastery—often in education, health care, or charitable work—and the latter involving a life of prayer inside a monastery. The term "apostolic" is often used instead of "active," as in an "apostolic sister" versus a "contemplative nun."

2. Sr. Michaela refers here to the tradition, originating in rabbinic literature and taken up in Christian tradition, that Jerusalem is at the center of the world.

3. Hardy, *Monastic Quest*, 27–28.

4. Nicolini-Zani, "Intermonastic Transmutatio," 1.

5. De Béthune, "Monastic Inter-religious Dialogue," 36.

6. Ibid., 35.

7. Arboleda Tamayo, "Aspects of Monastic Communion."

8. The phrase "monastic interreligious dialogue" has now become a rather technical term, referring to specific practices of dialogue occurring within a set of guidelines. The forms of interreligious dialogue that occur within the Judeocentric Catholicism discussed in this book, however, differ markedly from monastic interreligious dialogue as it is formally defined. To begin, in the context of a dialogue between Christians and Jews, it is not possible for both participants in the dialogue to be monastic, for there is no tradition of monasticism in Judaism. The interreligious encounters explored here, furthermore, rarely take the form of organized dialogues. Another notable difference between the interreligious encounters experienced by the participants in this study and the tradition of monastic interreligious dialogue lies in the very close theological and historical relationship between Christianity and Judaism, whereas the tradition of monastic interreligious dialogue often occurs between Christians and members of Eastern religious traditions.

9. The superior of the monastery then performs a ritual washing of the feet of the guest while reciting, "We receive your mercy, O God, in the midst of your temple" (Benedict, *St. Benedict's Rule*, chap. 53).

10. This is also seen in the opening line of the prologue to the rule, which addresses the reader with the instruction to "incline the ear of your heart." This suggests that the first step in monastic formation is opening one's heart in order to better hear the words of another; in other words, to adopt a position of spiritual openness and receptivity to the other. Indeed, the hospitality required in the rule is so radical that it is also seen as potentially dangerous, for disarming oneself entirely can also invite attack, whether physical or spiritual, and the rule also takes this into consideration, offering a precaution that must be taken: when a guest arrives, and is greeted by the superior and the community members, the "kiss of peace should not be given before a prayer hath first been said, on account of satanic deception" (ibid.).

11. Cornille lists humility, commitment, interconnection, and empathy as the other virtues essential for interreligious dialogue

(Cornille, *Im-possibility of Interreligious Dialogue*, 177).

12. Moyaert uses Paul Ricoeur's theory of the alterity of the self as a starting point, in which one's identity always retains an element of strangeness (Moyaert, *Fragile Identities*, 264).

13. Ibid., 263.

14. From my interview with Fr. Neuhaus.

15. In the Hebrew biblical text, the words *shem* and *sham* are identical without the diacritical marks.

Chapter 13

1. As early Christians developed their own theology of a Sabbath, arising directly out of the tradition of the Jewish Sabbath, they sought to differentiate their traditions and theologies while maintaining a degree of continuity with Judaism. The Jewish Sabbath was on the seventh day, but the Christian Sabbath was celebrated on the first day—or on the eighth day, if one continues to count ahead after the seventh day. In this tradition, the Christian Sabbath is both the first day of creation and also the last day; it is both the first and the eighth day. In Christian tradition, Sunday symbolizes a new creation that follows the memorial of God's rest on the seventh day, and patristic theologians also connected the Christian celebration of Sabbath on Sunday with the *eschaton*, the end of the world and the beginning of a heavenly reign.

2. The vicariate has congregations in Jerusalem, Jaffa, Haifa, and Beer Sheba.

3. In his interview, Br. Yohanan Elichai spoke of being the first person to celebrate the Catholic mass is Hebrew, in the Syrian rite, immediately upon his arrival in Israel in 1956. This is verified in the pastoral letter of the vicariate, "Sixty Years." When "Sixty Years" notes that as early as 1955, the Hebrew-speaking congregation of the St. James Association was using Hebrew as the "language of liturgy and community life," it refers to the use of the Hebrew language outside of the rite of the mass (Neuhaus, "Sixty Years," 12).

4. Neuhaus, "Sixty Years," 3.

5. Ibid., 6.

6. Ibid., 14.

7. Neuhaus served as the patriarchal vicar of the St. James Vicariate from 2009 until 2017. The current patriarchal vicar is Fr. Rafic Nahra, a Lebanese priest who holds a PhD in Judeo-Arabic literature.

8. From my interview with Fr. Neuhaus.

9. Neuhaus, "Sixty Years," 7.

10. Ibid., 13.

11. Kabbalat Shabbat is the Jewish Friday evening liturgical service that welcomes Shabbat.

Chapter 14

1. *Benei Noah* is literally "the sons of Noah." The phrase arises from the Noahide Laws, a rabbinic concept of a set of commandments that apply to all people, not only to Jews.

2. Catholic Church, "Gifts and Calling," 35.

3. Rist, "Interview with Pere Marcel Dubois," 195.

4. Yudelman, "Christian Theologian of Zion," 24–25.

5. Catholic Church, *Nostra Aetate*, 4.

6. Catholic Church, "Guidelines and Suggestions," 1.

7. Catholic Church, "Gifts and Calling," 40.

8. D'Costa, "What Does the Catholic Church," 613.

9. Ibid.

10. Pawlikowski, "Catholic Response," 639.

11. Ibid., 640.

12. Klein, "From Conversion to Dialogue," 399.

13. Catholic Church, "Gifts and Calling," 37.

14. Rennick, "Faith and Culture."

Altfelix, Thomas. "The 'Post-Holocaust Jew' and the Instrumentalization of Philosemitism." *Patterns of Prejudice* 34, no. 2 (2000): 41–56.

Arboleda Tamayo, Guillermo L. "Aspects of Monastic Communion in Latin America and the Caribbean." *Alliance Inter Monasteres*, Bulletin 102. http://www.aimintl.org/en/171-en /bulletin/bulletin-102.

Ariel, Yaakov. "A Different Kind of Dialogue? Messianic Judaism and Jewish-Christian Relations." *CrossCurrents* 62, no. 3 (2012): 318–27.

———. "'It's All in the Bible': Evangelical Christians, Biblical Literalism, and Philosemitism in Our Times." In *Philosemitism in History*, edited by Jonathan Karp and Adam Sutcliffe, 257–85. Cambridge: Cambridge University Press, 2011.

———. "Jewish-Christian Dialogue." In *The Wiley-Blackwell Companion to Inter-religious Dialogue*, edited by Catherine Cornille, 205–23. Malden, MA: Wiley-Blackwell, 2013.

———. *An Unusual Relationship: Evangelical Christians and Jews.* New York: New York University Press, 2013.

Assembly of Catholic Ordinaries in the Holy Land. "Relations with Believers of Other Religions." In *The General Pastoral Plan*, chapter 13. Jerusalem: Assembly of Catholic Ordinaries in the Holy Land, 2001.

Ateek, Naim Stifan. *Justice and Only Justice: A Palestinian Theology of Liberation.* Maryknoll, NY: Orbis, 1989.

———. *A Palestinian Christian Cry for Reconciliation.* Maryknoll, NY: Orbis, 2008.

Ateek, Naim Stifan, Marc H. Ellis, and Rosemary Radford Ruether, eds. *Faith and the Intifada: Palestinian Christian Voices.* Maryknoll, NY: Orbis, 1992.

Banki, Judith Hershcopf. "Some Reflections on Edith Stein." In *The Unnecessary Problem of Edith Stein*, edited by Harry H. Cargas, 43–59. New York: University Press of America, 1994.

Bauman, Zygmunt. "Allosemitism: Premodern, Modern, Postmodern." In *Modernity, Culture and "the Jew,"* edited by Bryan Cheyette and Laura Marcus, 143–56. Stanford: Stanford University Press, 1998.

Benedict, Saint. *St. Benedict's Rule for Monasteries.* Translated by Leonard J. Doyle. Collegeville, MN: Liturgical Press, 1948.

Berkman, Joyce Avrech. "Esther and Mary: The Uneasy Jewish/Catholic Dynamic in the Work and Life of Edith Stein." *Journal of Feminist Studies in Religion* 32, no. 1 (2016): 55–73.

Blée, Fabrice. *The Third Desert: The Story of Monastic Interreligious Dialogue.* Collegeville, MN: Liturgical Press, 2011.

Borden, Sara. *Edith Stein.* London: Continuum, 2003.

Bouwen, Frans. "The Churches of Jerusalem." In *Ecumenism: Present Realities and Future Prospects*, edited by Lawrence Cunningham, 37–49. Notre Dame: University of Notre Dame Press, 1998.

———. "The Churches of the Middle East." In *Ecumenism: Present Realities and Future Prospects*, edited by Lawrence Cunningham, 25–36. Notre Dame: University of Notre Dame Press, 1998.

Boys, Mary C. *Has God Only One Blessing? Judaism as a Source of Christian Self-Understanding.* Mahwah, NJ: Paulist Press, 2000.

———. "The Sisters of Sion: From a Conversionist Stance to a Dialogical Way of

Life." *Journal of Ecumenical Studies* 31, no. 1–2 (Winter–Spring 1994): 27–48.

Breger, Marshall J., ed. *The Vatican-Israel Accords: Political, Legal, and Theological Contexts.* Notre Dame: University of Notre Dame Press, 2004.

Burge, Gary M. *Jesus and the Land: The New Testament Challenge to "Holy Land" Theology.* Grand Rapids, MI: Baker Academic, 2010.

Burrell, David, and Yehezkel Landau, eds. *Voices from Jerusalem: Jews and Christians Reflect on the Holy Land.* Mahwah, NJ: Paulist Press, 1992.

Cargas, Harry J. *The Unnecessary Problem of Edith Stein.* New York: University Press of America, 1994.

Carroll, James. *Constantine's Sword: The Church and the Jews.* Boston: Houghton Mifflin, 2001.

Catholic Church. *Catechism of the Catholic Church.* 2nd ed. Vatican City: Libreria Editrice Vaticana, 2012.

———. "The Gifts and Calling of God Are Irrevocable: A Reflection on Theological Questions Pertaining to Catholic-Jewish Relations on the Occasion of the 50th Anniversary of *Nostra Aetate* (No. 4)." Vatican Commission for Religious Relations with the Jews, December 10, 2015. http://www.vatican.va/roman_curia /pontifical_councils/chrstuni /relations-jews-docs/rc_pc_chrstuni _doc_20151210_ebraismo-nostra-ae tate_en.html.

———. "Guidelines and Suggestions for Implementing the Conciliar Declaration Nostra Aetate, 4." Vatican Commission for Religious Relations with the Jews, December 1, 1974. http://www.vatican.va/roman_curia /pontifical_councils/chrstuni/rela tions-jews-docs/rc_pc_chrstuni_doc _19741201_nostra-aetate_en.html.

———. *Nostra Aetate.* Ecumenical Council Vatican II, October 28, 1965. http://www.vatican.va/archive /hist_councils/ii_vatican_council /documents/vatii_decl_1965102 8_nostra-aetate_en.html.

Cohn-Sherbok, Daniel. *Messianic Judaism.* London: Cassell, 2000.

Congregation Notre Dame de Sion. *Constitution.* 1984.

Connelly, John. *From Enemy to Brother: The Revolution in Catholic Teaching on the Jews, 1933–1965.* Cambridge: Harvard University Press, 2012.

Cornille, Catherine. *The Im-possibility of Interreligious Dialogue.* New York: Crossroad, 2008.

———. "Multiple Religious Belonging." In *Understanding Religious Relations,* edited by David Cheetham, Douglas Pratt, and David Thomas, 324–39. Oxford: Oxford University Press, 2013.

Crane, Richard Francis. "Heart-Rending Ambivalence: Jacques Maritain and the Complexity of Postwar Catholic Philosemitism." *Studies in Christian-Jewish Relations* 6, no. 1 (2011): 1–16.

Cunningham, Philip. *Seeking Shalom: The Journey to Right Relationship Between Catholics and Jews.* Grand Rapids, MI: Wm. B. Eerdmans, 2015.

Danon, Ruth. *Sister of Sion.* Jerusalem: Gefen, 2015.

Davies, James, and Dimitrina Spencer, eds. *Emotions in the Field: The Psychology and Anthropology of Fieldwork Experience.* Stanford: Stanford University Press, 2010.

D'Costa, Gavin G. "'Extra Ecclesiam Nulla Salus' Revisited." In *Religious Pluralism and Unbelief,* edited by Ian Hamnett, 130–47. London: Routledge, 1990.

———. "The Mystery of Israel: Jews, Hebrew Catholics, Messianic Judaism, the Catholic Church, and the Mosaic Ceremonial Laws." *Nova et vetera* 16, no. 3 (2018): 939–77.

———. "The New Catholic Zionism." *Mosaic,* September 9, 2019.

———. "Supersessionism: Harsh, Mild, or Gone for Good?" *European Judaism* 50, no. 1 (Spring 2017): 99–107.

———. "What Does the Catholic Church Teach About Mission to the Jewish

People?" *Theological Studies* 73 (2012): 590–613.

De Béthune, Pierre-Francois. "Monastic Inter-religious Dialogue." In *The Wiley-Blackwell Companion to Inter-religious Dialogue*, edited by Catherine Cornille, 34–50. Malden, MA: Wiley-Blackwell, 2013.

Deutsch, Celia. "A Journey to Dialogue: Sisters of Our Lady of Sion and the Writing of *Nostra Aetate*." *Studies in Christian-Jewish Relations* 11, no. 1 (2016): 1–36.

Dubois, Marcel. "Christian Reflections on the Holocaust." *SIDIC* 7, no. 2 (1974): 4–15.

———. "Israel and Christian Self-Understanding." In *Voices from Jerusalem: Jews and Christians Reflect on the Holy Land*, edited by David Burrell and Yehezkel Landau, 63–90. Mahwah, NJ: Paulist Press, 1992.

Edelstein, Alan. *An Unacknowledged Harmony: Philo-Semitism and the Survival of European Jewry*. Westport, CT: Greenwood Press, 1982.

Elihai, Yohanan. *Juifs et chrétiens: D'hier à demain*. Paris: Cerf, 2007.

Endelman, Todd M. *Leaving the Jewish Fold: Conversion and Radical Assimilation in Modern Jewish History*. Princeton: Princeton University Press, 2015.

Engberg, Aron. *Walking on the Pages of the Word of God: Self, Land, and Text Among Evangelical Volunteers in Jerusalem*. Lund: Lund University Press, 2016.

Feldblum, Esther. "Israel in the Holy Land: Catholic Responses, 1948–1950." *Journal of Ecumenical Studies* 12, no. 2 (1975): 199–219.

Fisher, Eugene. "Mysterium Tremendum: Catholic Grapplings with the Shoah and Its Theological Implications." In *Contemporary Christian Religious Responses to the Shoah*, edited by Steven Jacobs, 60–84. New York: University Press of America, 1993.

Friedman, Elias. "A Branch, Re-ingrafted into the Olive Tree of Israel." In *The Ingrafting: The Conversion Stories of Ten Hebrew-Catholics*, edited by Ronda Chervin, 15–30. Petersham, MA: St. Bede's Press, 1987.

———. *Jewish Identity*. St. Louis, MO: Miriam Press, 1987.

Fritz, Maureena. "An Ecclesial Copernican Revolution and the Bat Kol Institute." In *Coexistence and Reconciliation in Israel: Voices for Interreligious Dialogue*, edited by Ronald Kronish, 62–72. Mahwah, NJ: Paulist Press, 2015.

Frymer-Kensky Tikva, David Novak, Peter Ochs, and Michael Signer. "Dabru Emet: A Jewish Statement on Christians and Christianity." *New York Times*, September 10, 2000.

Galili, Lily. "An Unorthodox Aliyah." *Haaretz*, April 22, 2010.

Gera, Amir, dir. *Brother Daniel: The Last Jew*. Israeli documentary film, 2001.

Goldhill, Simon. *Jerusalem: City of Longing*. Cambridge, MA: President and Fellows of Harvard College, 2008.

Goldman, Shalom. "Christians and Zionism." *American Jewish History* 93, no. 2 (2007): 245–60.

———. *Jewish-Christian Difference and Modern Jewish Identity: Seven Twentieth-Century Converts*. Lanham, MD: Lexington Books, 2015.

———. *Zeal for Zion: Christians, Jews, and the Idea of the Promised Land*. Chapel Hill: University of North Carolina Press, 2009.

Gopin, Marc. *Holy War, Holy Peace: How Religion Can Bring Peace to the Middle East*. Oxford: Oxford University Press, 2002.

Greenberg, Gershon. "The Holocaust as a Source of Jewish-Christian Bonding." *Studies in Christian-Jewish Relations* 4, no. 1 (2009): 1–13.

Gregerman, Adam. "The Desirability of Jewish Conversion to Christianity in Contemporary Catholic Thought." *Horizons* 45 (2018): 1–38.

———. "Superiority Without Supersessionism: Walter Kasper, *The Gifts and the Calling of God Are Irrevocable*, and God's Covenant with the Jews." *Theological Studies* 79, no. 1 (2018): 36–59.

Gros, Marie-Dominique. "La congrégation Notre-Dame de Sion avant et après le concile Vatican II." *Sens* 271 (2002): 488–503.

Halsteda, Narmala, Eric Hirsch, and Judith Oakley, eds. *Knowing How to Know: Fieldwork and the Ethnographic Present*. New York: Berghahn Books, 2008.

Hardy, Gilbert G. *Monastic Quest and Interreligious Dialogue*. New York: Peter Lang, 1991.

Harris-Shapiro, Carol. *Messianic Judaism: A Rabbi's Journey Through Religious Change in America*. Boston: Beacon Press, 1999.

Hasson, Shlomo. "Territories and Identities in Jerusalem." *GeoJournal* 53 (2001): 311–22.

Hedt, Petra, and Malcolm Lowe. "Theological Significance of the Rebirth of the State of Israel: Different Christian Attitudes." *Immanuel* 22/23 (1989): 133–45.

Hussar, Bruno. *When the Cloud Lifted*. Dublin: Veritas, 1989.

Isaac, Jules. *The Teaching of Contempt: Christian Roots of Anti-Semitism*. New York: Holt, Rinehart and Winston, 1964.

Israeli Central Bureau of Statistics. *Statistical Abstract of Israel*. Jerusalem: Israeli Central Bureau of Statistics, 1998.

Jacob, Isaac H. "Preface to the Hebrew Translation." In *The Holy Rule of Saint Benedict*. Self-published, Tel Gamliel, 1980.

———. "The Rule of Benedict: Bridge to Israel." *American Benedictine Review* 45 (1994): 399–406.

Jenson, Robert W., and Eugene Korn, eds. *Returning to Zion: Christian and Jewish Perspectives*. Efrat, Israel: Center for Jewish-Christian Understanding and Cooperation, 2015.

John Paul II. "Proclaiming St. Bridget of Sweden, St. Catherine of Siena and St. Teresa Benedicta of the Cross Co-patronesses of Europe." Apostolic letter, October 1, 1999. http://www .vatican.va/content/john-paul-ii/en /motu_proprio/documents/hf_jp-ii _motu-proprio_01101999_co-patron esses-europe.html.

Judaken, Jonathan. "Between Philosemitism and Antisemitism: The Frankfurt School's Anti-Antisemitism." In *Antisemitism and Philosemitism in the Twentieth and Twenty-First Centuries: Representing Jews, Jewishness, and Modern Culture*, edited by Phyllis Lassner and Lara Trubowitz, 23–46. Newark: University of Delaware Press, 2008.

Kairos Palestine. Kairos Document. Jerusalem, December 15, 2009. https://www.kairospalestine.ps /index.php/about-kairos/kairos-pal estine-document.

———. "The Year of Painful Memories." June 5, 2017. https://www.kairospalestine .ps/index.php/resources/statements /the-year-of-painful-memories.

Karp, Jonathan, and Adam Sutcliffe, eds. *Philosemitism in History*. Cambridge: Cambridge University Press, 2011.

Katanacho, Yohanna. *The Land of Christ: A Palestinian Cry*. Eugene, OR: Pickwick, 2013.

Kavunguvalappil, Antony. *Theology of Suffering and Cross in the Life and Works of Blessed Edith Stein*. Frankfurt: Peter Lang, 1998.

Kelly, Mary. "Pioneers in the United Kingdom: A Positive Beginning." *SIDIC Review* 30, no. 2 (1997): 9–13.

Kenny, Anthony. *Catholics, Jews, and the State of Israel*. Mahwah, NJ: Paulist Press, 1993.

Khader, Jamal. "Christian-Jewish Dialogue in Palestine/Israel: A Different Dialogue." In *Coexistence and Reconciliation in Israel: Voices for Interreligious Dialogue*, edited by Ronald Kronish, 86–99. Mahwah, NJ: Paulist Press, 2015.

Khader, Jamal, and David Neuhaus. "A Holy Land Context for Nostra Aetate." *Studies in Christian-Jewish Relations* 1, no. 1 (2005–6): 67–88.

Khalidi, Rashid. *Palestinian Identity: The Construction of Modern National*

Consciousness. New York: Columbia University Press, 1997.

Kidron, Carol A. "Toward an Ethnography of Silence: The Lived Experience of the Past in the Everyday Life of Holocaust Trauma Survivors and Their Descendants in Israel." *Current Anthropology* 50, no. 1 (2009): 20.

Klatzker, David. "The Holy Land in Jewish-Christian Dialogue." *Union Seminary Quarterly Review* 28, no. 2 (1983): 193–201.

Klein, Charlotte. "From Conversion to Dialogue: The Sister of Sion and the Jews; A Paradigm of Catholic-Jewish Relations." *Journal of Ecumenical Studies* 18, no. 3 (1981): 388–400.

Korn, Eugene. "Jewish Reflections on Richard Lux's 'The Land of Israel (*Eretz Yisrael*) in Jewish and Christian Understanding.'" *Studies in Christian-Jewish Relations* 3, no. 1 (2008): 1–5.

Kronish, Ronald, ed. *Coexistence and Reconciliation in Israel: Voices for Interreligious Dialogue.* Mahwah, NJ: Paulist Press, 2015.

Landau, Yehezkel. "The Land of Israel in Jewish-Christian-Muslim Relations." *Studies in Christian-Jewish Relations* 3, no. 1 (2008): 1–12.

Langer, Ruth. "Theologies of the Land and the State of Israel: The Role of the Secular in Jewish and Christian Understandings." *Studies in Christian-Jewish Relations* 3, no. 1 (2008): 1–17.

Levenson, Alan T. *Between Philosemitism and Antisemitism: Defenses of Jews and Judaism in Germany, 1871–1932.* Lincoln: University of Nebraska Press, 2004.

Levenson, Jon D. "Must We Accept the Other's Self-Understanding." *Journal of Religion* 71, no. 4 (1991): 558–67.

Lindbeck, George. *The Nature of Doctrine: Religion and Theology in a Postliberal Age.* Philadelphia: Westminster, 1984.

Lux, Richard C. *The Jewish People, the Holy Land, and the State of Israel: A Catholic View.* Mahwah, NJ: Paulist Press, 2010.

———. "The Land of Israel in Jewish and Christian Understanding." *Studies in Christian-Jewish Relations* 3 (2008): 1–18.

Manuel, Frank E. *The Broken Staff: Judaism Through Christian Eyes.* Cambridge: Harvard University Press, 1992.

Markowitz, Fran, ed. *Ethnographic Encounters in Israel: Poetics and Ethic of Fieldwork.* Bloomington: Indiana University Press, 2013.

McGarry, Michael. "A Contemporary Religious Response to the Shoah: The Crisis of Prayer." In *Contemporary Christian Religious Responses to the Shoah,* edited by Steven Jacobs, 124–38. New York: University Press of America, 1993.

———. "The Land of Israel in the Cauldron of the Middle East: A Challenge to Christian-Jewish Relations." In *Seeing Judaism Anew: Christianity's Sacred Obligation,* edited by Mary C. Boys, 213–24. Lanham, MD: Rowman & Littlefield, 2005.

———. "One Christian Perspective on Land and the State of Israel." *Studies in Christian-Jewish Relations* 3, no. 1 (2008): 1–8.

———. Preface to *Coexistence and Reconciliation in Israel: Voices for Interreligious Dialogue,* edited by Ronald Kronish, xi–xiv. Mahwah, NJ: Paulist Press, 2015.

McGuire, Meredith B. *Lived Religion: Faith and Practice in Everyday Life.* Oxford: Oxford University Press, 2008.

Merkley, Paul Charles. *Christian Attitudes Towards the State of Israel.* Montreal: McGill–Queen's University Press, 2001.

Miller, Elhanan. "The Zionist Monk Who Teaches Israelis How to Speak Arabic." *Tablet,* May 9, 2016.

Minerbi, Sergio I. *The Vatican and Zionism: Conflict in the Holy Land, 1895–1925.* Translated by Arnold Schwartz. Oxford: Oxford University Press, 1990.

Moore, Brenna. "Philosemitism Under a Darkening Sky: Judaism in the French Catholic Revival, 1900–45." *Catholic Historical Review* 99, no. 2 (2013): 262–97.

Moyaert, Marianne. *Fragile Identities: Towards a Theology of Interreligious Dialogue.* Amsterdam: Rodopi, 2011.

Moyn, Samuel. "Antisemitism, Philosemitism, and the Rise of Holocaust Memory." *Patterns of Prejudice* 43, no. 1 (2009): 1–15.

National Conference of Catholic Bishops. "Bishops' Conference for Ecumenical and Interreligious Relations." April 24, 1987.

———. "Catholic Teaching on the Shoah: Implementing the Holy See's *We Remember*." Washington, DC: United States Catholic Conference, 2001.

Neuhaus, David. "Jewish-Christian Dialogue in Israel Today." In *Coexistence and Reconciliation in Israel: Voices for Interreligious Dialogue*, edited by Ronald Kronish, 73–85. Mahwah, NJ: Paulist Press, 2015.

———. "Jewish-Christian Relationships in West Asia: History, Major Issues, Challenges, and Prospects." In *The Oxford Handbook of Christianity in Asia*, edited by Felix Wilfred, 368–78. Oxford: Oxford University Press, 2014.

———. "Sixty Years." Pastoral letter, August 9, 2015. http://catholic.co.il/index .php?option=com_content&view=ar ticle&id=11368:sixty-years-a-pastoral -letter&catid=28&Itemid=134&lan g=en.

Neusner, Jacob. "Toward a Zionism of Jewish Peoplehood." *Reconstructionist*, November 1972, 14–21.

Nicolini-Zani, Matteo. "Intermonastic Transmutatio: Monastic Identity Molded by Interreligious Dialogue." *Dilatato Corde* 6, no. 1 (2016). https://dimmid .org/index.asp?Type=B_BASIC &SEC=%7B58154A1C-2E50-46E5 -9932-4FE094828651%7D.

Novak, David. "Edith Stein: Apostate Saint." *First Things*, October 1999, 15–17.

Orsi, Robert A. *Between Heaven and Earth: The Religious Worlds People Make and the Scholars Who Study Them.* Princeton: Princeton University Press, 2006.

———. "Is the Study of Lived Religion Irrelevant to the World We Live In? Special Presidential Plenary Address, Society for the Scientific Study of Religion, Salt Lake City, November 2, 2002." *Journal for the Scientific Study of Religion* 42, no. 2 (2003): 169–74.

Oz, Amos. *The Amos Oz Reader.* Boston: Houghton Mifflin Harcourt, 2009.

Palant, Paula. "I Do Not Look Jewish." *Commonweal*, February 28, 1997, 31.

Palestinian Bureau of Statistics. "Demography of the Palestinian Population in the West Bank and Gaza Strip." *Current Status Report*, no. 1 (December 1994).

Pawlikowski, John T. "A Catholic Response to Gavin D'Costa." *Theological Studies* 73, no. 3 (2012): 629–40.

———. "The Re-Judaization of Christianity: Its Impact on the Church and Its Implications for the Jewish People." *Immanuel* 22/23 (1989): 60–74.

———. "The Shoah: Continuing Theological Challenges for Christianity." In *Contemporary Christian Religious Responses to the Shoah*, edited by Steven Jacobs, 140–65. New York: University Press of America, 1993.

Perron, Gregory. "Dwelling in the Heart of the Desert: On the Dialogue of Religious Experience and Monastic Interreligious Dialogue." *Dilatato Corde* 2, no. 1 (2012). https://dimmid .org/index.asp?Type=B_BASIC &SEC=%7BB1C79CDB-2E25-40D8 -B746-541EDCEFDB79%7D.

Prior, Michael. "The State of Israel and Jerusalem in the Jewish-Christian Dialogue: A Monologue in Two Voices." *Holy Land Studies* 3, no. 2 (2004): 145–70.

Racionzer, Leon Menzies. "Christianity in Modern Israel." *International Journal for the Study of the Christian Church* 5, no. 4 (2005): 167–81.

———. "Hebrew Catholicism: Theology and Politics in Modern Israel." *Heythrop Journal* 45, no. 4 (2004): 405–15.

Raheb, Mitri. *I Am a Palestinian Christian.* Minneapolis: Fortress Press, 1995.

Ramey, Steven. "When Acceptance Reflects Disrespect: The Methodological Contradictions of Accepting Participant Statements." *Method and Theory in the Study of Religion* 27, no. 1 (2015): 59–81.

Rennick, Paul. "Faith and Culture Gold Medal Presented to Maureena Fritz NDS." Assumption College, November 21, 2010. https://www.notredame desion.org/archived/www.notre damedesion.org/en/news3176.html ?caso=view&id=104.

Reuther, Rosemary Radford. "Christian Zionism and Mainline Western Churches." In *Comprehending Christian Zionism*, edited by Goran Gunner and Robert O. Smith, 179–90. Minneapolis: Fortress Press, 2014.

Rioli, Maria Chiara. "A Christian Look at the Israeli-Palestinian Conflict: Bruno Hussar and the Foundation of 'Neve Shalom/Wahat Al-Salam.'" *Quest: Issues in Contemporary Jewish History* 5 (2013): 22–49.

Rist, Anna. "An Interview with Pere Marcel Dubois OP Superior of the Maison St. Isaie, Jerusalem, and Professor Emeritus at the Hebrew University." *New Blackfriars* 78, no. 914 (March 1997): 187–97.

Ronning, Halvor. "The Land of Israel: A Christian Zionist View." *Immanuel* 22/23 (1989): 120–32.

Rosenthal, Gilbert S., ed. *A Jubilee for All Time: The Copernican Revolution in Jewish-Christian Relations.* Eugene, OR: Pickwick, 2014.

Rubinstein, William D., and Hillary L. Rubenstein. *Philosemitism: Admiration and Support in the English-Speaking World for Jews, 1840–1939.* London: Palgrave Macmillan, 1999.

Rutishauser, Christian. "'The Old Unrevoked Covenant' and 'Salvation for All Nations in Christ': Catholic Doctrines in Contradiction?" In *Christ Jesus and the Jewish People Today: New Explorations of Theological Interrelationships*, edited by Philip A. Cunningham, Joseph Sievers, Mary C. Boys, Hans Hermann Henrix, and Jesper Svartvik, 229–50. Grand Rapids, MI: Wm. B. Eerdmans, 2011.

Sabbah, Michel. "Reflections on the Presence of the Church in the Holy Land." Pastoral letter, December 3, 2003. http://eohsj.net/LatinPatriarchTheo logicalCommission.html.

Sabella, Bernard. "Comparing Palestinian Christians on Society and Politics: Context and Religion in Israel and Palestine." Paper presented at the Meeting of the Middle East Studies Association, San Francisco, 2001. https://www.ispionline.it/it/docu ments/Religioni2011/Sabella_Com paring%20Palestinian%20Christian sin%20Society...pdf.

Sa'di, Ahmad H. "Catastrophe, Memory and Identity: Al-Nakbah as a Component of Palestinian Identity." *Israel Studies* 7, no. 2 (2002): 175–98.

Said, Edward W. *Orientalism.* New York: Pantheon, 1978.

Sand, Shlomo. *The Invention of the Jewish People.* Translated by Yael Lotan. London: Verso, 2009.

Sandford, Michael J. "Is Jesus Palestinian? Palestinian Christian Perspectives on Judaism, Ethnicity and the New Testament." *Holy Land Studies* 13, no. 2 (2014): 123–38.

Sartre, Jean-Paul. *Anti-Semite and Jew.* Translated by George J. Becker. New York: Schocken Books, 1978.

Saxon, Wolfgang. "Father Bruno Hussar, 84, Dies; A Font of Jewish-Arab Amity." *New York Times*, February 16, 1996.

Shapiro, Faydra. "Autobiography and Ethnography: Falling in Love with the Inner Other." *Method and Theory in the Study of Religion* 15, no. 2 (2003): 187–202.

———. *Christian Zionism: Navigating the Jewish-Christian Border*. Eugene, OR: Cascade Books, 2015.

———. "Jews for Jesus: The Unique Problem of Messianic Judaism." *Journal of Religion and Society* 14 (2012): 1–17.

Shuali, Eran. "Why Was the New Testament Translated into Hebrew? An Introduction to the History of Hebrew Translations of the New Testament." *Open Theology* 2, no. 1 (2016): 511–22.

Silverman, Emily Leah. "On the Frontiers of Faith: Edith Stein Encounters Herself as a Burnt Offering." *Hebrew Studies* 51 (2010): 375–78.

Solle, Dorothee. *The Silent Cry: Mysticism and Resistance*. Translated by Barbara Rumscheidt and Martin Rumscheidt. Minneapolis: Fortress Press, 2001.

Soloveichik, Meir. "How Not to Become a Jew." *Commentary*, July 2006, 40–45.

Soulen, R. Kendall. *The God of Israel and Christian Theology*. Minneapolis: Fortress Press, 1996.

Spickard, James V., Shawn Landres, and Meredith B. McGuire, eds. *Personal Knowledge and Beyond: Reshaping the Ethnography of Religion*. New York: New York University Press, 2002.

Steinsaltz, Adin. "Is There Such a Thing as the Jewish People?" *Moment*, July–August 2012, 46.

Stern, Frank. *The Whitewashing of the Yellow Badge: Antisemitism and Philosemitism in Postwar Germany*. Translated by William Templer. New York: Pergamon, 1992.

St. James Vicariate for Hebrew Speaking Catholics in Israel. "Gabriel Grossman OP." N.d. http://www.catholic.co.il/index.php?option=com_content&view=article&id=282:gabriel-grossman-op&catid=38&lang=en&Itemid=145.

Swanson, Karna. "Israeli Priest Father David Neuhaus Reflects on His Vocation." *Zenit*, November 6, 2009. https://www.ewtn.com/catholicism/library/serving-christ-in-the-holy-land-9224.

Tapie, Matthew. "Christ, Torah, and the Faithfulness of God: The Concept of Supersessionism in 'The Gifts and the Calling.'" *Studies in Christian-Jewish Relations* 12, no. 1 (2017): 1–18.

Tec, Nechama. *In the Lion's Den: The Life of Oswald Rufeisen*. Oxford: Oxford University Press, 1990.

Thomas, David. "Arab Christianity." In *The Blackwell Companion to Eastern Christianity*, edited by Ken Parry, 1–22. Oxford: Blackwell, 2007.

Visotzky, Burton L. "Some Aspects of Rabbinic Literature on Holy Land and Covenant." *Studies in Christian-Jewish Relations* 8, no. 1 (2013): 1–13.

Werblowsky, R. J. Zwi. "The Meaning of Jerusalem to Jews, Christians, and Muslims." In *Jerusalem in the Mind of the Western World, 1800–1948*, edited by Yehoshua Ben-Arieh and Moshe Davis, 7–21. Westport, CT: Praeger, 1997.

Whalen, Robert K. "'Christians Love the Jews!' The Development of American Philo-Semitism, 1790–1860." *Religion and American Culture: A Journal of Interpretation* 6, no. 2 (1996): 225–59.

Wilken, Robert L. *The Land Called Holy: Palestine in Christian History and Thought*. New Haven: Yale University Press, 1992.

Yudelman, Jonathan. "The Christian Theologian of Zion." *First Things*, February 2014, 23–25.

Zerubavel, Yael. *Recovered Roots: Collective Memory and the Making of Israeli National Tradition*. Chicago: University of Chicago Press, 1995.

Zubrzycki, Geneviève. "Nationalism, 'Philosemitism,' and Symbolic Boundary-Making in Contemporary Poland." *Comparative Studies in Society and History* 58, no. 1 (2016): 66–98.

CPSIA information can be obtained
at www.ICGtesting.com
Printed in the USA
BVHW030605281020
591972BV00002B/16